PENGUIN BOOKS

THE MONEY GODDESS

Paula Hawkins was deputy personal finance editor of *The Times*. She has worked in journalism for ten years, writing for a variety of publications and media on a range of subjects, from money to art and science.

The Money Goddess

The Complete Financial Makeover

Paula Hawkins

PENGUIN BOOKS

PENGUIN BOOKS

Published by the Penguin Group
Penguin Books Ltd, 80 Strand, London WC2R 0RL, England
Penguin Group (USA) Inc., 375 Hudson Street, New York, New York 10014, USA
Penguin Group (Canada), 90 Eglinton Avenue East, Suite 700, Toronto, Ontario, Canada M4P 2Y3
(a division of Pearson Penguin Canada Inc.)
Penguin Ireland, 25 St Stephen's Green, Dublin 2, Ireland
(a division of Penguin Books Ltd)
Penguin Group (Australia), 250 Camberwell Road, Camberwell, Victoria 3124, Australia
(a division of Pearson Australia Group Pty Ltd)
Penguin Books India Pvt Ltd, 11 Community Centre, Panchsheel Park, New Delhi – 110 017, India
Penguin Group (NZ), 67 Apollo Drive, Mairangi Bay, Auckland 1310, New Zealand
(a division of Pearson New Zealand Ltd)
Penguin Books (South Africa) (Pty) Ltd, 24 Sturdee Avenue, Rosebank, Johannesburg 2196, South Africa

Penguin Books Ltd, Registered Offices: 80 Strand, London WC2R 0RL, England

www.penguin.com

First published by Michael Joseph 2006
Published in Penguin Books 2007
1

Set in 11.25/14 pt Legacy Sans
Typeset by Rowland Phototypesetting Ltd, Bury St Edmunds, Suffolk
Printed in England by Clays Ltd, St Ives plc

ISBN: 978-0-141-02134-8

Contents

Author's Note

All the rates quoted in this book, for savings, current accounts, personal loans, mortgages and credit cards, are correct at the time of writing. However, since interest rates move frequently, and since banks regularly change their rates even when interest rates are not moving, they are unlikely to be identical at the time of publication; they are given for illustrative purposes only. The same goes for insurance quotes, annuity rates and any other prices. The tax bands and rates quoted are for the year 2006/7.

Although I am a financial journalist and have written for the finance pages of various magazines and newspapers for a decade, I am not a financial adviser. Anyone who is planning to invest sums of money needs to be aware of the risks of those investments, and should take appropriate advice where necessary.

Acknowledgements

In writing *The Money Goddess* I have drawn on the expertise and advice of colleagues in the media and contacts in the financial services industry. Without their help, support, insights and analysis this book would not have been possible. I would like to thank the Money team at *The Times*, and in particular *The Times*'s brilliant personal finance editor, Anne Ashworth. My thanks also to Melanie Bien at Savills Private Finance, Justin Modray at Bestinvest, Mark Dampier and Tom McPhail at Hargreaves Lansdown, Jason Hollands at Isis Asset Management, Philippa Gee at Torquil Clark, David Hollingsworth at London & Country, Paul Ilott at Bates Investment Services, Roddy Kohn at Kohn Cougar, Ray Boulger at John Charcol, Patrick Connolly at John Scott and Partners, Karen Ritchie at Financial Planning for Women, Tim Cockerill at Rowan & Co., Kevin Carr at Lifesearch, James Stewart at Reynolds Porter Chamberlain, Mike Warburton and Ian Luder at Grant Thornton and Anna Bowes at Chase de Vere.

1. Wedding Belles: Women and Their Money

'That,' Kate remarked, settling into the back of the taxi, 'is quite the most patronizing thing I have ever heard in my entire bloody life.'

'Cheers,' I replied, clambering in after her. I had just been telling her about my brilliant new idea: to write a book for women, all about how to manage money.

'Why a money guide for women?' she asked. 'Because girls are too dumb to understand pensions?'

'No,' I said evenly, trying not to get annoyed with her, 'not because they're too dumb. Listen for a second – why shouldn't there be one? Why is a book about money patronizing? There are plenty of books around telling women how to do other things, like understand Martians or snag the perfect husband or be good in bed, which is, OK, arguably a more important skill than balancing a budget, but you know what I mean.'

'Maybe you're right.' She smiled at me. 'For while I am fantastic in bed, I am also completely broke and unable to afford to buy myself a home to live in, so, hey – maybe I should be reading your book rather than the Kamasutra or whatever the hell it was Alex gave me for my birthday.'

'My point exactly.'

We were heading over from my flat in south London to a little restaurant just off Bond Street to meet a bunch of girlfriends. The taxi was a bit of an extravagance but it was a nasty, wet, bitterly cold November evening and we were both wearing impractical heels, so it seemed fair enough. The occasion was the celebration of an engagement – that of a mutual friend, Amy, to a rather dashing Nigerian investment banker by the name of Ade – although celebration may, in Kate's case, have been something of an exaggeration.

'Another one bites the dust,' she sighed, staring mournfully out into the wet and miserable south London streets. 'And she's so young. If you have to get married you really shouldn't do it before you're thirty. I just know it's going to be a disaster.'

'Could you please not say that to Amy?' I asked. 'Because I honestly don't think that's what one says to the newly betrothed. Congratulations. You say, "Congratulations and I'm sure you'll be very happy." Or, "You up the duff, then?" or something like that.'

'Natasha! I'm not completely insensitive, you know. Of course I won't say anything. But it's going to be nauseating. All that talk of who's wearing what, or Wang or Choo, and what colour the bloody flowers are going to be. Hell,' she muttered darkly, 'is other people's wedding plans.'

We were stuck in near-gridlock at Waterloo. The rain was pounding down so hard you could barely see the car in front of you, let alone the river. Kate was reapplying glittery stuff of some description to her eyelids.

'So,' she said, squinting at herself in a grubby make-up mirror, 'apart from the fact that I'm flat broke, why should I, as a woman, need to read a book about money? I mean, any more than Alex should need to read a book about money? He's just as useless as I am.' (Alex is Kate's boyfriend, or 'life partner', as she likes to call him.) 'I mean, is financial planning really any different for women than it is for men?'

*

It is and it isn't. Apart from in a handful of instances, the advice that one would give to a man of a certain age, in a certain wealth bracket, with certain prospects, would be identical to the advice that one would give a woman in the same circumstances. The reason I know this is because I am, for my sins, a personal finance journalist. Sometimes it does feel like an admission of guilt, since most people have a very dim view of personal finance. They think it's dull (it isn't – you should read some of the letters we get), or just 'writing to fill the space around the adverts' (it most definitely is not – many a financial scandal has been uncovered by the more hard-nosed money hacks). In any case, over the course of my career, writing for a couple of national newspapers, as well as the odd magazine, I've noticed a worrying trend among women of all ages to neglect their finances.

Consider a few alarming facts and figures which show that, at some level, women's finances are different. One in four single women pensioners live in poverty. The average retirement income of a single woman is just over half that of men. Because of their working patterns, only half of women qualify for a full state pension, compared with nine in ten men. Newspapers may be full of stories about supergrans, illustrated with pictures of Jerry Hall and Joan Collins looking fabulous, but the reality is less glamorous.

It is not just in retirement that woman are falling behind in the financial stakes. The average woman has 20 per cent less money saved in cash than the average man. And around twice as many women as men say they find investing in the stock market a daunting experience.

This is not to say that women are no good at investment. Quite the contrary – studies suggest that they are better at playing the stock market than men. In 2005 Digital Look, a financial information website, surveyed 100,000 investment portfolios and discovered that ordinary women often outperform some of the best-salaried suits in the City. It found that in the year to May 2005 the average woman's portfolio rose by 17 per cent, beating not just the FTSE All Share Index, which rose by 13 per cent, but the average man too: their portfolios rose by an average of just 11 per cent, the poor dears. This is not a one-off result: similar surveys have shown that women consistently outperform men; indeed, Barclays Stockbrokers even hosts a seminar on investment psychology entitled 'Why Women are More Successful Traders Than Men'.

The reason women tend to do well is simple. Talk to independent financial advisers – an overwhelmingly male profession – and you will hear plentiful praise for the feminine investment style. Women are cautious and pragmatic; they are less gung-ho than men; they don't try to be too clever. They don't kid themselves that they are going to be able to make a fast buck. To put it simply, they aren't macho investors.

Some experts say there is a Darwinian explanation for the differences in investment approach between the genders: while the male has evolved from a hunter-gatherer, whose survival hinged on risk taking, women have always cared for children, and looking after children requires caution. Others suggest it has something to do with feminine intuition. Nicola Horlick, a famous 'superwoman' of the City, has had a twenty-year career in fund management as well as five children. No mean feat. She believes that women are 'shrewder judges of character, enjoy more common sense and can read a situation more clearly and instinctively than men'. These, she says, are ideal qualities for making a success of share dealing.

But if we're all so brilliant at investing, why aren't we building up comfortable nest eggs via the stock market? The answer is that most of us lack confidence. We feel patronized by bankers, financial advisers and stockbrokers, and as a result we tend to avoid stock market investment altogether. This is a mistake. We need to take greater risks with our money, and we need to do it while we are young, while we still have time to recover should we suffer any setbacks. Savings accounts are all very well, but history shows us that it is by investing in the stock market, as well as in property, that real wealth is created.

Female poverty in old age has more complex causes than just our investment approach. The pay gap remains a key factor. More than three decades after the passage of the Equal Pay Act, there is still a 20 per cent hourly pay gap between men and women who work full time. A staggering 4.7 million women – that's 43 per cent of all female employees – earn less than £5 an hour, statistics from the Fawcett Society, an organization which campaigns for women's rights, show.

So women are poorer because we earn less and so have less money over to save. We have irregular work patterns, are more likely to take career breaks and do a great deal more unpaid work than men do. Many women are left on their own to care for children, meaning that they have less money to spare and less time to go out to work. And where women do have spare income, they are more likely to spend it on their children than to save it. Alarmingly, research has shown that a mere 2 per cent of 21–45-year-old women are saving for retirement.

The tabloid press may be awash with stories of wives 'fleecing' their high-earning husbands, but the reality is that women do very badly out of divorce. Around 40 per cent of divorced women over the age of sixty-five are poor enough to qualify for income support, compared with 23 per cent of divorced men. Few manage to win a share of their husband's pension on divorce, even though they have not been able to provide for their own retirement because they have been looking after children.

'It's funny that you think it's a patronizing idea, Kate,' I said, 'because the response I've had from the men I've told about my plans has been quite different. They've all said, "Oh, you mean how to screw him for 75 per cent in the divorce", or "You mean a guide to snagging a millionaire." It's been really annoying. Men don't seem to get the concept of women just earning, saving and managing their own money.'

'Really?' (I knew that would bug her.)

'Absolutely. And then you have all these patronizing surveys coming out telling us that all women who do earn their own money just fritter it away on booze, fags and high heels.'

'Well, some do,' Kate said with a shrug. 'Just look at Nikki.'

'Yeah, OK, some do, but there are plenty of us who don't. You, for example. But the thing is that when you look at all the facts and figures, and when you talk to women in the office or wherever, we aren't helping ourselves enough. As much as I don't like to use the word empowerment, since these days that seems to be associated with taking your top off or doing lap dance classes, knowing where you stand financially really is empowering. It puts you in control. You of all people should believe in that.'

The taxi pulled up to a courtyard just outside the restaurant. I flung the door open, hopped out and fell into an ankle-deep puddle of muddy water.

Kate laughed. 'And you of all people should stop being so bloody sanctimonious and watch where you're going.' She hopped over the puddle and left me to pick up the cab fare.

The others had already arrived and were installed at the bar, knocking back champagne.

'All right, girls?' Jackie called out, proffering a couple of overflowing flutes. She was wearing one of those diaphanous frocks that always used to make her look so beautifully ethereal in her hippie days, but now, two pregnancies and several years of comfortable married life later, just look like a flimsy tent.

'Hi, Jacks, you look fantastic,' I lied, giving her a kiss on the cheek and accepting the champagne. I took a sip, then Kate and I did the rounds.

Kate, who lived in Oxford and didn't get to see everyone as much as I did, was greeting Nikki as though the two had been apart for years.

'Hello, you. You look great,' Nikki said, when released from Kate's vice-like grip. She, of course, looked fantastic as usual in an exquisite silk chiffon Chloé top and vertiginous heels. She also looked impossibly thin and glamorous standing next to poor old Jackie, who, I noticed, had a spot of baby sick on her tent dress.

I said hi to Mel, while Kate moved on to smother Amy. 'You really don't waste any time, do you?' she was saying, spilling generous quantities of champagne down the back of Amy's dress.

It was true. Amy and Ade had been together a mere matter of ten months. But then again, Ade is six foot four and drop-dead gorgeous, he's clever and successful (does something very high-powered at Merrill Lynch), and he treats Amy as though she is the most beautiful, funny woman he has ever met in his life. Honestly, he laughs at all her crap jokes.

'Do you think I'm completely insane?' Amy asked earnestly.

'Certifiable,' Kate muttered, not quite under her breath.

'Kate . . .' we chorused. (Kate's views on marriage are well known. She thinks it is a nasty, misogynist institution, a throwback to the era when women were passed from father to husband as chattels. She wears black to weddings and has been known to long for the time 'when the first round of divorces starts'. Nikki reckons she's just pissed off because Alex has never asked her to marry him.)

The group of us – Amy, Mel, Jackie, Kate, Nikki and I – go back quite a way. Nikki and I have known each other longest – we met at school in Wimbledon when we were seven. Nikki's parents lived just around the corner from mine and we were inseparable throughout our teens, even going to the same university together. At Manchester we'd met Jackie and her now husband, Sam, as well as Kate, Mel and Amy. Despite a few rocky patches, and some vicious personality clashes, we'd somehow managed to remain friends throughout our twenties and into our thirties.

That was partly due to us all moving back to London after college. Nikki did a law conversion, while Jackie started teacher training and Kate was working appalling hours in the hell that is casualty at Charing Cross Hospital. I, meanwhile, got a job with a successful magazine publisher, earning virtually nothing writing about privatization in Bulgaria. Mel dabbled in fashion before going into graphic design, a field she hated then and still does, while Amy, who looks a bit like Kate Hudson and has the dress sense of Sarah Jessica

Parker, found her natural home to be the world of glossy magazines. She is paid next to nothing but gets the best freebies in the business – that woman's bathroom holds more cosmetic treasures than Space NK. And aside from Kate, who moved to Oxford with Alex once she was fully qualified, in London we all remain.

Despite the majority of us being just the wrong side of thirty, Amy is only the second of the bunch to tie the knot. The first was Jackie, who married Sam the year after we left college. Their eyes met across a steamy, sweaty, smoke-filled room on the second night of freshers' week and they never looked back. They are now the proud parents of two little terrors – four-year-old Roman and baby Lila. Sam and Jackie's wedding was a laid-back affair on a beach in Cornwall in July. Jackie wore a diaphanous kaftan over her bikini and most of the guests, including Sam's grandmother, were completely stoned.

Amy's nuptials were going to be a little different.

'We're going to get married in Wales,' she announced. 'Next December.'

'Christ, you actually are certifiable,' Jackie laughed. 'Call out the men in white coats. Wales? In December?'

'Told you,' Kate said through a mouthful of olive.

'It's going to be gorgeous,' Amy insisted.

It appeared the wedding plans were already fairly advanced. There would be a lovely wintry ceremony at her parents' local village church (she was thinking of a holly arrangement in her blonde hair), followed by a reception in an isolated country house in Snowdonia.

'The place is huge – it's a sort of manor house – so most of the guests will be able to sleep there. We can stay the whole weekend, sit around the fire getting drunk, go horse riding in the hills, have snowball fights. It's going to be gorgeous,' she said again, all misty-eyed.

'What are you wearing?' Nikki asked, cutting to the chase. 'Because I know it costs, but you really, really can't go wrong with Vera Wang. And Jimmy Choos.'

I didn't even have to look at Kate to know that she was, at this point, rolling her eyes dramatically.

'Or maybe Gucci. Is Gucci vulgar at a wedding?' She turned to me.

I shrugged. 'Not quite in your shopping league, Niks,' I said, 'but what I will say is that the whole thing gets horribly expensive. The average wedding costs around something like eighteen grand these days – and that's not including Welsh country houses and Vera Wang.'

'Oh, God, you always have to be so bloody sensible,' Nikki snapped. She turned back to Amy. 'I know it's not really politically correct, but I think in Wales, in winter, for your wedding, you might be able to get away with a real fur stole.'

Kate was almost choking on her champagne.

'We are going to pay for it ourselves,' Amy said, starting to look a little nervous. 'Well, Ade is, I suppose, since I really don't have much in the way of savings. I can put a bit on my credit card.'

Ade, I could tell, was clearly going to be in for a shock, particularly if Nikki was playing wedding planner. Because the fact is that unless you start saving very early, you can end up with a mountain of debt once the honeymoon is over. And then – well, the honeymoon really is over.

Relationship counsellors say money problems are one of the most common causes of arguments between couples, not because we value money over everything else, but because money problems tend to reflect other conflicts, over power, control, rights and responsibilities. But couples who are constantly struggling to make ends meet are likely to have problems that those who have a balanced family budget are not. That is not to say that wealthy couples do not argue over money: how rich you are is not the issue, the important point is that you should feel in control. And having huge, unserviceable debts is not likely to make you feel in control of your life.

And although we all like to be in control, we don't prepare financially for life's big events. We don't start saving for weddings years before the proposal and we don't start saving for children years before conception. There used to be a time when people saved just in case, for a rainy day, but we've fallen out of that habit. These days, the spending comes first and the hard part comes later.

'I know this is really, really dull of me, Amy, but the one thing you must do is get your wedding insurance as soon as possible,' I said, ignoring Nikki's exasperated look.

'Really? Already? Will it cover my engagement ring? Because I'm terrified someone's going to steal it,' she said, blushing charmingly and holding out her delicate little hand so that we could all admire, not for the first time, her square-cut diamond on platinum.

'Now that is what I call a rock,' Nikki breathed, awestruck.

Kate rolled her eyes heavenwards.

'Nope, it won't cover that,' I said, 'so call whoever covers your home contents to make sure it is included in your policy. But you should have wedding insurance in place before you start booking venues and that sort of thing.'

'So it covers everything else, then? Like the marquee, the honeymoon, the expensive exotic flowers?' Amy asked.

'Well, there are exclusions,' I said. 'There always are with insurance policies. You need to look through the fine print. Don't do any dangerous sports between now and then, because if you break your leg and can't walk up the aisle, they won't want to know. But knowing you, Ames, you weren't planning on going skydiving in the near future.' There was general amusement at the very thought. 'And of course you're not protected for disinclination to marry,' I added, *sotto voce*.

'Disinclination?' Amy gave me a look.

'Getting stood up,' Kate interrupted with a grin. 'You know, I've always wanted to go to a wedding where someone is left at the altar,' she went on, to our collective horror. 'I've always wondered what everyone does afterwards. Would it be like in films, where you all have a huge party anyway, and the jilted bride snogs the best man, whom she's always secretly been in love with anyway, or do you think everyone just goes home all miserable and embarrassed?' she mused.

Amy looked distraught.

'Oh, not you, Amy!' Kate said quickly. 'I don't mean I hope that happens to you. Just someone. You know. It would be interesting.'

'Christ, Kate, will you shut up?' Mel cut in. 'You are unbelievable! This is supposed to be a celebration of Amy's engagement and you're just giving her the fear.'

'I think I can already feel it coming on,' Amy said in a small voice.

As the drinks flowed, Nikki hit her stride. Before long, she had Amy and Ade dressed in coordinated Gucci going-away outfits, flying first class to the Seychelles. Or perhaps St Kitts . . . Meanwhile, Kate's pick of topics for discussion took a turn for the worse.

'Do you think he'll make her sign a pre-nup?' she asked me and Jackie in a stage whisper that could probably be heard halfway across London.

'No, of course he won't,' Amy said, looking hurt.

'They're actually a really good idea, you know,' Kate went on. 'Aren't they, Natasha?' I kept my mouth shut. 'Just so everyone knows where they stand.'

'You don't even want to get married, Kate!' Nikki sighed, exasperated. 'And anyway, they're not legally binding.'

'I know that, but if I were to get married, I would insist on a pre-nup. Absolutely. You have to make sure that when it all goes wrong, you're going to be OK.'

'Well, we don't, we . . .' Amy began to protest.

'Rubbish! One in two marriages ends in divorce, Amy. One in two! What are the chances of you being the one that doesn't? I mean, really?'

'Right, and how many cohabiting couples split up?' Nikki snapped at Kate, starting to get annoyed. 'Statistically the chances of breaking up if you live together are higher than if you marry. Have you and Al signed a cohabitation agreement? Have you decided who gets to keep the Smiths CDs?'

Kate drained her glass, preparing for a fresh assault.

'My aunt and uncle might be getting divorced,' Mel piped up, doing a really bad job of trying to defuse the situation, 'which is a shame because they always seemed really happy.'

Amy was looking more and more miserable.

I began to babble. 'Some things just don't turn out, I suppose, after a while, once the kids have gone, you know, and you realize that perhaps you don't have quite as much in common as you used to. That happens to some couples, but probably not so much any more, since we all get to know each other a great deal better before we tie the knot.' I paused for breath.

'Ade and I have only been together ten months,' Amy said in a small voice.

'It wasn't that anyway. Apparently Uncle Ed's been shagging some colleague for ages,' Mel said cheerily.

'You see?' Kate slurred triumphantly at no one in particular. 'You see?'

Nikki and I poured disconsolate Amy, thoughtful Mel and very nearly unconscious Kate into a cab. I went home alone, relieved that Kate had decided to spend the night before the get-together at my place rather than the night after. I left Jacks and Nikki, who both live north of the river, standing on the pavement discussing the best place to have wedding lists. Nikki was wondering whether it was rude to expect people to shell out at Liberty or Harvey Nicks.

I suspected that it probably was. I wondered how annoyed Amy really was with Kate, and whether they'd kiss and make up in the morning, for as luck would have it, it was on Amy's sofa that Kate would be spending the night, unless of course Amy threw her out into the street. I was pretty sure Amy would forgive her. Kate may not put things in the most diplomatic of terms, but her wariness of hopeless romanticism is not altogether misplaced. We – Nikki, Jackie, Mel, Amy, Kate and I – come from a generation of independent women who did not actually have to fight for that independence. All the really hard work was already done for us, by our mothers and grandmothers. We could still get angry about unequal pay or the glass ceiling, but a lot of us are too busy trying to do it all and have it all to really bother any more. Sometimes I think we take it for granted, we do not always protect that hard-won independence with the requisite vigilance.

Despite decades of feminism, young women starting work

today are likely to be just as poor in old age as their grandmothers were. That is not to say that no progress at all has been made. There are now more than 360,000 women in the UK with net worth of over half a million pounds. Women now account for 13 per cent of company directors, compared with fewer than 10 per cent five years ago, and almost a third of managers are now women, compared with just 2 per cent in 1974.

But the high-fliers remain the exception rather than the rule. There are still women out there who have never had their own bank account or applied for a credit card in their own name, women who are completely without a credit history, which means that they are very vulnerable. Moreover, women tend to lag behind men when it comes to knowledge of financial matters. A 2003 poll by Charcol Meehan, a financial adviser, found that while more than 60 per cent of men knew the correct level of interest rates and inflation, less than half of women did, and as a result the women had completely unrealistic expectations about the level of return they should be getting on their savings.

There are women who take no interest in personal finance simply because they do not find it very interesting. Well, no, and neither is cleaning the car or doing the ironing, but someone has to do it. One adviser told me that she was amazed when a successful small business owner who happened to be female related that she had no idea where the marital savings were invested. 'I leave all that to my husband!' she quipped.

I remember my own shock at reading a column by a journalist in a national newspaper in which the author, a woman, discussed modern marriage and 'traditional wifely attitudes'. She wrote: 'Mortgages are anathema to me, and I'm happy to let my husband do the research, deal with the broker and make the decisions.' She acknowledged that she was aware of how 'horribly 1950s' it sounded. Well, yes, it does. It also sounds more than a little naive.

Romantic realism is a better philosophy than hopeless romanticism. Face facts: almost half of all marriages end in divorce. Unmarried couples who live together are even more likely to split up. And even if you do have a happy relationship that lasts a lifetime, the chances are that your lifetime will be longer than his, just because women live longer. It is foolish to believe that you will never be alone, that you will never have to do the research, deal with the broker and make the decisions. It is foolish to believe that there will always be someone else around to sort the money problems out. Financial ignorance leaves you vulnerable and dependent. Not a desirable state for anyone.

That is not to say that you need to know in great detail the latest trends in the money markets and how these are likely to affect fixed-rate mortgages. Because, let's face it, life is much, much too short. My personal bugbear is pensions, which I find both boring and scary – an unpleasant combination. The upshot is that at the grand old age of thirty-two (and I'm afraid to say that that really is quite old in pension planning terms) I have no pension plan. But I'm working on it. At present, I'm vacillating between doing the sensible thing, taking out a private pension plan, and making alternative pension provision. I quite fancy investing in French property. Or perhaps vintage cars . . .

I arrived home shortly before two. There were three messages on my answer phone. Yes, I am one of those old-fashioned sorts who still has an answer phone, largely because my mobile is a work phone. Plus I don't like mobiles and I love the answer phone. I like its little red light blinking at me when I get home, full of promise.

Dad had called to remind me that it is Gran's birthday on Wednesday, and also to give me the number of his financial adviser (he is determined that I'm going to go down the sensible pension planning route). Ben rang, said hello a few times, checking to see if I was screening, and then hung up. The third call was a hang-up. Ben again. Probably.

2. Shopaholics Anonymous: Debt and How to Survive It

A few days after Amy's fateful soirée, Nikki rang me in floods of tears.

'Bastards. They're bloody bastards,' she snivelled.

'Oh, I know,' I replied, settling back on the sofa. 'What's he done now?'

'Won't bloody give me any more money.'

I was a little taken aback. Trying to sound sympathetic, I said warily, 'Really? Oh. That's . . . Oh. I didn't know he was giving you money actually, Niks, because you're doing OK now at Charles Russell, aren't you? Do you mean for shoes and stuff, or does he owe you money . . .' I tailed off.

'What the hell are you talking about?' she snapped.

'Andrew – giving you money . . .'

'Not Andrew, for God's sake, he earns about half what I do,' she snapped again. 'Bloody Barclays, the bloody personal relationship manager or whatever the hell they call it now, won't extend the overdraft. What do I do? How do you get them to give you more cash? I'm totally run out of credit! At this rate I'm not going to be able to pay the rent next month and I'll be falling behind on all my cards and then they'll fine me and then Andrew will have to give me money. Oh, God. The humiliation . . .' She started sobbing again.

Nikki has a spending problem. She's always been a keen shopper, but the odd thing is that it is only since she qualified as a solicitor and began making decent money that the problem started spinning out of control. Back at college she spent her student loan on clothes while everyone else spent theirs on beer, but if anything that just made her seem healthier and more in control. In her twenties she took full advantage of her bank's generous policy of granting enormous graduate loans to customers who, they believed, would one day justify the bank's faith by earning large amounts, but again that did not seem too problematic, since one day she would indeed earn serious money.

Unfortunately, it was precisely then that she began developing delusions of being Carrie Bradshaw and the serious spending started. I imagined, the first time that I saw it, that the Luella buckle bag was a fake. I thought that the six bottles of champagne in the fridge were left over from a party. But when she turned up to the pub sporting real Jimmy Choo slingbacks (to the pub! They cost around 300 quid!) I knew we were in trouble.

But I didn't quite realize she had got to the rent default stage until now. So I told her to come round that afternoon, armed with bank and credit card statements, as well as details of any other outstanding debts, and that we would go through it together. Reluctantly, she agreed.

I began to understand her reluctance shortly after she arrived. Sheepishly, she pushed a pile of unopened bank and credit card statements towards me across the dining-room table.

'You really ought to open those when they arrive,' I said, somewhat redundantly.

She ignored me.

'I could do that thing like that girl on the Internet, couldn't I?' she asked hopefully.

'I think that in order to auction your virginity on eBay you would, um, need to be, you know, a virgin,' I replied, trying to be tactful.

She raised an eyebrow. 'Not her, for God's sake. The one who ran up all those shopping debts – in America, you know – and then just appealed for help over the Internet and loads of people pledged money and it all got sorted out. She probably made a profit.'

'I think you might find a few problems with that.'

'For example?'

'First, it's been done before and I don't think it will work again. Second, you aren't American. And I think you'd probably need to be American to get away with that sort of cheek. Third, it's just . . . wrong. People shouldn't be pledging money to well-heeled – incredibly well-heeled – London lawyers. They should be pledging it to shoeless, Jimmy Choo-less children in the Third World.'

She poured a couple of glasses of wine and handed me the smaller one.

Is Debt an Addiction?

The twelve-step programme was originally developed by Alcoholics Anonymous. But these days it is used by everyone – Crystal Meth Anonymous, Overeaters Anonymous, Sexaholics Anonymous and, yes, Debtors Anonymous. The first step is to admit that you are powerless over (insert addiction here) and that your life is unmanageable. In other words, you must accept that you have a problem. In order to do so, you need to open your statements, take several deep breaths, then have a close look at just how bad things really are.

Things were really bad for Nikki. A couple of hours of sifting through her statements and I was almost in tears myself. The overdraft was not a problem, just above £2,000. Personal loan debt stood at £13,000 – again, nasty, but not the end of the world. But the credit and store card debts! She was maxed out on the lot. There was £5,500 on the Barclaycard, £10,000 on Morgan Stanley Platinum, £10,000 on the Amex Blue, £20,000 divided up between the Harvey Nichols and Liberty cards, and smaller amounts on a host of other bits of plastic. It added up to almost £60,000. I was aghast. The minimum repayments on the credit card debts would be more than £2,000 a month. She had been meeting repayments by using her other cards, but the credit line had – at last – run out. The last three applications she had made had been declined.

'Have you applied for every single credit card that has ever been offered to you? Christ! Do you have any idea what the rate on a Liberty store card is?' I asked.

'No, because I'm not a boring personal finance geek,' she replied sulkily.

'It's about 20 per cent!' I yelled. 'Which means that on your debt of eight grand you'll pay more than two grand in interest this year alone. Nikki, it really is stupid. Unbelievably stupid.'

She poured us both some more wine.

Nikki is not stupid at all. She's a very bright girl. She's also pretty, funny and well liked. But she is the third of four very pretty, very bright sisters and she did grow up in a home where competition for attention was fierce. And then there is her problem with men. None of her friends – and that includes me – has ever been able to fathom why Nikki seems to have such appalling taste in men. Andrew, who is kind and funny and absolutely adores her, is very much the exception.

Throughout her late teens and twenties, she had her heart broken by complete idiots on a regular basis. There was Jerry the cheat, Simon the paranoid control freak and worst of all was Evil Tom. He put her down in public, tried to seduce her younger sister and had a violent temper. We all hated him, but for some reason she stuck at it for two years. By the end, her already fragile self-esteem had taken quite a battering.

People with low esteem tend to use something to fill the gap between their real and ideal selves. Some people drink, some gamble, some go on wild spending sprees. Obviously it is not just people with a poor self-image who get into debt. Some people overspend because they think they deserve it. Some are almost proud of it, adopting Oscar Wilde's maxim that 'anyone who lives within their means suffers from a lack of imagination'.

Chronic debtors are often ignorant of both their own financial situation and personal finance in general. This might be through choice: they simply do not want to know about money. Which is understandable. Given a choice between reading my bank statements and flicking through *Heat*, I know what I'd choose. Reading your bank statements is not just dull, it can cramp your style. Knowing how much, or how little, you have in your account makes it harder to justify those extra indulgences, those weekends away, that fantastic pair of wedge heels.

But remaining in ignorance is not only foolish, it is uncomfortable. You are constantly left with that oh-God-I-think-I-might-have-left-the-cooker-on feeling. A vague malaise pervades your thoughts. Every purchase – no matter how inconsequential – is greeted with a nasty stab of guilt.

Living in debt is also dangerous, since it means that you are unable to save. You have no emergency funds should something go wrong, no safety net should you lose your job, or fall ill, or get divorced, or fall pregnant.

'Three hundred pounds at Daisy & Tom! Christ, you're pregnant, aren't you?'

Nikki raised her eyes to heaven and took another deep drag on her cigarette. 'God, no. I bought some stuff for Sal's baby. They have the sweetest baby Dior dresses in there. You would not believe . . .'

And off she went. The thing about Nikki is that she does not just spend money on herself. She is almost – though not quite – as generous with everyone else.

'Yes, OK!' I was starting to get a little snappish now myself. 'Concentrate. You need to think about priorities.'

Prioritize Your Debts

Remember that not all debts are created equal. The second task of the debtor, after admitting the size of their problem, is to sort out which creditors must be paid on time and which can wait. Step eight on the twelve-step programme (yes, I know I've missed out two to seven, but many of them have odd religious overtones – deciding to turn your will and life over to the care of God, for example – and are not particularly relevant here) is to make a list of all persons you have harmed and become willing to make amends to them all. For debtors, this boils down to making a list of your creditors and ranking them in order of importance, and for our purposes this is step two of the programme.

Mortgage and rent should get top billing, then other essentials such as ground rent, utilities bills and council tax. Your friends and family are at the very bottom of the list, unless of course your family are Corleones. Credit card and personal loan repayments can wait until you have paid the basics. But the first thing you need to do is to inform your creditors of your situation.

SERIOUS TROUBLE

If you are in very serious debt trouble – perhaps you face eviction or repossession, perhaps you have lost your job and have no money at all coming in – then you should not attempt to tackle your debt problem alone. Your first call should be to the debt counsellor. The Consumer Credit Counselling Service (CCCS), a debt charity, and National Debtline, a national telephone helpline, both offer free counselling. If you would like to speak to someone in person, you can set up an appointment through the CCCS (*www.cccs.co.uk* or 0800 138 1111) or National Debtline (*www.nationaldebtline.co.uk* or 0808 808 4000). Alternatively, Citizens Advice Bureaux or the Federation of Independent Advice Centres should be able to help.

Since Nikki and I had by now polished off the best part of a bottle of wine I decided that this was perhaps not the right moment to draft letters to creditors.

'Why don't you come round on Saturday morning and we'll get this all properly sorted?' I asked her.

'OK, then. Thanks so much for helping me. Can I buy you –'

'No, you can't!' I interrupted. 'You can't buy me anything. You can't buy yourself anything. You can't buy anything full stop. You can't afford it,' I said sternly.

'OK, OK,' she said with a small smile. 'But what are you doing tonight? Do you want to come round and have dinner – or are you seeing Ben?'

I sighed. I would have to admit it some time. 'I'm not seeing Ben. Ben's being posted to Moscow,' I added flatly, shuffling bits of paper around the dining-room table.

'What? When? Soon? Are you going?'

'No. I mean, yes, soon, I suppose. There's still some stuff to sort out. I think he'll be moving just after Christmas. Visas permitting and all that. I don't really know. But no, I'm not going.' I sighed again. 'I didn't want to say anything before, but we decided to split up. He'll be gone for a couple of years at least and I'm not doing the long-distance thing.'

'Why didn't you tell me?' she yelled. 'When did this happen? Why didn't you tell me?'

'I didn't –'

'I can't believe you didn't tell me!' she yelled again, interrupting. 'When did this happen?'

'He rang the day of Amy's thing. In the afternoon. He said they'd offered him the job and he couldn't say no and he was all excited, blah blah. Anyway, I didn't want to rain on Amy's parade and spoil what was – I'm sure you'll agree – a delightful evening, so I just didn't say anything.'

'But that was three days ago! You should have called me. Did you ever think about going with him?'

'He didn't ask. Even if he had, I don't know if I'd have wanted to. So that's that now.' I surprised myself by how sanguine I sounded about the whole thing.

'I can't believe I've just been whining about my bloody money all evening . . . I'm so sorry, darling.'

I thought she was about to start crying again.

'I'm fine actually. I'm completely fine. Weirdly fine.' I was just starting to realize that I actually was fine. I had hardly thought about him all day.

A few minutes later Andrew came up to pick Nikki up. I had promised not to tell him the full extent of her debt woes, and she promised that they would stay in that night, and that they would not call Deliverance and pay £40 for a couple of curries and a bottle of wine.

'What will we eat?' Andrew asked, slightly alarmed.

'I'll make something,' Nikki said.

He looked really frightened then.

Lead Us Not into Temptation

Closing the door behind them, I glanced through the junk mail I hadn't yet bothered to open that week. There were a few credit card offers among the letters, as there are most weeks. Usually I head straight for the shredder with these (never straight into the bin! ID fraudsters are everywhere!), but having just endured the afternoon I had, I opened them.

The first came from a credit card company. The promotional leaflet featured brightly coloured photographs of hot-air balloons, a plate of sushi and some dinky red and blue high heels. 'It's my card . . .' reads the blurb, 'and I'll go where I want to, eat what I want to, dress how I want to . . . You could too if we gave one to you.'

Very tempting. Now read the small print. *Fancy swapping a month's salary for a fortnight in the Maldives?* What a marvellous idea. After all, with an APR (interest rate) of just 19.9 per cent – yes, that's right – just five times the Bank of England base rate – your £2,500 holiday will end up costing you a mere £3,000 once the interest payments have been met, provided that you manage to pay the whole lot off within twelve months. What a bargain. Over the week, I had received three credit card offers. In total, I was being offered £6,000 of credit. In a single week. This is not unusual in the run-up to the Christmas period, when card issuers know we're all thinking about presents and skiing holidays.

There's no denying that credit cards are extremely useful so long as you use them sensibly. However, what is worrying in the UK today is the extent that credit culture has taken hold. No one saves for anything any more - no one needs to. Why wait three months for an iPod when you can have one now? Instant gratification is so much more, well - gratifying. Why go to Bognor when you could go to Bali?

The British have become very comfortable with debt. Between us, we now owe more than a trillion pounds. That's a thousand billion pounds. If you find it difficult to get your head around that figure, think of it as enough to buy 4 million Rolls-Royces. Most of this is made up of mortgage debt, so it is at least backed by assets which have also grown rapidly in value. However, unsecured debt - borrowing on credit cards and personal loans - has also mushroomed over the past few years. Between January 2000 and January 2005 credit card and loan debt rose by around 65 per cent - from £38 billion to £63 billion, an increase of £25 billion. We are now so indebted that the average Briton spends over a month's worth of wages just paying loan and credit card interest each year. Think about that. One whole month's worth of nine to fives, deadlines, commuting and hassle from your boss and all your hard-earned wages are going to the credit card company.

Credit card companies tempt us with fantasies of exotic holidays and to-die-for shoes, but no one mentions the very real misery of debt. Nowhere in the leaflet does it say, 'Spend

£2,500 on a holiday in the Maldives that you really cannot afford and by next year you will owe around £3,000, and the year after that £3,500 and that debt will just keep on growing, by larger and larger amounts, the longer you are unable to repay the original sum.'

Nowhere does it explain that, even for people like Nikki, with good incomes and good support networks, getting out of debt can be a difficult, painful and drawn-out process. And Nikki is in a relatively strong position. For many others, debt is truly terrifying, a nightmare of county court judgments, late-payment fees, debt collection agencies, bankruptcy and the threat of repossession.

There Is a Way Out

Nikki turned up on Saturday morning in a black mood. She was not enjoying curbing her spending. Nor was she enjoying being forced to stay home and prepare her own food, rather than go out and have it served to her, or at the very least brought to her doorstep by a man on a moped. The previous evening Andrew had suggested she make risotto on the basis that it was 'impossible to mess up'. Yet somehow Nikki's risotto had been all but inedible, and a nasty domestic had ensued.

'All the more reason to get this debt thing sorted, so that you can go back to eating out when you feel like it,' I said brightly.

She lit a cigarette and glared at me, all post-breakup sympathy seemingly evaporated. 'Let's just bloody get on with it.'

Budgeting

When you contact your creditors, you need to give them an accurate picture of your financial situation, as well as offering a realistic payment schedule for your debts. Realism is the key here. The more times you have to renegotiate your debts, the less patient the bank or building society is likely to be. Step three of our debt programme, then, is to draw up a realistic budget. Many websites contain sample budget forms – Credit Action's financial statement is a particularly detailed one. But essentially, drawing up a budget means calculating your earnings after tax (in Nikki's case £30,000) and subtracting essential outgoings (in Nikki's case £22,000). Anything left over – £8,000, or around £670 a month, in Nikki's case – is there to cover debts. If there is nothing left over at the end of the month, then you have to start making cutbacks straight away (see the end of this chapter for some tips – it's easier than you think).

ESSENTIAL OUTGOINGS

This does not include a clothing allowance, unless you have children, in which case you had better keep them properly clothed. Essential outgoings include rent or mortgage repayments, gas, electricity and water, rates, council tax, TV licence, phone, home and car insurance, transport costs, pension contributions, endowment policy payments and basic groceries (including, if you really must, cigarettes).

Nikki's Budget

Income

Monthly salary	£2,500

Outgoings	
Rent	£1,000
Water	£14
Council tax	£100
Contents insurance	£35
Electricity	£24
Gas	£14
Phone/Internet	£50
Mobile	£20
TV licence	£10
Transport costs	£80
Pension contributions	£250
Food and groceries	£150
Cigarettes	£150
TOTAL	**£1,897**
Plus	
Minimum credit card repayments	£1,770
Personal loan repayments	£395
Total outgoings:	**£4,062**
Monthly deficit:	**£1,562**

There was a sharp intake of breath from Nikki's side of the table.

'Oh, my God. I can't do it. Without more credit cards I just can't afford it!'

'No, you can't, but the last thing you need is more cards. You've got to stop thinking that you can borrow your way out of this. But don't panic. Some of your creditors are just going to have to wait. What we need to do is have a look at all your cards and target the ones with the highest rates. Those are the ones we want to pay off first.'

Of Nikki's many cards, the most expensive were the store cards – Liberty and Harvey Nichols. Barclaycard and Amex came next, followed by Morgan Stanley, egg and Virgin. If we could get the last four to hold off for a bit, while trying to reduce the monthly payments on her personal loan and at the same time making a few cutbacks, we might be able to get somewhere.

Consolidation

You might be thinking at this point that there is an easier way to get around all this: debt consolidation. This is the process of taking all your existing, disparate debts and putting them together in the form of one loan, with one company. There is a huge market for consolidation now. If you've ever taken a day off work and watched a bit of daytime TV, you'll know what I mean. Channel 5 is particularly enlightening – advert after advert featuring some C-list celebrity entreating you to switch all your credit debts to a company with a forget-about-your-troubles name like Ocean Breeze, so that you can make 'just one low monthly payment'.

You should not be seduced by these people – they're evil and those C-listers should be thoroughly ashamed of themselves. Evil may sound like a strong word, but what debt consolidation companies frequently do is lower your monthly payments and then encourage you to borrow more – now that you can afford it! All they are doing is tempting you ever deeper into the mire, and making a pretty profit out of it.

The way that they cut your monthly outgoing is simply by restructuring your debts so that you pay them off over a far longer period. In most cases, the interest rate will be higher than the rate you are currently paying and over the long term you will pay thousands of pounds in extra interest.

The other drawback, hinted at but never made explicit outside of the fine print, is that you put your home at risk. Debt consolidation is always offered to homeowners – for a reason. What you do by consolidating your debt in this way is transfer it from unsecured to secured debt. So that if you fail to keep up repayments, you run the risk of repossession.

That is not to say that it never makes sense to secure your debt. If Nikki had been a homeowner, I might have suggested that she remortgage to pay off at least a part of her credit card debt. But you do not need a debt consolidation company to help you do this. All you have to do is find a decent mortgage and make sure that you can afford the higher repayments without getting into trouble.

However, you must remember that you are extending the term of your debt to the term of your loan, which could be anything up to twenty-five years. And this can be very costly. Say, for example, you had personal loan debt of £10,000 charging a reasonable loan rate of 8.9 per cent over three years. Over the loan period, the total interest that you pay back is £1,374. However, if you decide to secure your debt, adding it in to your twenty-five-year mortgage, which charges 5 per cent, then over the whole of term of the mortgage, the interest you would pay on your £10,000 loan is a whopping £12,500.

So the trick is, once you have remortgaged and once you are on a more even keel financially, to make regular overpayments on your mortgage to ensure that you clear the extra debt as quickly as possible.

SAMPLE LETTER TO CREDITORS

Credit Card Company
2 High Street
London

Ref. Card number 4563 8797 5406 7822

Dear Sir

I write to advise you that, due to financial difficulties, I am temporarily unable to meet my financial commitments in full.

I am taking steps to rectify my financial situation and I do take my responsibilities seriously. I hope to be able to repay my debts in due course, but will need some assistance from my various creditors.

I enclose a list of my creditors, details of my outstanding debts, as well as my income and expenditure. You will see that, of my monthly disposable income of £2,500, I spend £1,897 on essentials, leaving me a monthly balance of £633 to repay my debts. However, the minimum monthly repayments on my debts come to £2,165 a month.

I propose to divide the balance between my three largest creditors for the time being. These are also the companies charging me the highest rate of interest. Once I have managed to pay off these debts, I will turn my full attention to other creditors. I propose to review the situation with you, and with my other creditors, on a quarterly basis.

I would be most grateful if you would consider freezing interest on my outstanding debt, and if you would be so kind as to forgo charging fees for failure to meet minimum repayments.

Yours faithfully,

Nikki Rooke

'What happens if the card companies say no?' Nikki asked, quite reasonably.

'Then we write again with another offer. If they still do not accept that, then they can take steps to recover the debt,' I told her.

She looked nervous. 'They send round the bloke with the baseball bat?'

'Much worse. They can take you to court.'

'Oh, my God. I'll be declared bankrupt!' Nikki looked genuinely horrified for a few seconds. Then an idea came to her. 'Actually . . . that wouldn't be so bad . . . Bankruptcy's not that terrible these days, is it? Not so much stigma attached. In fact, in some circles I would imagine it's considered quite glamorous, in a decadent sort of way. And then I wouldn't have to pay back anything!' She grinned, cheering up straight away.

'Oh, yes – bankruptcy's a total party. You lose your assets, your home – if you had one – quite possibly a large slice of your salary and you can never get a decent mortgage offer! In any case, you, my dear, are not exactly what one would term an "honourable bankrupt".'

'What do you mean?' she cried, looking really quite affronted at that.

'In fact,' I went on, rather unkindly, 'you might even be seen as a reckless spendthrift, in which case it's the poorhouse for you.'

Bankruptcy and Individual Voluntary Arrangements

It is true that bankruptcy does not carry the stigma that it used to. In many cases, you can now be discharged from bankruptcy after one year, instead of three. It is becoming more and more common: in 2004 there were over 46,000 personal insolvencies – the highest number ever recorded. The increase, a leading accountancy firm says, is 'the result of more and more people amassing excessive debt on their credit and store cards'.

But bankruptcy is not an easy way out. You still lose control of your financial affairs and you could still lose most of your assets, including your home. You could lose your job, though that depends on your employer. But even if you keep your job, you are likely to lose a slice of your salary for up to three years. And although you may be discharged after twelve months, the bankruptcy order will remain on your credit file for several years, and you will probably never be able to get a mortgage or a loan from a high street bank. You will have to go to a specialist lender and pay higher rates.

Reckless spendthrifts suffer harsher penalties (though they aren't actually sent to the poorhouse). In most cases people like Nikki, who have run up high credit or store card debts, might not be seen as honourable, but nor would they be deemed reckless.

The alternative to bankruptcy for those unable to reschedule their debts with their creditors on a casual basis is an individual voluntary arrangement (IVA). This is a formal, legally binding agreement with your creditors to pay off an affordable amount of debt each month, usually over a period of five years. IVAs have obvious advantages over bankruptcy: you will not usually have to sell your home, though you are likely to be asked to remortgage in order to pay your creditors at the end of the five-year arrangement period; you need not inform your employer; and there is no provision preventing you from running a business, as there is with bankruptcy. However, IVAs can be very expensive, in some cases costing thousands of pounds to set up, and debt counsellors stress that they are appropriate in only a minority of cases.

Dealing with Creditors

Any creditor wanting to pursue you for your debts will appoint a collection agency. Debt collectors won't come round with baseball bats, but they may send you lots of nasty letters and bombard you with phone calls. In some cases they do send bailiffs, but you are not obliged to let them into the house. Debt collectors are not allowed to harass or threaten you. If they do, write them a letter of complaint and send it by registered post. After that, they are not allowed to contact you unless they intend to take you to court.

Nikki looked at me apprehensively.

'So what happens in court?'

'The judge will order you to pay them an amount which the court deems reasonable. In a lot of cases this is actually lower than the offer of the debtor, so creditors are actually quite reluctant to go down the legal route. Having said that, defaults and county court judgments stay on your credit file for six years, so we'll do anything we can to avoid that.'

Credit Records

A stain on your credit file is a pain: you may struggle to get credit in the future and, when you do, you will have to pay more for it, so try to keep as clean a file as possible. If you wish to assess the current state of your file, write to one of the credit reference agencies – Experian, Equifax or Checkmyfile – for a copy. They cost just £2.

Your credit file records your financial history, your residential history (where you have lived and with whom) and, if you are registered to vote, your electoral roll entry. You can instantly improve your credit rating by making sure that you are on the electoral roll and by making sure that you are not being linked with another person, perhaps via your address, with whom you have no financial link. You can also ask the credit agency to add a Notice of Correction, a statement of up to 200 words explaining why, for example, you fell into mortgage arrears or were unable to pay a bill on time.

These agencies should also be your first port of call if you have had a debt problem which has now been sorted out, as they can ensure that this fact is recorded.

Nikki and I spent the afternoon drafting letters to her various creditors, and she promised to pursue a more monastic lifestyle over the next few months: no eating out, no calling out for expensive takeaways, no lottery tickets, no taxis – public transport only.

'Try staying in for a few weeks,' I said.

'God, it's horrible being poor,' she moaned.

'Oh, please, go to the Third World and then come back and talk to me about poor. In fact, go visit a bloody council estate ten minutes down the road and then come and talk to me about poor.'

'But what about Christmas?' she wailed.

She had a point. There were less than thirty shopping days to go till the big day and she did have quite a large family.

'You'll just have to make stuff this year,' I said.

She looked as though she was going to cry.

'Your family will understand.'

'The kids won't! They won't understand why I haven't bought them fabulous things this year, the way I always do. Miranda will buy fantastic stuff because she's so bloody loaded and then she'll be the favourite aunt.'

'Just think creatively,' I said rather weakly.

She looked so forlorn as she turned away and shuffled off down the street I almost wanted to cry myself. Then I thought about how it was actually all her fault in the first place and she didn't really deserve my sympathy. It wasn't like anyone had forced her to buy thirty-seven pairs of shoes in twelve months, was it? Thankfully, though, her creditors were relatively sympathetic. Over the next couple of weeks there was a bit of toing and froing, but eventually we managed to reach agreements more or less acceptable to all parties, which meant that legal wrangling has – so far at least – been avoided. But I was still annoyed with her – if we'd just caught the problem a little earlier, all this could have been avoided.

If you find yourself sinking a little deeper into the red at the end of each month, if you find the amount you owe on credit rising a little each month, if you find yourself able to meet only the minimum repayments on your cards or if you find yourself using credit to pay for your essentials, then you have a debt problem and you need to address it as soon as possible. If you do so now, you can avoid all the pain that Nikki is currently having to go through.

Use Credit Wisely or Not at All

If you want to make clever use of credit cards and personal loans you need to be boringly careful and responsible, and you need to get wise to the way that lenders operate. Remember that it is not in the card issuer's interest for you to be a perfect customer who remains well within her credit limit and pays off her balance in full each month. You are no use to the lender if you pay off your personal loan early. The finance boys at the care company want you to be reckless, late, on the very verge of default. That's how they make a profit. And once you've got to your credit limit, they'll extend it, to reel you in just a little bit more.

Pick the Right Card for You

In the couple of years to summer 2005 there was an abundance of 0 per cent offers on the credit card market. These were great deals: in many cases, you could transfer debts from other cards and make purchases for up to a year without paying any interest at all. But these are few and far between. As customers became better and better at exploiting 0 per cent offers, so card issuers felt the bite in the bottom line. You will still find 0 per cent offers around, but most have stings in the tail – they charge fees for balance transfers, for example.

The right card for you will depend on what you use it for. The best place to look for the right card is online. Go to Moneyfacts (*www.moneyfacts.co.uk*), an independent financial information provider. It lists the best-buy cards should you want to transfer a balance, find the lowest standard rate or the highest cash-back offer. If you are a sensible card user and you do pay off your balance in full each month, go for cash back – this way, you can actually make money out of the credit card company. But keep an eye on the details. Some cards – including Lloyds TSB Advance Mastercard and Halifax Flat Rate Visa – will charge you interest from the day on which you make a purchase – even if you clear your balance each month.

Do More Than Just the Minimum

Never imagine that just by keeping up the minimum repayments on your credit card that you are managing your debt well. You are not. In the old days credit card companies used to insist that you pay off at least 5 per cent of your outstanding balance each month as your minimum repayment. But today many have lowered that percentage to just 2 per cent per month. Isn't that good of them, asking for a little less of your hard-earned cash each month? Well, no, not really. Moneysupermarket (*www.moneysupermarket.com*), a financial website, has figured out that if you have a typical card with an APR of 13.9 per cent and a balance of £2,200, it will take eight years to settle the debt by repaying 5 per cent each month. Now, eight years may seem bad enough, but if you reduce your repayments to 2 per cent each month, that measly debt will last for twenty-six years. Twenty-six years!

Shun Store Cards

There are a staggering 22 million store cards in circulation, which quite frankly is a disgrace, given that their average rate is more than 25 per cent and that only 60 per cent of cardholders pay off their full balances. Outstanding balances on store cards run in the billions, meaning that we're wasting millions of pounds on them each year.

Don't believe the sales patter. Even if you took advantage of every single discount or special offer they dangled in front of you, you would still come out the loser. Just take a look at the rates on these cards: Harvey Nicks charges 26.5 per cent, Oasis 29 per cent, and they aren't even the worst of the bunch.

Compare this with the best standard rates on the market, which are less than 10 per cent, excluding introductory offers – it's a no-brainer.

Loans and Car Loans

OK, you've had your eye on the VW Beetle cabriolet for a while. I don't blame you – they're beautiful to look at, zippy, sturdy . . . just the thing. Not cheap, though – £16,000 is a bit much to stick on the credit card. And even *I* don't expect you to save for several years before you buy a car. I do realize that some people actually need cars, especially those who live out in the sticks.

So once you have your heart set on a particular motor, your options are to take out a personal loan or a car loan or to remortgage. I wouldn't recommend the last, unless you have other reasons to remortgage as well as the car purchase. It isn't free, and the difference between good loan rates and mortgage rates is no longer sufficient to justify the extra expense.

Between car loans and personal loans there is relatively little to choose. Car loans often come with incentives such as free car inspections and discounts on spare parts and tyres, which can be quite valuable so long as you think you will take advantage of the added extras. Personal loans have slightly more competitive rates, but the difference really is marginal – we're talking fractions of a percentage point. You'll find the best deals these days hovering around 6 per cent, assuming a loan of £15,000 over five years. Anything over 10 per cent is too expensive. Again, for the best deals, check Moneyfacts.

There are a couple of other factors to bear in mind when shopping for personal loans. The first is that the majority of lenders charge a fee of up to two months' interest should you want to repay early. There are a handful of lenders who do not, however, and most charge very competitive rates. They include egg, Nationwide, Morgan Stanley and Northern Rock.

The second is that you should not be persuaded to buy payment protection insurance from the lender. Payment protection insurance covers you in the event that you are unable to meet your loan repayments: for example, if you fall ill or are made redundant. It is expensive and, in the majority of cases, unused. Many people would rather put aside a small amount each month into a savings account than spend the money on insurance. However, if you do want cover, shop around. Specialists such as Goodfellows offer cheaper cover than the lenders themselves.

For example, you borrow £5,000 over three years from Tesco Personal Finance at 7.7 per cent. Your monthly premiums are £155.47. Over three years, the loan costs you £5,597. If you take Tesco's own payment protection insurance, your premiums rise to £173.31. Over three years, the loan costs you £6,239. If you buy insurance from Goodfellows, your premiums are £167.13. Over three years, the loan costs you £6,016 – and you are just over £220 the richer.

Stuff Oscar Wilde – Learn to Live within Your Means

The phone rang around one thirty in the morning the day after Nikki and I had done the letter drafting.

'I've had a bloody genius idea!' she chirped at me.

'Fantastic,' I said, rolling over, turning on the light and steeling myself for her next ludicrous get-out-of-jail-free scheme. 'What now?'

'The Internet!'

'Haven't we already been here? We've already been over the fact you have to be a virgin, haven't we?'

'Oh, do shut up about that. Do you know how many pairs of shoes I have?' she asked. 'Or how many handbags? Or belts? Or dresses that I've worn once and completely hate?'

'I shudder to think,' I replied.

'Boxes full. Boxes upon boxes full. You told me to think creatively – I'm thinking eBay. I can flog everything over the next few weeks and – presto – I'll have the cash to buy the nieces presents. Plus something for Mum if she's really lucky.'

I was impressed. It was a good idea, although the idea of Nikki running amok in shoppers' cyber-paradise did have me a little worried.

'Just don't buy anything on eBay, OK?'

'God, of course not!' she replied, a sneer in her voice. 'Some people might call it vintage. I call it second-hand.'

I smiled, relieved. 'Oh, and don't become obsessed by it. Some people get totally hooked. I had a boyfriend who was obsessed by eBay once. He had this weird thing about buying toast racks and butter dishes.'

A lot of the stuff flogged on eBay might be a load of old tat, but if you're looking to declutter your home or to pick up books, DVDs and CDs on the cheap, it is very useful, and is just one of a host of ways to save money, and perhaps make a little if you have stuff worth selling. As with any online shopping, you need to learn the rules to make sure that you're not getting ripped off. The 'Help' and 'Community' sections of the eBay website have plenty of tips for successful eBaying.

*

In any case, Christmas came and went, and Nikki's nieces were delighted with their gifts – she actually made enough to buy all the family presents, as well as a pretty decent bottle of champagne on New Year's Eve. Apart from New Year's, she'd been staying in and behaving herself, which frankly she was finding a little dull. On a particularly bitter and miserable January afternoon, I decided the time had come to treat the poor love, so I rang up to ask her out to dinner – my treat. (I had to admit this was not a purely altruistic move. I loathe the prevailing tendency to quit everything immediately after the Christmas break – like January isn't depressing enough without having to give up drinking and smoking and eating chips cooked in duck fat.)

So off we went, to a great French place in Farringdon – perhaps not the ideal location to suggest, as I did, that Nikki made a few more cutbacks in order to expedite her escape from the debtor's mire.

'What do you mean cutbacks?' she spluttered incredulously. 'I've been taking the tube, not taxis, I haven't bought any clothes or shoes for a month, I've been cooking! Christ, forget Atkins – try the Nikki diet. Just cook your own food – it's revolting and you won't want to eat it!'

She did look a little frail, I had to admit.

'I'm not spending anything,' she insisted.

'You've been brilliant, and I know that January is a rubbish time to do this, so do it next month,' I said in a conciliatory tone. 'You could always quit smoking . . .'

'No!' she snapped, snatching her cigarette packet from the table top and holding it to her as though it were a precious jewel, or a small child. 'No – really, I draw the line there. I have *no* pleasures left at all. You can't take my cigarettes from me!'

I had expected that reaction. In fact, it was part of my

plan: allow her to keep her cigarettes in exchange for a few other concessions.

It is amazing how much money you can save by making relatively minor adjustments to your everyday lifestyle. Making your own lunch instead of buying a sandwich to eat at work will save you something in the region of £700 a year – more if you have a weakness for Pret a Manger sushi. Skipping your morning grande latte will save you just under £500 a year. Having said that, smoking really is the big one. All you impoverished pack-a-day smokers out there, take a couple of minutes to ponder the utter futility of spending roughly £1,800 a year to yellow your teeth, age your skin, render foul your breath, fur up your arteries and blacken your lungs.

However, if you cannot face giving up any luxuries, other changes can also pay dividends. Use websites such as Uswitch (*www.uswitch.com*) or Buy.co.uk (*www.buy.co.uk*) to find out whether you are using the cheapest gas, electricity and phone suppliers in your area. There are plenty of good deals out there and you can save hundreds of pounds a year by taking advantage of them.

Shop around for insurance too. Most people get routinely ripped off simply because they cannot be bothered to research the best home, travel and motor deals. Yet the Internet really does take the hassle out of finding the most competitive policies. Use it. Even if you do not have a computer at home or at work, nip out to an Internet café. You do not have to buy online (although this is often a method of making additional savings), but the Internet is the best place to do your homework.

Living within your means is not just about making cutbacks, it's about maximizing your income too. When was the last time you had a raise? Do you deserve one? If you believe you do, go to the boss and go prepared. You need to have an ideal salary in mind, a bottom line (the minimum you'll accept) and somewhere in between (a realistic goal). Arm yourself with useful facts and figures – evidence to show that you've been doing your job well. Perhaps sales figures are up, for example.

Make sure that you are not paying too much tax. There's no point throwing money at the government. And while you're at it, check if they owe you anything – every year billions of pounds of benefits go unclaimed. If you are on a low income, if you have children or if you care for an elderly or sick relative, you might be eligible for state help in the form of benefits (see Chapter 8 for details).

If you have a tendency to make impulse buys, leave your credit card at home. In extreme cases try freezing your assets. Put your card in a plastic bag, pop it into a mug full of water and stick it in the freezer. That way you cannot make any rash decisions – you have to wait for your card to thaw out (this may not work if you own a microwave). Remember that credit seen from another point of view (i.e. yours) is debt. If you can handle it, go ahead. If you know that you can't – and you really should know by now – just do without. The simplest way to deal with problem credit cards is to cut them. You can manage without them. We all used to, didn't we?

3. Useless Bankers: Current Accounts

'He is *such* a bastard.'

Nikki was on the phone again. Not in tears this time, just furious.

'What?' I cried, alarmed. 'What's happened? Did those people from Barclaycard call you again? Because we've already talked about this . . .'

'Not the bank! Andrew!'

Sometimes it's hard to keep up.

A few weeks had passed since our dinner in Farringdon and I was under the impression that all was going swimmingly. Nikki had switched phone and gas suppliers, saving herself a modest sum each month, and was continuing to streamline her wardrobe via eBay. Apparently there had been quite a bidding war for the Gina boots she had worn just once and found too uncomfortable to wear again. But I was concerned that it would not take much of an upset to send her off the rails.

'So you two have had a fight, I take it?'

'You could say that. He promised ages ago that we could go to La Mamounia for Valentine's Day and it was all booked, and I know we're supposed to be on this whole live-frugally-or-go-to-jail thing, but I was so looking forward to it. Anyway, he's just cancelled it. Says there's no way he could afford it all by himself – which I know is true – but

. . . I was really looking forward to it! And he just cancelled it! Without even asking me what I thought!'

'Oh, Nik. I feel really bad now. He's only doing this because I said you couldn't spend anything. I'm sorry. What's La Mamounia?'

'Oh, how can you be so bloody out of it? It's a hotel in Marrakesh. And it's just supposed to be amazing. Kate Moss goes there.' There was a short silence. Then she added sulkily, 'And you're right, you know. It is all your fault. I blame you. Completely.'

'I'm sorry your trip's been cancelled,' I said, feeling like Little Miss Killjoy Bitch, out to ruin everyone's fun. 'But it could be worse. You could be me,' I pointed out, 'spending Valentine's Day at home drinking Jack Daniel's on my own till I pass out.'

'Oh, rubbish,' she said. 'You'll meet some man and be taken out somewhere glam. You always fall on your feet.'

Totally untrue, of course, but I sensed that there wasn't much point in arguing.

She went on, 'I know Andrew's right. And I know you're right. It's the right thing to do. It's the stupid, boring right thing to do.'

'It is,' I agreed solemnly.

'But I was just so disappointed . . .'

There was a plaintive note creeping into her voice now, one I wasn't sure I liked the sound of.

'And?'

'Well, I was just feeling so down . . .'

'What did you do?'

'There was a card that arrived the day after we went through everything you remember that Saturday when I was so upset and anyway it was just offered to me it was from Ryanair and I vaguely remember signing something a while ago it was some sort of special offer after a flight and I didn't mean to use I just put it in a drawer and I was so good until yesterday and then I went to Harvey Nichols and bought a belt.'

The words came rushing out, like a confession on speed.

'A belt?' I asked, somewhat relieved. 'Just a belt?'

'Just one. One belt. Then I came home. I'm so, so, so sorry.'

Her remorse was quite sweet actually, so much so that I was moved to volunteer to give her the belt as an early birthday present on condition that she cut up the Ryanair card. She was a little miffed that I insisted she do this in front of me, and I was a little miffed that she hadn't told me the belt was from Chloé and cost £219, but we settled our differences over a few drinks in the pub, and all was well, particularly since Andrew had promised her an alternative, admittedly cheap, Valentine's Day surprise.

The day after Nikki's shopping slip-up, I had to do a BBC radio interview. It went badly. The presenter of the radio show, an old hand with something of a reputation, clearly had no interest whatsoever in the debt crisis. He asked me the same question at least four times and, try as I might to vary the answers, I ended up sounding like a complete idiot. He didn't listen to my answers and he didn't laugh when I made amusing remarks. It was mortifying.

I left in a foul mood, desperate for a drink, and headed straight for the nearest bar. I was just about to leave, two gin and tonics down, when I heard a voice behind me.

'I heard you'd been dumped, but I didn't know it had come to this.' It was Michael – an old boyfriend of Mel's. He gestured towards my almost-empty glass. 'Drinking alone, are we? Bit sad, innit?'

'Oh, shut up, you bastard,' I said, and gave him a kiss on the cheek. 'I've had a horrible day. I had to do this disastrous thing on Radio 2. It was absolutely horrendous.'

'I'm sure you were great,' he said, pulling up a bar stool next to mine. 'Another drink?'

Michael is very good-looking and rather rakish. He works in the City (something in derivatives trading), makes quite a bit of money, spends it as though it were water and has only one true love - West Ham. Mel met him about four years ago, fell madly in love, got her heart spectacularly broken, cried for about a year, then - bizarrely - decided that they could still be friends. He is quite hard to resist.

'Go on, then,' I said, settling in for another drink. 'So what've you been up to lately?'

There followed a long and complicated tale of his attempts to seduce Lisa, a former lingerie model (I kid you not) he'd met in some less than salubrious East End pub. He had taken her to a very expensive Japanese restaurant, only to find that she had never eaten sushi and nor did she want to try it. Then things got worse.

'I had a bit of a shocker,' Michael admitted. 'She bored me bloody stupid talking about cosmetic surgery all night and then, just to top it all, my card didn't work and I only had the one with me, because my credit card was nicked a couple of weeks ago. Anyway, I ended up having a row with the manager, and then with the bank over the phone, and in the end she had to pay anyway.' He reddened with shame at the very memory. 'Don't think I'll be seeing her again.'

'How appalling,' I said. 'Hope you gave the bank hell. Which one is it?'

'NatWest.'

'Oh, right, and let me guess, you've banked with them

since you went to Middlesex Poly back in '78 because they offered you a free Our Price voucher?'

'I did not go to Middlesex Poly and I was not at college in 1978, Natasha. Jesus, how old do you think I am?'

I shrugged demurely.

'But I think you're right – there may have been record tokens involved,' he admitted.

'But you've been completely happy with the bank's customer service ever since, I take it. Well, at least until the other night.'

'Of course not. They're rubbish. Drive me up the bloody wall. I've been a good customer for – I don't know – fifteen, twenty years – and I'm pretty much always in credit. Got my mortgage with them too. So you'd think they'd be grateful.'

Oh, the naivety.

'But try and speak to them about a problem – like the other night – and no one knows who the hell you are or what's going on. And this is not the first time I've had hassle with cards. Seems like every time I go on holiday, they cancel it, just in case I'm a thief. Plus there are always terrible queues in the branch on Whitechapel High Street.'

'Never thought of switching banks, then?'

'Oh, I can't be arsed. It's just too much hassle.'

Is Breaking up So Hard to Do?

That made me laugh. Michael, who was constantly dodging the hostile attentions of women he had split up with, thought it would be too much trouble to break up with his bank manager. People stay with their banks for lots of reasons, none of them very good. Like Michael, they believe that switching will be too time-consuming. Or they imagine that, like politicians, banks are all the same. They believe that all banks offer pretty much the same products, and the same level of service, so there is little point in moving from one to another. Some people even have a totally irrational sense that by leaving the bank they have stuck with since student days, or since they first began working, they are in some way being disloyal. It's ridiculous.

The Hassle Factor

In my experience, it is a great deal easier to ditch your bank than it is to lose a bunny boiler. OK, I don't have much experience of the latter, but I'm using my imagination. There was a time when moving from one bank to another was a hugely bureaucratic and time-consuming exercise, but these days switching is much simpler.

All you need to do is contact the bank to which you want to move and make your application. You will need to provide two pieces of ID – one to prove who you are (a driver's licence, passport or certified copy of either will do) and one to prove where you live (a recent utilities or council tax bill, for example.) Your new bank will contact your old bank for a list of all your direct debits and standing orders, and they will do all the work for you. It may take several weeks to complete the switch, so you do need to keep funds in both accounts for a while. You may even want to run two accounts at the same time for the first few months, just to make sure that you are happy with the new bank. You will also need to contact your employer, and anyone else who pays you money on a regular basis, to let them know about the switch.

They're All the Same Anyway . . .

They aren't, you know. Switching really can pay dividends. The average current account balance in the UK is more than £1,500. Now, a standard current account from Barclays pays 0.1 per cent interest, while the best account on the market – from Alliance & Leicester – pays around 5 per cent provided you meet a few key criteria. Assuming you held your current account for thirty years, you would waste more than £5,000 by remaining loyal to Barclays, rather than switching away. There are huge differences in overdraft rates too. Barclays charges almost 10 per cent more than A&L should you sink into the red. Most banks levy punitive charges if you should make a mistake. NatWest and Royal Bank of Scotland, for example, charge a whopping £28–£58 for going into unauthorized overdraft and a £30 'paid transaction' fee.

What about Captain Mainwaring?

The idea that you have a bank manger, a rather stern, curmudgeonly figure who may scare you but always has your best interests at heart, is, like *Dad's Army*, unbelievably outdated and should now be laid to rest. Let's just get something straight. You don't have a bank manager. You have a call centre in Solihull, or perhaps Mumbai. If your bank does assign you a 'personal relationship manager', you will soon find that this is bank-speak for 'someone who will try to sell you life insurance'. Do not imagine that when you leave your bank there is a little moustachioed man in an office somewhere, wringing his hands and wondering what he's done wrong.

Banks for Rich and Poor

Accounts with Fees

Packaged or 'premier' accounts usually charge an annual fee of around £100–£200, although some simply impose a minimum salary requirement. In many cases, these are high – some insist that you earn as much as £100,000 a year, or have a similar sum to invest.

In return for your hefty salary, or your fee, you are given access to a better class of service than the average punter. You will be assigned your very own bank manager – usually called a 'relationship manager' or something of that sort – to oversee your affairs and deal with any problems. In addition, there will be a host of other add-ons, such as a share-dealing service, portfolio management, mortgage broking and so on. Many banks also offer free breakdown cover, travel insurance and a concierge service which will sort out travel bookings or arrange for a plumber to come round if the boiler goes on the blink.

Packaged accounts have become very popular. Mintel, the market research group, estimates that we spend around £870 million a year on current accounts. But are they worth it? Much depends on whether you will take advantage of the add-ons offered. The Consumers' Association claims that around 40 per cent of customers use none or just one of the extras. So most people are probably getting a pretty poor deal.

Basic Bank Accounts

At the other end of the scale you have basic bank accounts, which were devised for those who do not meet the credit checks run by banks and building societies and so are unable to open ordinary current accounts. These are no frills accounts: you cannot go overdrawn, you do not get a debit card or cheque-book and you receive minimal, if any, interest. Some accounts offer access through post office branches.

Fifteen banks and building societies offer basic accounts, including the big high street banks and Nationwide, Co-operative Bank, Bank of Ireland and Yorkshire Bank. Nationwide pays 0.5 per cent on balances in credit, while NatWest, Royal Bank of Scotland and Norwich & Peterborough Building Society pay 0.1 per cent. The rest offer no interest at all.

Remember that your apathy, your cynicism or your deference plays neatly into the hands of the big high street banks. These used to be Barclays, Lloyds, Midland and NatWest. A few mergers and takeovers later, they are Barclays, Lloyds TSB, HBSC, Royal Bank of Scotland, which owns NatWest, and HBOS, which was formed by the merger of Halifax and Bank of Scotland. These five dominate the banking sector, sharing 80 per cent of the current account market. Together, they made profits of £29 billion in 2004.

'I'm well aware of the profits the banks make,' Michael said, and sighed. 'Right, if you're sure that I won't have to spend the better part of a day on the phone to a call centre in order to switch, then I'll do it. That'll teach 'em to mess up my dates.'

'Bravo,' I said, and drained the rest of my drink.

'Now, all I need to do is to decide which bank will be the beneficiary of my custom. D'you fancy some dinner while we figure it out?' he asked.

'Sure. Shall we get a table here?'

'No. Come back to my place. I'll cook.'

'You can cook?' I was more than a little surprised.

'I can. I like to think of myself as a chef in the Gordon Ramsay mould,' he said. 'None of your Jamie Olivers for me.'

'Right. I'm impressed.'

'You should be. Now, let's go, and you can bore me to tears with this banking business.'

Michael lives in the East End, just behind the East London Mosque. His early-morning slumbers are punctuated by the call to prayer, he tells me. He reckons it gives the place an exotic feel. Nevertheless, he's thinking of moving.

'I think I've outgrown it,' he said, as we hopped into a cab on Aldwych. 'I've been there for ten years now and I quite fancy going south of the river actually.'

'You are joking,' I said, amazed. I like south of the river, but no one else seems to.

'Not down your way! Not in nappy valley . . .' He grimaced at the very thought. 'Christ, no. I mean somewhere around Borough, Southwark – somewhere like that. It's nice round there these days. Edgy. And I could pretty much walk to work. I've been thinking that now would be a good time to sell. Then I could rent for a year and buy again once house prices have come off a bit more.'

'You think prices will keep falling?' I asked. 'Because I was thinking about looking into buy-to-let. I think I prefer property to a regular personal pension plan.'

Michael did that sharp-intake-of-breath thing that builders do when you've called them round to take a look at a leaky room and they tell you that you've got subsidence.

'Very risky. I'd go for the plain old pension plan option. Yeah, it's dull, but you already own a home, so you're already vulnerable to any fall in house prices. Just be dull.' He smiled at me. 'It suits you.'

Back at Michael's flat, I lived up to my dull reputation by doing a quick Internet search for all the latest rates and account details while Michael rustled up a mean cottage pie. Over dinner, I gave him a quick run-through of his options. These are numerous, because the current account market in the UK has never been so competitive. There really is something for everyone.

How to Pick a Current Account

You will find that if you stick to branch-based banking, you will not be able to get quite such a good rate as you would if you were prepared to bank on the Internet or by phone. If you are nervous of banking in cyberspace, you really shouldn't be: hacking incidents are widely reported but rare. Don't be put off by the silly names Internet banking operations have either: IF, Cahoot and Smile are owned by HBOS, Abbey and the Co-operative Bank – big, established financial institutions all. Real technophobes should check out rates offered on telephone bank accounts, since these are often better than those offered on standard, branch-based accounts.

Watch out for the strings attached to great-looking rates. For example, Alliance & Leicester's Premier Plus account pays 5 per cent, but in order to qualify you must pay at least £1,000 a month into the account and have an email address, because the bank does not send out paper statements. Similarly, Lloyds TSB pays 4 per cent on its Classic Plus account, but you must jump through hoops to benefit from its rate too. You must pay at least £2,000 a month into the account and you must log on to your account via the Internet at least three times every three months. Moreover, if you have more than £5,000 in your account, the rates on the excess falls to 0.1 per cent. Many accounts will pay a higher rate if you agree to forgo a chequebook.

Some of the best accounts have relatively high minimum income requirements (or minimum monthly funding requirements, which amounts to the same thing, since low earners will not be able to pay £2,000 a month into their account). However, do not be discouraged: Citibank, Alliance & Leicester and Cahoot all offer good accounts with low or no minimum salary requirements.

If you are always in the red, in-credit interest rates will not be of much interest to you. You should instead scrutinize overdraft rates and charges. The days when banks could get away with charging extortionate overdraft rates are over. You needn't be fleeced simply because you are overdrawn: Alliance & Leicester charges nothing for a year, then levies a rate of 7.9 per cent, while Nationwide's Flex Account charges 7.75 per cent a year.

HOW SAFE IS CYBERSPACE?

Banking on the Internet freaks some people out because they believe that it is fundamentally unsafe. Every now and again, you read stories in the papers about how a bank's security system was breached, revealing customers' account details to the Internet community at large. In fact, Internet banking is fairly safe. Entering your credit or debit card details into a website is generally a great deal safer than reading those details out over the phone, since it is much easier to listen in on a phone line (either physically or through a phone tap) than it is to hack an encrypted website.

That said, there are some risks associated with Internet banking. Systems breaches do occur. When they do, however, rest assured that the bank is responsible: you will not lose any money.

That is no reason to let down your guard. There are scammers out there, and they may try to target you directly. The most common scam is known as 'phishing': you receive an email purporting to be from your bank or credit card company usually saying that there has been some sort of problem on your account, or that they are carrying out a security check, and that you need to resend your bank details, along with passwords, in order to reset the system. The message may even say that your account will be closed unless you do so. Never, ever reply to these emails. Your bank will never ask for your details in full, either over the phone or in an email. Note down the address of the sender, then report the email to your bank before deleting it.

Identity Fraud

This is a far more dangerous threat. ID theft and ID fraud are among the fastest-growing crimes in the UK. ID fraudsters use your identity in criminal activity, while ID thieves misappropriate your identity, which they then use to obtain goods and services in your name. ID theft is scary because it can be months or even years before you realize that it is going on. The thief may apply for loans and cards in your name, running up huge debts in the process, but it is only once that person defaults, or once you are refused credit, that you know something is wrong.

There are ways to protect yourself. The best is never to throw anything with your name and address on it into the bin without first destroying it. Ideally, you should invest in a shredder – you can buy them for less than £25. Alternatively, just tear everything up into very small pieces and throw it out with your rubbish (not with the recycling, as this is easier to sift through). You could put the pieces in with a bit of rotting veg or your baby's dirty nappies in order to ensure that only the most committed of thieves will be able to get their hands on them.

Always check your bank and credit card statements, and get a copy of your credit file once a year to make sure there are no nasty surprises there. If you have bank accounts that you no longer use on a regular basis, close them. An easy time for ID thieves to strike is when you move home, so make sure that your mail is redirected and that you inform relevant institutions of your change of address.

Prevention is very important, since it takes on average sixty hours for victims to sort out their affairs and clear their names once their ID has been stolen. Cifas, the fraud prevention service, says that in cases where a 'total hijack' has occurred, where as many as thirty lenders might be involved, it can take the victim up to 400 hours and cost as much as £8,000 before everything gets back to normal. Any financial losses will be recouped by you, but this can take months, leaving you up to your eyeballs in debt in the interim. You can suffer serious, if temporary, damage to your credit status too.

What about Service?

Getting a decent rate is all very well, but there is more to choosing a current account than simple number crunching. The most common causes of bank rage are, after all, not poor current account rates. Research shows that customers are most likely to switch banks following an experience such as a statement error or an encounter with a rude staff member than they are in protest over poor rates.

Customers resent the fact that they can never get to speak

to an actual person, are enraged by the inefficiency with which complaints are handled and resent the high charges that are levied for minor infractions. This is particularly infuriating when you are struggling with debt and, by accident, drift above your overdraft limit, only to be charged £15 for a letter from the bank informing you that you have done so, in the process taking you even further into the red. We loathe the fact that it takes just as long to clear money transferred electronically as it does when paying in a cheque. We hate the way our banks are forever trying to sell us stuff. Entrust your money to a bank and are they grateful? No! They simply try to take more of your money by flogging you substandard life assurance, investment accounts or travel insurance.

The problem for the customer is that it is clearly a great deal more difficult to compare the quality of service offered by different banks than it is to compare their rates. However, *Which?*, the magazine of the Consumers' Association, has done some research into customer satisfaction with various banks. It found that, on average, just over 30 per cent of customers were satisfied with the service offered by the Big Four. Best for service, *Which?* says, are Smile, the Internet bank owned by Co-operative Bank, First Direct and Nationwide.

The *Guardian* and *Observer* newspapers run an annual Consumer Finance Awards poll, in which they ask readers which banks they believe deliver great service. The winner in the current account category in 2005 was First Direct, which scored 4.28 points out of 5.

First Direct claims to be recommended by a customer every five seconds. Its rates are not table-topping (the in-credit rate is 2 per cent, the overdraft rate is cheap at 9.9 per cent), but they are still a vast improvement on those offered by many high street banks. First Direct's closest competitors in the Consumer Finance Awards were Smile, the Co-operative Bank,

Nationwide and Alliance & Leicester, which also appeared in the top five.

Ethics

Sceptics might argue that the appearance of an ethical bank (the Co-operative Bank and its Internet spin-off, Smile) and of a building society (Nationwide) might reflect the leftist tendencies of *Guardian* and *Observer* readers. But these did feature in the *Which?* research too.

If you are interested in ethical banking, your choice is fairly restricted. Aside from the Co-op Bank and Smile, there are just two main ethical institutions, Triodos Bank and the Ecology Building Society, and neither of these offer current accounts, though they do offer savings and mortgages. The Co-operative Bank and Smile have the same ethical policy, which is spelt out in detail on the Co-op Bank's website (*www.co-operative bank.co.uk*). You can obtain a full ethical policy information pack by calling 0845 714 2128. In short, the bank seeks through its investments (or lack thereof) to promote human rights, corporate social responsibility, environmental awareness, social enterprise and animal welfare, and to curb the arms trade and genetic modification.

The Co-op Bank's current account rates are not impressive. It pays no interest on balances in credit and its overdraft rate is almost 20 per cent. Smile's rates are much better. It pays 3.25 per cent on balances in credit and charges 9.9 per cent if you go overdrawn.

Muslims can also find a bank to suit their ethical and religious standpoint. The Islamic Bank of Britain opened its doors in September 2003, offering savings and current accounts, and is soon to launch a mortgage, as well as business accounts and a credit card. Islamic banking hit the mainstream in February 2005, when Lloyds TSB became the first of the big banks to introduce a current account compatible with sharia law.

Mutuality: Are Building Societies Better?

Mutuals do not offer the best rates on current accounts (although their rates are definitely worth checking out when it comes to mortgages and savings), but there is an argument that belonging to a mutual is inherently better than being the customer of a bank. The reasoning goes that building societies are owned and run for the benefit of their members, rather than for the benefit of shareholders, therefore building society customers – who are its members – get a better deal than bank customers. Because banks have to pay dividends to shareholders, their costs are around 35 per cent higher, the Building Societies Association (BSA) says, and ultimately it is customers who have to cover these costs. However much the mutual movement claims moral superiority over the PLC, building societies are not above reproach. Many could be run a great deal more efficiently. Few allow their members the right to vote on directors' pay and there are plenty of fat, or at the very least fairly corpulent, cats around as evidence.

Dinner with Michael ended up being a long night. He didn't make any final decisions about banks, although we narrowed it down to two or three. Then we spent a long time moaning about our respective relationship troubles. Michael told me that I always went for safe, slightly boring types and then obviously resented them for being safe and boring.

'Ben isn't boring!' I protested.

'Oh, please. He was always talking about his batting average.'

I was a bit miffed. Michael was not the first person to have revealed if not a dislike of, then at least a certain disdain for, Ben (in a drunken moment, Nikki had admitted that she thought he looked a bit funny, and complained that he was always talking about himself). It was all a little harsh. The poor boy hadn't even left the country yet (administrative problems, apparently) and they were already dancing on his grave. I said that I thought Michael was talking rubbish and that, anyway, I wasn't going to take relationship advice from someone who tried to sleep with former lingerie models.

'What d'ya mean tried to?'

I got home around two. There were a couple of messages on the answer phone. The first was from Mel, who for some bizarre reason had been listening to Radio 2 mid-afternoon and had heard the disastrous interview. She, of course, found it hilarious. Then she said we ought to go for a drink before she topped herself (something about hating her job), and also that her aunt wanted to talk to me about getting divorced. Cheerful.

There was a message from Dad, saying he'd been to see Gran and that she wasn't looking great. The liar (Gran that is). I spoke to her three days ago and she said she was on top form. You can't trust that woman. And then there was a message from Kate, asking me to go up to their place for the weekend. This didn't seem odd at the time, but when I woke up the next morning, just a trifle hungover, I rang her straight away.

'You want me to come and stay with you on Valentine's weekend? That's just . . . weird.' I was a bit suspicious.

'Oh, for Christ's sake, Tasha, you know I don't believe in all that crap. Alex and I don't do Valentine's. It's just ridiculous commercial tosh. But I know all the other saddos do, so I thought you might want to come and see Alex and me and just hang out. Mel's going to be in Oxford too – she's seeing that aunt who's getting divorced. What's her name?'

'Susannah.'

'Yeah, that's the one.'

'OK. Lovely. I would love to come and stay,' I said, secretly relieved to have an excuse not to be sitting on the sofa drinking all alone. If anyone asked what I did for Valentine's Day, I could say I'd been away for the weekend, all mysterious-like.

'Hang on,' I said. 'How did you know I wouldn't have plans for Valentine's Day?'

'I just . . . I don't know.'

'You thought because I was so hideous that no one would ever ask me out again.'

'Yup.'

Kate was waiting on the platform when I got to Oxford. She looked exhausted.

'Double shift in A&E,' she explained as we walked to her car.

'I don't know how you do it,' I said.

'Well, we were short-staffed. Not much of an option really.' She smiled wearily.

'God, you should have just spent the weekend sleeping, Kate, instead of inviting guests over.'

'Oh, I don't intend to entertain you,' she said, slinging my bag on to the back seat of her rather battered-looking Peugeot. 'I was rather hoping you might do the cooking, so that Alex and I can spend the weekend in bed.'

I gave her a filthy look.

'No, darling. I wanted to see you! I felt bad about the whole engagement party debacle – you know, insulting your book idea and then giving poor Ames such a hard time.'

'Oh, yes. Did she forgive you for that, then?'

'Of course she did. Actually, you know what Amy's like – total lightweight – I don't think she could remember half of it.'

'Probably for the best,' I said. 'God – was that the last time I saw you? Amy's thing? It's been ages . . .'

Kate filled me in on her Christmas news. They were with Alex's parents up in Leeds, which was delightful except for Alex's mother point blank refusing to accept that they had still not tied the knot.

'"It's all very well now it's just the two of you," she kept screeching at me, "but my grandchildren are not going to be bastards!"' Kate rolled her eyes. 'Of course, it's just assumed that the grandchildren are on the way any time now and that I'm going to stop working. I shudder to think what will happen if we actually do have kids eventually and I insist on carrying on.'

'*If* you have kids?' I asked.

'Mmmmm. I'm not totally convinced, you know. Neither is Al. And at the moment we're struggling to get our own lives together. We are both so bloody sick of living in crappy rented accommodation. We're desperate to buy somewhere.' She jammed on the brakes to avoid a cyclist swerving out in front of us. 'Bloody students!' she yelled at a frightened-looking young man. 'The prices in this place are just as bad as London,' she went on. 'It's not going to be easy to afford anything on our salaries.'

Kate and Alex lived in a decidedly ramshackle terraced place in Jericho. Its previous occupants had been not just students but male physics undergraduates, so the place had been in a pretty awful state when they moved in. Unsurprisingly, the landlord didn't want to know. But it was dirt cheap and they had done an awful lot of work on it, so it looked fairly decent these days.

'No more slugs and mice in the bathroom, then?' I asked gingerly. I'd had a nasty shock while taking a bath one morning soon after they'd moved in.

'Nope. We're living slug-free these days. And I haven't seen a rodent for months.'

Alex was already home when we arrived.

'Just opening a bottle of red,' he called out as we negotiated the bicycles in the hallway. 'Fancy a glass?'

'Fantastic,' we said in chorus.

Kate nipped upstairs to change and I settled down at the dining-room table for a chat. Al is probably my favourite of the girls' other halves. He's clever, laid-back and self-deprecating, with a wit as dry as a tinder box.

'Haven't seen you for bloody ages,' he said, handing me a glass of wine and giving me a peck on the cheek. 'You look well. And you're single again! Excellent!'

'Mmm,' I mumbled.

'I always thought Ben was a bit of a tool,' Alex said, a bit too honestly.

'Oh, right.' I didn't really know how to reply to that.

'Mmm. Bit of a wanker,' he elaborated.

'Oh, well, it's a good thing he dumped me, then, isn't it?' I replied rather grumpily. I was actually starting to feel a bit sorry for Ben.

'He didn't dump *you*,' Alex said. 'But even if he had it wouldn't matter, because he's a wanker.'

The conversation was starting to get a bit circular, so

I was relieved to hear Kate clattering down the stairs. She had changed into jeans and boots, with a snugly fitting low-cut top.

'We going out?' I asked.

'Yes!' Kate smiled. 'We're going to meet a friend of Al's for dinner.'

'Oh, I knew it!' I cried. 'This is a bloody set-up!'

'Of course it is.' Alex grinned at me. 'Go jump in the shower, then put on something slinky. We've got a booking at Gee's for eight.'

I tramped upstairs, calling them both many different types of bastard as I went.

A few minutes later I was standing in Kate and Al's spare room, wrapped in a towel, glaring at the paltry selection of clothes I had brought for the weekend. Slinky, my arse. Why didn't I bring the other, more flattering jeans? Ones without a stain of some sort on the right thigh would have been an improvement too.

'Kate!' I yelled. 'I need to borrow something to wear!'

I ended up in a pair of Kate's jeans (Topshop, nice cut) and my own top (Paul & Joe, floaty and interesting) and some very high heels (glamorous, but deeply uncomfortable).

'I wish you hadn't done this bloody fixing-up thing,' I complained as I hobbled out to the waiting minicab, concentrating hard on not falling over. 'You do know that Ben is still in England?'

'So what?' Al asked callously.

'So . . . I don't know. Who drew the short straw, then, anyway?'

Kate looked at me blankly.

'Who's the poor unfortunate you're fixing me up with?'

'His name's Mark and he works in the City,' Kate said,

settling into the back seat, 'so you should have plenty to talk about.'

'I met him on my brother's stag do last year,' Alex said.

'You don't like your brother,' I said warily.

'No, I know, and his friends are tossers,' Al said.

'Great.'

'No, I mean complete idiots. Apart from this one bloke, Mark, who is a City boy but was also quite civilized and a good laugh. Since then we've played squash a couple of times – he comes down to Oxford quite a lot, as his parents live near Witney.'

'Oh,' I said, definitely not loving the sound of this. 'So the guy you're fixing me up with is someone you met once at a stag do and then played squash with twice.'

'Well, we only played squash once actually,' Alex admitted.

'Right.'

'Never mind that!' Kate interrupted. 'Jeez. The point, Tasha, is that he is very good-looking and he earns a fortune!'

'Not that you think I'm shallow or anything.'

'I know you are, darling. You're obsessed with money.'

Kate never could get her head around the fact that just because I write about finance does not mean I am obsessed with money. I pointed out none of my past three boyfriends had been well paid at all.

'They weren't much to look at either,' Kate mused unkindly.

Gee's is a lovely place housed in a giant Victorian conservatory on the Banbury Road. It's been a favourite haunt for Kate and me ever since she moved down here – many a sunny summer afternoon has been misspent over a long, lazy, boozy lunch. Nevertheless, I wasn't really looking forward to this dinner.

'I wish you hadn't fixed me up,' I grumbled as we arrived.

But I changed my mind almost immediately on entering the restaurant.

'This is Mark,' Al said, introducing me to the very tall and extremely attractive man leaning on the bar.

'Hi,' I said, grinning hugely. 'Lovely to meet you.'

And it was. He was charming, witty and obviously very clever. And about six foot four, blond-ish and athletic-looking. ('At least he's not dark and emaciated, like yours usually are,' Kate hissed at me when he'd disappeared to the loo. Actually, I like 'em dark and emaciated, but blond and athletic makes a nice enough change.)

Conversation fairly rattled along, which was a huge relief, as I'd been fearing a stilted evening. But we had loads to talk about. He knew quite a few journalists, having worked for a short spell on the *Telegraph* before going into investment banking, he'd travelled loads and – surprisingly for a City boy – he had done a bit of work for the Labour Party.

'I wrote some stuff for them on ways to get people on lower incomes to save more for retirement,' he said. 'Stakeholder and all that, you know?'

'And did the government take your advice?' I asked.

'Uh . . . not really.'

'So that's why stakeholders have been such a failure, then?'

He laughed. 'Well, perhaps not a failure, but . . .'

'Actually, I should get one,' I admitted.

'You don't have a pension plan?' He looked aghast. I must have too, because he went on, 'Sorry . . . sorry. That is a really boring thing to say, but I'm genuinely surprised. Personal finance people are always banging on about how you have to start a pension plan by the time you start teething, aren't they?'

I nodded. 'They are, but we're all hypocrites. Do as we say, y'know? Anyway, I was thinking maybe about buy-to-let, instead of just a straight pension plan. Not straight away, obviously, as I have to save up a bit more, but a few years down the line.'

Mark looked dubious. In fact, his reaction was exactly the same as Michael's had been. Stick to the boring stuff, don't rely too much on property. He had some good suggestions of funds and fund managers I should be thinking about. So, clever, attractive and useful. A winning combination.

'Could you two stop jabbering on about pensions?' Alex asked eventually. 'Christ.'

We all went on to some nasty little basement bar on Walton Street for a few more drinks before staggering home to Alex and Kate's. Mark called a taxi to go back to Witney, and we shyly exchanged contact details in front of an openly gloating Kate. He promised to call soon.

I woke up to a text from him wishing me Happy Valentine's. Although he sent it at seven thirty – rather earlier than I would have liked to be woken on a Saturday morning – it still put me in a good mood for the rest of the day, which Kate and I spent mooching around our old Oxford haunts.

Back at Kate's, we chopped vegetables in anticipation of Mel and Susannah's visit. Kate had invited them around for dinner that evening. The likelihood of it being a swinging time were slim. Mel had already called to warn us that Susannah was in a bad way but really needed some advice and Mel was at a bit of a loss. Plus, she was trying to take Susannah's mind off the fact that it was Valentine's Day and her husband of twenty-one years was at an expensive hotel in Barcelona with Kim, thirty-five, a vivacious redhead.

I had met Susannah a couple of times before – she and Mel were very close. Mel had a quite spectacular falling-out with her parents when she was about sixteen and ended up moving in with Susannah and Ed for a few months. Susannah, being arty and laid-back, was a little more understanding of Mel's teenage traumas than her parents had been. I think everyone has (or should have) an older relative like Susannah. Perhaps ten years or so younger than your parents and much, much cooler. The relative who will (guiltily) share a cigarette with you when you're fifteen and you hate everyone and life just isn't fair.

Life certainly did not seem particularly fair for Susannah right now. Sitting at Kate's kitchen table, she looked smaller than I remembered and certainly more frail.

'I feel very lost,' she said to me. 'He moved out about six weeks ago and last week he rang to say that we needed to do something about bills. You see, because I haven't worked – well, I've never had a real job – I've never had my own account.' She looked embarrassed. 'I know it must sound odd to you, but I moved straight from my parents' home to our home, and then I had the kids almost straight away, so . . .'

'It isn't odd,' I said. 'It's quite common actually.'

'Well, Ed always paid all the bills, so I didn't open my own bank account. He just gave me money when I needed it – it's never been a problem. I don't even have my own credit card! But now . . . Well, he's living in a flat in Bristol now and I don't think he sees any reason why he should carry on paying my gas bill and my phone bill. Not sure how I'm going to pay them, but there you go!' She laughed nervously. 'I went up to the Alliance & Leicester in Chipping Norton on Saturday and it was just a nightmare. I had my passport with me, but they said I needed another piece of ID, one which proved where I live. But my name isn't on any of the bills, and they wouldn't accept a mobile phone bill because apparently that can be sent to any address, it doesn't have to be your home one. I just felt really stupid.'

Who Are You and How Do You Prove It?

These days you must provide two proofs of ID if you want to open a bank account. In fact, you may even find that your bank asks for ID years after you opened your account. This is because the money-laundering laws were tightened up following the 11 September attacks, so some banks are retro-identifying their customers. It may be annoying, but it's the law now, so you have to put up with it.

When you buy a financial product, you need to prove who you are and where you live. For proof of identity, a passport, driver's licence, Inland Revenue tax notification or benefits book is the best bit of documentation to provide. To prove your address, you should take along a recent council tax or utility bill, or a recent bank statement. Banks and building societies will accept alternative proofs, however, but there is no standard list, so you'll have to ask the bank in question if you do not, for example, have a utility bill in your name. In some cases, a letter from a professional, such as a lawyer or doctor, will be accepted.

If you are simply trying to open a current account, then having no credit history should not be a problem. However, it is helpful if you are on the electoral roll, so if you haven't registered to vote, do so. However, without any credit history you will struggle to get a credit card or a loan. The best way to proceed is to open your current account first. Once you have an established record with the bank, you will find it increasingly easy to buy other financial products.

But it wasn't just current accounts that were getting Susannah down. Since her children had now left home, there was no need to keep a four-bedroom house for just her to live in. Ed was determined to sell the family home they had lived in for the best part of twenty years. And then there was the problem of what she would do for money. She had no savings of her own, no credit cards, nothing. Obviously she would get something – presumably a pretty substantial amount from the divorce settlement – but that was still some way off. And even if she did get a decent settlement, she would still need to think about getting work. She looked utterly terrified. I really felt for her. It can't be easy entering the labour market in your late forties.

I was on the train on my way back to London on Sunday when the phone went. It was Michael.

'So, you all man-hating again?'

'Huh?'

'I hear you had dinner with Susannah last night. I spoke to Mel this morning.'

'Why is that you always know everyone's business? You're such a gossip. Are you sure you're not gay?'

He was chuckling to himself on the other end of the line.

'Anyway, the answer to your question is yes.'

'What question?'

'The man-hating one. You're all scum. What do you want, anyway?'

'Well, I think in the end I've decided to go for convenience and rate. I just thought I'd let you know that I have completed my online application for a Cahoot account.'

'Bravo.'

'I think the name's good, actually. Cahoot. In cahoots. It sounds sort of sneaky and underhand. That appeals to me.'

'That's because you're a man,' I replied.

The train entered a tunnel and Michael was unceremoniously cut off.

Back in London, for the first time in for ever, I checked my emails before my phone messages.

And there it was!

To: *Me@hotmail.com*
From: *MarcusGray@mlim.co.uk* (Hang on. His name is Marcus?)
Re: pensions

Hi
How are you?
I've attached the pensions info we talked about. There was clearly no great urgency in me sending you this, but I'm using it as a lame excuse to get in touch and ask you out to dinner. How are you fixed Thursday? Let me know.
Fingers crossed,

Mark

I danced around the room briefly (who cares if his name is Marcus!) and poured myself a large glass of Pinot Grigio. This was fantastic. A new man already and the old one was barely cold in the ground, so to speak. Feeling loads better, I sat back on the sofa, put my feet up on the coffee table and flicked on TV.

There was a re-run of *Sex and the City* on Channel 4. Suddenly, I was gripped by fear. What the hell was I going to wear?

Dinner went well. Very well indeed. (And I wore one of Nikki's cast-off Diane Von Furstenberg dresses, since you ask.) So well, I was tempted to invite Mark to Amy and Ade's engagement party, but since Ben had not been officially uninvited, I felt that I really couldn't. Not that he would turn up, of course. Would he? He didn't, but that didn't stop me spending the whole evening watching the door, waiting for him to show.

4. Rainy Days: Saving and Investing

Jackie rang me – way too early – the day after the party.

'Just because you have children doesn't mean everyone is up at bloody nine fifteen on a Saturday,' I bitched at her.

'Oh, God. Sorry. Were you asleep?' Sometimes I wonder about parents. They really do behave as though they cannot remember what it was like to be child-free.

'I have a terrible hangover,' Jackie said quietly. 'I haven't drunk that much in ages.'

'I don't feel so bad actually,' I said. 'But it could be that I'm still drunk.'

There was a pause.

'You OK, Jacks?' I asked.

'I am. I was just wondering if I could trouble you for some advice. Would you mind if we came round?'

My heart sank. Much as I love Roman and Lila, I had been looking forward to a day of lying on my sofa, wading through the Saturday papers and watching rubbish TV. But I said that was fine, of course, dragged myself into the shower, made a hasty attempt to child-proof the flat and put on some coffee. I was just starting to feel human when the phone rang again.

Oh, please be cancelling, I thought. But it wasn't Jackie.

'It's me.' It was him. Ben.

'Oh, hi,' I said, all casual, heart pounding. Suddenly I think I can feel that hangover coming on after all.

'I just wanted to tell you that the permits are all sorted.

I'm leaving on Tuesday. I wanted . . . to make sure you were OK.'

'I feel like death warmed up actually,' I said. 'I was out celebrating last night.'

'Right.'

'It was Amy and Ade's engagement party. You were invited, remember?' I said tetchily.

'Oh, right, yeah. Sorry. Good, was it?'

Like you're interested.

'I'm fine, Ben. I'll be fine. You're fine, aren't you?'

'Yes, I –'

'So there you go, we're both fine.'

'I'm sorry.'

'Yes, I know. Look, I have to go. Jackie's coming round with the kids. I hope it all goes well for you over there.'

We hung up. I thought I was going to cry, but I didn't. I just felt guilty.

Jackie arrived within an hour. Since it was unseasonably warm and sunny for late February, we decided to take the kids to Clapham Common. Lila, who had woken the moment the car engine was turned off, had begun to wail. Roman was kicking up his heels in his pushchair. 'Go, go, go, go, GO!' he was yelling. Oh, yes, the hangover was definitely kicking in now. Thankfully Lila had dozed off again by the time we had reached the common, a ten-minute walk. Roman was still yelling, but once we had let him out of the chair to play in the sandpit (and dog shit, no doubt), he seemed happy enough. Jackie, on the other hand, seemed very worried.

'This is not very easy for me,' she said quietly, fidgeting with the fringe of Lila's blanket.

'What is it, Jacks?' I was suddenly struck by the fear. She

was going to tell me something terrible. Sam was having an affair. Or she was having an affair. Or someone had contracted a terrible disease.

Jackie took a deep breath. 'I think we're going to have to send the kids private,' she said softly, still staring at her fidgeting fingers.

You would have thought she had just told me she was planning to sell them into the white slave trade from the look of guilty anguish on her face.

'It's awful, I know,' she rushed on before I could say anything. 'It's terrible, but the local places are just . . . awful. Really poor. We just couldn't . . .' she tailed off.

'Jackie! It isn't that bad! You don't have to justify yourself to me. If the schools round your way are no good, then . . . Well, any parent with the means would do the same. I mean, it's either that or move house, isn't it?'

'We've thought about that. But we love the house and all our friends are here. We really don't want to have to go. But, as you say, it's a question of means.'

I could see where this was going now.

'You have anything saved up?' I asked.

'Not really. So I wrote off to the Independent Schools Council last week for some info and I got the stuff through the post this morning. Christ, I got a shock! You're looking at something like £3,000 a term for day pupils – and that's now! Imagine what they'll be charging by the time Lila is eleven!'

'It is horribly expensive,' I agreed. 'Ideally, if you want your kids to go to private school you have to start saving around the time you conceive. But all is not lost. If you start putting decent amounts aside now, you can at least ease the pain for when the time comes.'

It is mightily weird to discuss private school fees with

Jackie. If you had known her a decade ago, you would understand. She and Sam were the archetypal hippie couple at college: dreadlocked, tie-dyed and permanently stoned. They banked with the Co-op, went hunt-sabbing on the weekends, travelled to London to march against racism and student loans or for the whales and the rights of Third World farmers to sell their coffee beans at realistic prices. After we left college, Jackie became a teacher and Sam went to work in marketing for Fair Trade. They were doing all right, but any money they had back then was spent on holidays in Goa or Vietnam. They maintained a deep distrust of financial services companies, so very little was saved. But if a child is a hand grenade thrown into a marriage, it can torpedo the firmest of principles too. There was no way that darling Roman and precious Lila were going to be educated at some ropy north London comprehensive.

'OK, then, Jacks,' I said, when she had returned from persuading Roman not to beat the little blonde girl with whom he was sharing the sandpit with a spade, 'what we need to do is think strategy.'

'Right,' she said, breathing in deeply. 'I'm ready to soak up knowledge. Assume I know nothing. Because I don't. Know anything, I mean.'

Got a Dream?

Fretting over whether or not you are going to be able to afford to send your children to private school is, admittedly, a problem of affluence. But do not believe that those of us of more modest means and dreams should not develop a strategy too. Don't believe for a second that just because you're young, poor and would sooner open your veins than subject your kid to Eton you do not need to undertake a bit of financial planning.

You might believe that you cannot afford to save. Perhaps you have nothing left at the end of the month, once the rent has been paid and the essentials bought from the supermarket. Perhaps you have nothing left over once you have bought three pairs of shoes and some DVDs. Not everyone wants to make sacrifices in order to save money. Not everyone is prepared to give up nights out on the town or dinner with their husband in their favourite restaurant a few times a month.

Nor should you be forced to live on bread and water simply in order to save money. Saving and investing are activities that are supposed to improve your quality of life, not ruin it. There is no point in making yourself miserable by giving up everything you enjoy most in life to save for some theoretical rainy day. Having said that, there is no point in burying your head in the sand either. If you want to maintain anything like the standard of living that you have when you are working once you are retired, then you will have to save. The state will not keep you in the style to which you are accustomed. Deal with it.

It is always surprising how much you can save by making minor, and sometimes painless, changes to your lifestyle. Switching electricity and gas supplier can save you a couple of hundred pounds a year in some cases. Hunting down cheaper motor, home and travel insurance will save you tens, and perhaps hundreds, of pounds a year too. If you have a mortgage, you can save thousands by switching to a better deal, particularly if you pay your bank's standard variable rate. A pack-a-day smoker who decides to quit has an extra £1,800 or so at her disposal each year. Running in the park, rather than at the gym, could save you from £360 a year upwards, depending on how swank or shabby your gym is. Most people can find room in their budget to make some savings, however small.

Once you've scraped together a few pennies to save, you need to consider four essential factors that will determine where you put your money.

Goals

These can be long or short term, specific or vague. There are likely to be many of them, so draw up a list. Maybe you would like to go on holiday to Croatia next summer, to buy your own flat within the next five years, to be able to afford to have kids within ten years, to retire at fifty-five . . . You may find it easier to think in broader terms: perhaps you want to build up one fund for short-term emergencies or spending sprees, and one to meet future goals yet to be decided on.

Short-term goals are likely to take priority, and so they should. But do not let the short term obscure the long. Try not to let longer-term projects slip out of view, since before you know it the short term will have become the long term and you will be up the proverbial creek.

Resources

How much you save depends on two things: the amount you can afford to save and the amount you need to save. For most of us, what we actually put aside is determined by how much is left over at the end of the month, if anything, rather than what we need to put aside in order to reach some specific goal by some specific date. But if – like Jackie and Sam – you do have to meet a specific goal by a specific date, you will have to think about things in terms of need. You may need to make additional sacrifices.

Remember that even if you want to invest in the stock market, you do not have to have enormous amounts to put aside. Regular savings plans allow you to put as little as £50 a month into an investment fund. That's £1.70 a day – less than a cup of coffee from Starbucks.

Risk

If you plan to do more than simply stash cash in a savings account, you need to think about risk. Any investment involves an element of risk, so what you must ask yourself is how much of an appetite for risk you have. The interesting thing is that most people believe their appetite for risk is quite large, until they lose all their money and then realize that, after all, they are quite cautious really. So the question you need to ask yourself is what you can afford to lose. If you really cannot stand to lose any money at all, then you must stick to saving, not investing. But bear in mind that the downside of this is that your money will not grow in the way that it might if it were invested in shares. It will deliver a steady return, the size of which depends on the level of interest rates, but there is no scope for huge capital growth.

Timing

Risk and timing are linked. In theory, the longer your timescale, the more risk you can afford to take, since the longer the time you have to recover from any setbacks. As your deadline nears, the more cautious you should become, in order to protect your gains and minimize the risk of losses. So – again in theory, since this will depend on other factors – the young can afford to take risks that the old cannot. Unless you have at the very least five and preferably ten years to invest, you should steer clear of the stock market altogether. On a shorter timescale, you will find yourself at the mercy of market volatility. Your money needs time to grow, and if the market falls, it will need time to recover.

'So,' I said, teeth starting to chatter slightly (the weather had taken a sharp turn for the worse), 'we know what your goal is – to send the kids to private school. We have a timescale. Eight years for the first tranche of Roman's fees, and then a series of other deadlines will follow that – term after term, year after year. Because you can stagger payments, we should be able to get a nice mix of investments. So what we need to talk about is how much you've got to save and how much you can afford to lose.'

'OK,' said Jackie, shivering. 'But could we do that back at the flat, cos it's bloody freezing out here and my children are starting to turn blue?'

Jackie shoehorned a decidedly grubby Roman into his pushchair and we set off, with Lila just starting to stir in her papoose, which was slung around my shoulders. By the time we got halfway home she was announcing, in no uncertain terms, that she felt it might be time for lunch. Back at my place, I made tea while Jackie fed Lila and gave Roman a quick wash and a sandwich. We placed him in front of a *Shrek 2* DVD and persuaded Lila to play with some incredibly interesting empty cardboard boxes that I found in my study. Outside, the sky had darkened and it was starting to rain.

Before You Start . . .

Before you start investing, there are a few things you should do. First, you should clear any significant debts you have, aside from your mortgage. Second, if you haven't already, you should start making provision for retirement, through a pension plan or in some other way. And finally, if you have children, you must buy life insurance.

How Risk-averse Are You?

We're all risk-averse. No one wants to lose money. But many of us will accept some level of risk if that means that the potential rewards are boosted. Jackie, like many women, had decided that any risk was too much.

When I started to protest, she snapped, 'This is my kids' education we're talking about!'

'And you stand a much better chance of building up the kind of fund that you need to put two children through private education within the next fifteen years if you take on some risk.'

I wandered off into my study in search of some evidence and returned brandishing a fascinating-sounding document, the Barclays Equity Gilt Study. Jackie wrinkled her nose at me.

'It analyses the returns produced by various assets, such as cash, shares and bonds,' I explained, flicking open my laptop. 'Now, pay attention. I'm going to show you something.'

Greater Risk = Greater (Potential) Reward

The Barclays Equity Gilt Study shows that over the past twenty years cash has produced a real return averaging 4.4 per cent a year. Equities – or shares – have produced an average return of 8 per cent. So, assuming that twenty years ago you had taken the decision to put £100 a month into the average cash savings account, you would now be sitting on a fund of more than £38,000. That doesn't sound too bad, does it? However, if you had invested the money in a stock market fund producing the average return of 8 per cent, you would now have almost £60,000.

Jackie looked impressed. 'OK. So maybe the risk element isn't so bad.'

'Mmmm, well, don't get too excited, because an average return of 8 per cent a year from shares is pretty good, and just because it happened over the last two decades does not mean it's going to happen for the next two decades. In fact, there are plenty of good arguments why that won't happen.'

Many economists and investors believe that the gains seen from shares in the 1980s and 1990s in Britain and America were unusually high, and that we are now likely to see lower returns over the medium to long term. That doesn't mean that shares aren't worth investing in, it just means that no one should count on 8 per cent growth each year, every year.

How Much Can You Afford to Save?

In some cases, it makes sense to work backwards on this one. If, say, your goal is to go travelling for a year in two years' time and you estimate that you will need at least £3,000 to cover the trip, then it's easy. Three grand over twenty-four months is £125 a month. But sometimes working backwards is impossible, or simply too daunting. Jackie's case was one of those.

'I'm not even going to try to hazard a guess as to what school fees for two children might be in around ten years' time, since I think the figures will get too depressing as well as being wildly inaccurate,' I told Jackie. 'I think what we should do is establish how much you think you and Sam could realistically put aside each month for the next decade.'

'That's impossible, Natasha!' Jackie protested. 'I can tell you what we can put aside for the next twelve months or so, but after that . . . Well, we might have another baby, I might or might not go back to work, Sam might get promoted . . .'

'Sure – I know this is going to have to be vague. Let's be conservative and assume that you'll have to make the savings on one salary.'

I grabbed a pen and paper, and Jacks and I did a few quick calculations.

Monthly Income		**Monthly Outgoings**	
Sam's net salary	£2,300	Pension plan	£350
Child benefit	£120	Life insurance	£45
		Mortgage	£800
		Home insurance	£35
		Car insurance	£80
		Bills	£150
		Groceries	£350
		Clothes	£100
		Entertainment	£150
		Childcare	£150
TOTAL	£2,420	TOTAL	£2,210

Jackie totted up her calculation. 'That leaves us with £210 a month!' she said, looking impressed.

'Not bad at all,' I said.

'So what could we save up over ten years?' she asked eagerly. 'What are we talking about?'

I went back to the laptop.

'Let's be a bit more conservative. We'll predict that shares give an average return of 6.5 per cent a year instead of 8, shall we? In which case, if you save your £210 a month you could be looking at a sum of £35,363.'

'Brilliant!' she enthused.

'Remember that that's still fairly optimistic,' I pointed out. 'But just watch this. Let's say you manage to find another £40 a month to invest – perhaps take it out of your entertainment budget?'

Jackie frowned at me.

'Just hear me out, OK? Say you invest £250 a month. Then you would be left with £42,100.'

'Wow! That's quite a difference.'

'Mmm-hmm. And if you managed to find an extra £90 a month, you could build up a fund of over £50,000.'

'Bloody hell!'

It's amazing how small changes in your savings habits can dramatically affect the outcome over time.

'It's all about compound interest, you see.'

'I don't think I do see, actually,' Jackie said with a small sigh.

Compound Interest

There is a formula for calculating compound interest, but unless you are good at maths, it isn't likely to be much use to you. If you have access to the Internet, you will find compound interest calculators on the web – *www.moneychimp.com* has a good one. What you will notice if you do a few calculations is that relatively small differences in the amounts you invest, and in the rate of growth, have a dramatic impact on the outcome.

For example, if you invest £100 a month over ten years at a

growth rate of 5 per cent, your final pot is £15,528. If you invest £125 a month over ten years at a growth rate of 5 per cent, your final pot is £19,410. The difference in your contributions is £3,000, but the difference in your final pot is almost £3,900. If you are investing £125 and the growth rate rises to 7 per cent, your final pot becomes £21,635. If the growth rate is 10 per cent, your final pot is £25,605.

The other point to note is that starting early really helps. The difference between saving £100 at 5 per cent over ten years and saving the same amount over seven years is almost £5,500, despite the fact that the difference in contribution levels would be just £3,600.

Now, while all these figures look fantastically juicy, we are glossing over a rather important point: that the value of shares can go down as well as up.

'Let's go back to the scenario in which you invest £250 a month. Remember, we were assuming that you might end up with a fund of £42,100? But, if the market were to fall by an average of 3 per cent a year – and this is certainly not impossible, though it is unlikely over a ten-year timescale – you would end up with a fund of just under £26,000.'

'That doesn't sound so terrible,' Jackie said.

'But it is, Jacks! Because your contributions alone over that time would add up to £30,000! So you would have lost about four grand! You would have been better off putting the money under the mattress!'

'Why are you telling me this?' Jackie asked unhappily. 'I was just getting all excited.'

It is important not to get carried away with the thought that you might make a killing on stocks and shares. Remember that in the first few years of the twenty-first century, most people's

FTSE 100 Performance 1990–2005

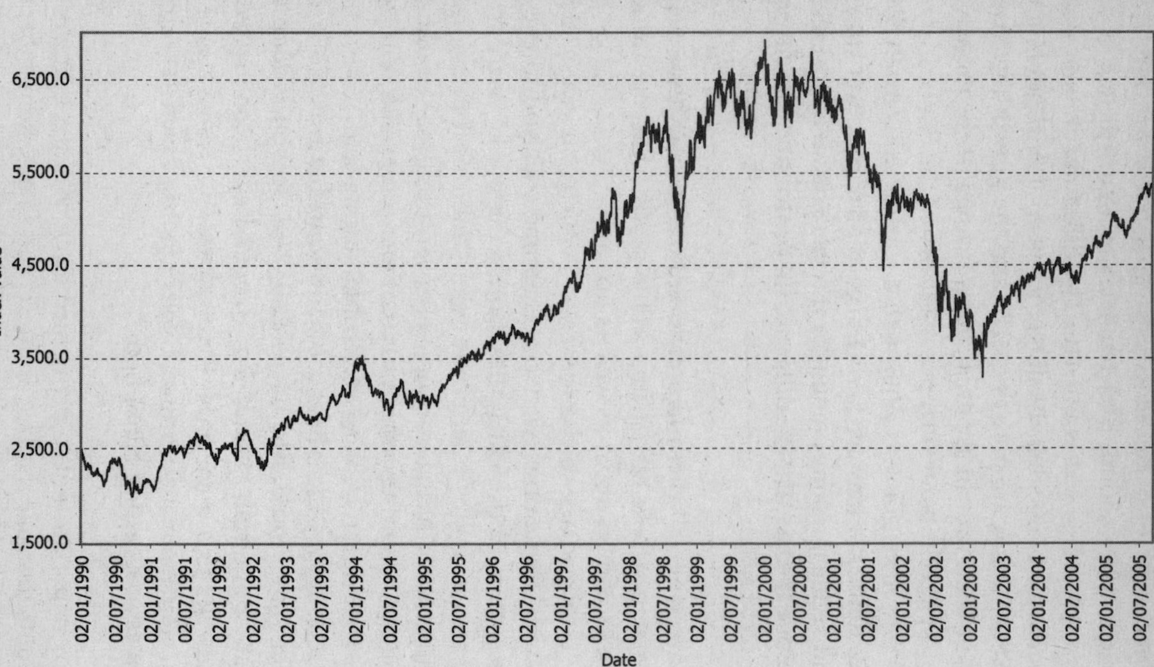

Source: FTSE Group

experience of the stock market was not a happy one. Take a look at a chart of the FTSE 100, which charts the share prices of the 100 largest companies listed on the London stock exchange. It was first developed in 1984, starting from a base level of 1,000 points. In 1989 the index reached the 2,000 mark and by 1995 it had hit 3,000. Then the real boom times came. On 31 December 1999, on the last day of the last century, the FTSE 100 reached its highest-ever closing point of 6,930 points. Since then, times have been leaner, with the market suffering falls in 2000, 2001 and 2002, although rises were recorded in 2003 and 2004. The point is that the value of shares can go up as well as down, and a series of traumatic world events – the bursting of the dot-com bubble, the terrorist attacks of 11 September, a war involving two of the world's largest economies – can have a dramatic and long-lasting impact on share price performance.

Diversify, Diversify, Diversify

There are various ways to ensure that, even if the market does perform badly, you do not lose all your money. The most obvious is to make sure that you do not have all your eggs in one basket, that you have a wide mix of asset classes.

If you're wondering what the hell an asset class is, it isn't really complicated. For the purposes of most small investors, there are four main ones to consider. Some are best suited to providing a regular income, others offer the chance for capital growth. Some do a bit of both.

Cash

This includes savings and current accounts, National Savings products and the money you keep hidden under the mattress. It is very important to keep cash as a rainy-day fund for emergencies. You should also have enough to cover medium-term expenditure – things like holidays, for example. There are three drawbacks to keeping large sums of money in cash. First, the return is relatively low – at the moment, you should be looking to earn 4 to 5 per cent. There is no opportunity for capital growth. And in times of high inflation (now is not such a time), the value of your money will be eroded.

Equities

These are shares in companies which are traded on the stock market. Equities are volatile, but historically they have produced the best returns over the longer term. Many shares pay a dividend, which can be used to provide a regular income. The easiest way for beginners to invest in equities is not directly in the shares of individual companies, but through an investment fund which itself puts money into a range of companies. There are two main types of fund: investment trusts and OEICS (that's pronounced oik, but stands for Open-ended Investment Company – of these, more later).

Fixed Interest

Fixed-interest securities include gilts and bonds. When you buy a corporate bond or a gilt (which is a government-issued bond), you are lending money either to the firm in question or to the government. They represent an easy way for governments and companies to raise money by borrowing from institutional investors, such as pension funds, and private investors, like you and me. As their name suggests, fixed-interest securities pay a fixed amount (known as the 'coupon') on maturity. As such, they are best suited to providing an income. Bonds tend to be less volatile than equities, but this does not mean they are all low risk. Some are: gilts, for example, because they are backed by the government, carry no risk at all. Others, such as high-yield corporate bonds, are very risky. The easiest way to buy bonds, like equities, is through an investment fund.

Property

Many of us already have significant exposure to the property sector through our own homes. However, there are other ways of investing in property. Buy-to-let has become extremely popular over the past decade, since the opportunities for both income and growth have been excellent. However, residential property is difficult to buy and sell quickly, so it is highly risky. Investing in commercial property is simpler, because it can be done through commercial property funds.

Jackie was wrinkling her nose at me. She looked exactly like Roman does before he's about to throw a tantrum.

'I don't know anything about commercial property and I'm still not sure I understood that bit about gilts,' she said. 'They sound boring anyway.'

'Never mind that,' I reassured her. 'Not many newbie investors are going to start dabbling in property. Hell, most experienced investors don't hold property. In fact, very few people hold anything but some cash and perhaps some shares. So let's start with the simple stuff. Cash, first. You should have at least three months' salary in cash savings.'

'I don't have a salary, Tasha. I'm a full-time mother,' Jackie pointed out.

Lila squirmed in her arms to emphasize the point.

'Well, based on what you used to earn, or what Sam earns. Whatever. The point is that you need a cash buffer – at least three, ideally six, months' money in a good, accessible savings account.'

Cash Is King

Everyone needs to build up a cash buffer. This is the money that keeps the wolf from the door, should you notice him lurking in the garden, sizing up the chickens. Six months' money is ideal, three months is good, but it will take some time to build up this level of savings. Don't worry if it takes you a while, and don't feel that you have to put all other spending or investing on hold until you have achieved this; just make sure you keep building up your fund, slowly and steadily. Set up a direct debit from your current account. If you know that you are the type to dip into savings whenever you spot a desirable item in a shop window, stash the money in a notice account so that you can't use it for impulse buys.

Here are a few good accounts in which to stash your emergency money (these are the best rates as I write, but for the very latest rates, check the personal finance pages of the newspapers, or go to *www.moneyfacts.co.uk*):

Cahoot. Cahoot's introductory savings account pays 5.1 per cent on £1 or more, with no notice required. The account is operated by phone or Internet.

ING Direct (don't be concerned by the unfamiliar name. ING stands for International Netherlands Group, and is a large, well-respected international Dutch bank – the one that bought Barings for £1 after Nick Leeson lost $1.3 billion (£730 million) and then went awol). ING Direct pays 4.7 per cent on £1, with no notice required. You can bank by phone or Internet.

Chelsea Building Society. Guarantee 50 is the best notice account on the market, paying 5 per cent. The minimum deposit is £500 and you need to give fifty days' written notice if you wish to withdraw money. You can access the account via a branch or by post.

In general, the best rates tend to be offered on telephone and Internet accounts. This is because accounts offering access through bank and building society branches are more expensive to run, so tend to offer poorer rates. If you do not already have Internet access, it really is worth considering. In all areas of financial services, web access is a godsend. A word of warning: when you scour the best-buy tables, you will find that many accounts offer 'introductory bonuses'. The reason they do this is to artificially inflate their headline rate of interest so that they will be included in the best-buy tables. Introductory bonuses, which usually range from a half to a full percentage point, are paid for a temporary period, generally six to twelve months, after which time the rate falls. Dedicated rate chasers, or rate tarts as they are sometimes known, will flit from account to account, taking advantage of the introductory bonuses before moving their money to the next 'boosted' account. If you cannot be bothered to move your money around every six months or so, ignore bonus-paying accounts and go for one with a good track record for paying a decent rate of interest.

In addition to your easily accessible cash fund, you may want to hold other cash savings. You could choose a fixed-rate account, which is likely to pay a higher rate of interest than a notice or instant-access account, the drawback being that you must leave your money invested for a given term, from one to five years. At the time of writing, the best one-year fix comes from National Counties Building Society. It pays 5.1 per cent. The best five-year fixed rate, available from MBNA Savings, pays 5.15 per cent, on £2,500. The risk attached to putting your money into a fixed-rate account is that interest rates might suddenly rise, leaving your money languishing in a relatively uncompetitive account.

National Savings

An alternative way of holding cash is through National Savings & Investment (NS&I) products. Being backed by the Treasury, NS&I bills itself as 'the safest home for your money', safer even than a deposit account at the bank, since – although this is highly unlikely – it is possible for a bank to go bust. NS&I was once the nation's favourite savings institution, although it has become rather unfashionable of late. Its rates are not the most competitive on the market.

However, it does have other advantages, notably its tax-free accounts. NS&I's index-linked certificates offer the best value. Index-linked certificates pay a fixed amount plus the rate of inflation, and the interest is paid tax-free. Confusingly, certificates are still linked to the old measure of inflation (the Retail Price Index).

Say, for example, that the NS&I's three-year index-linked certificate pays 1.25 per cent plus the RPI index and that inflation is 3 per cent. This gives you a rate of 4.25 per cent. However, since the interest is paid tax-free, this is equivalent to earning 4.56 per cent on your money if you are a basic-rate taxpayer, or 5.08 per cent if you are a higher-rate taxpayer. You are allowed to save a whopping £60,000 tax-free in index-linked certificates.

Individual Savings Accounts

A less generous tax break is offered on Individual Savings Accounts (ISAs), which exist in various forms, one of which is a cash mini-ISA. These are offered by most banks and building societies. They often pay better rates than other deposit accounts and the advantage is that interest is tax-free. However, in the 2005/6 tax year, you are allowed to save no more than £3,000 in a cash mini-ISA. The other drawback is that if you opt to put cash in an ISA, you restrict the amount of money you can invest in shares, also through an ISA.

It's a little complicated, so I'll explain. Essentially, what an ISA does is to provide a tax-free wrapper for your money. What you put inside the wrapper is, to a certain extent, up to you. ISAs come in three forms and two different sizes (I told you it was complicated). The forms are these: equity ISAs, cash ISAs and life insurance ISAs. The two sizes are mini and maxi. Each tax year, you are allowed to choose either one maxi-ISA or up to two mini-ISAs (it used to be three, but the life insurance element has now been combined with shares).

You may not choose a maxi and a mini in the same year. Until 2010, when the ISA allowances will be reassessed, if you choose a maxi ISA you are allowed to invest either up to £7,000 in shares or up to £3,000 in shares, up to £1,000 in cash and up to £1,000 in life insurance.

If you choose to invest in mini-ISAs, you can invest up to £3,000 in shares and £1,000 in life insurance (these used to be separate but have now been combined) and up to £1,000 in cash. Each mini component can be bought from a different provider.

Interest Rates, Tax and Inflation

A quick word about rates. The interest rate paid on savings (or indeed charged on mortgages and loans) is determined by the base rate of interest, which is set on the first Thursday of each month by the Bank of England's Monetary Policy Committee (MPC). The MPC's aim, when it sets rates, is to control inflation. The government has an inflation target – usually something like 2 per cent or 2.5 per cent – and it is the MPC's job to ensure that rates are set a level which makes it likely that the target will be met. If the MPC believes that inflation is rising, it will raise rates. This makes it more expensive for everyone – individuals and businesses – to borrow money, therefore they will be less likely to spend it. Thus inflation falls. But if inflation is too low, this suggests that the economy is sluggish. If the Bank feels that the economy needs a boost, it will cut rates to lower the cost of borrowing.

In most cases, the rate you will see quoted is the annual equivalent rate (AER). This is in fact a notional rate – the total interest that would be paid on your money if it were paid and compounded annually. Rates are also quoted gross, before tax is paid.

Tax and inflation need to be taken into consideration when you are choosing a savings account. For example, if you are a basic-rate taxpayer and you put £1,000 into a Barclays Reward Saver account, which pays 2.75 per cent, you are actually losing money. Once you have deducted inflation of 2.3 per cent, and basic-rate tax on savings (20 per cent), you are no longer seeing a positive real rate of return. At the moment, in order to see a break-even, a non-taxpayer must earn at least 2.3 per cent on their savings, a lower-rate taxpayer must earn 2.56 per cent, a basic-rate taxpayer 2.88 per cent and a higher-rate taxpayer needs to find an account paying 3.83 per cent.

To work out whether you are earning a real rate of return (ROR) on your money:

non-taxpayers:	ROR = savings rate minus inflation
lower-rate taxpayers:	ROR = (savings rate minus inflation) × 0.9
basic-rate taxpayers:	ROR = (savings rate minus inflation) × 0.8
higher-rate taxpayers:	ROR = (savings rate minus inflation) × 0.6

'So my Halifax Liquid Gold account paying 0.4 per cent really isn't doing anyone any favours, is it?' Jackie asked as she put down her pen. She had filled half a notebook with her scribblings and was looking exhausted. Roman had by now finished *Shrek 2* and was starting to grizzle. She picked him up in her arms and he gently pulled her hair.

'I think I ought to get them home. I'm not sure who looks more knackered – Roman or you.'

'I think I am personal-financed-out for the day,' I admitted. 'But why don't you get a babysitter one night this week and then you and Sam and I can go over some of the investments you might want to look at? Because he's going to need to be involved in the decision-making, isn't he? It is his money we're investing after all.'

'Pah! I look after his kids, I can decide what to do with his bloody money,' Jackie said with a smile. 'But you're right. Let's do something on Wednesday. My sister does yoga at the gym down the road so she can come over and watch them afterwards when she's all calm and blissed out.'

'Wednesday it is.'

*

We met at a trendy pub in north London packed with annoyingly attractive, willowy girls in Seven jeans and expensive coats thrown over tiny tops. Sam was sitting alone at a table, eyeing up a particularly svelte brunette when I arrived.

'Oh, hello!' he said, jumping up to give me a kiss. 'Didn't see you there.'

'No,' I replied, 'you were just admiring the view.'

He smiled sheepishly. 'Jacks is at the bar getting drinks. I'll just go and catch her. Gin and tonic?'

'Thanks.'

Sam returned empty-handed. 'I think she might be there a while. There's quite a crush.' He settled back into his chair and lit a cigarette. 'So how's Mark?'

'Fine,' I said warily.

'Investment banker, is he?'

Oh, here we go.

'Pink pinstriped shirts? Rugger? Hunting at the weekends?'

'Oh, shut up.'

OK, so he had worn a pink pinstriped shirt to lunch last week but he'd come straight from work. That's what they wear. And, yes, maybe he does like rugby. So what?

'He does not hunt,' I said emphatically, though I was pretty sure he thought anyone who wanted to had the right to do so. 'He once did some work for the Labour Party!' I blurted out, a little too stridently.

Sam laughed. 'Just winding you up. I'm sure he's a great bloke. Can't be worse than that last one! Bring him over for dinner. I'll crack open the Pétrus '88 and we'll have venison.'

'I look forward to it.'

'Anyway, Jacks has been talking about money non-stop since you saw her,' he said, mercifully changing the subject.

'She really has her heart set on this private school thing,' I said.

'Don't.' He rolled his eyes at me. 'I can see where she's coming from, but it's humiliating to be such a sell-out, you know? I used to be so right on. Look – I drink bitter, for Christ's sake.' Jackie was approaching with the drinks. 'And I let my wife buy the drinks. In fact I insist on it. I'm a beardie, new-man, *Guardian*-reading, sandal-wearing liberal sell-out. Can we buy shares in big tobacco and oil, just to complete my misery?'

'No, we bloody won't,' Jackie said firmly as she sat down. 'I was just reading a piece in the paper on Sunday and apparently ethical investment funds do just as well as the normal, unethical ones.'

'See?' Sam turned to me. 'She reads the money pages now. You've created a monster.'

'We do need to decide where you're going to invest this spare cash of yours,' I said, ignoring Sam's pained expression. 'Jackie and I talked about cash, and you're more or less OK with that, though you must make sure you've got your savings in good accounts. I gave Jacks some ideas on where to look. But now we're talking about this £210 a month that you're going to put aside.'

'Actually,' Jackie interrupted, 'we talked about that, and we've decided that Sam can give up his ludicrously expensive gym membership, so we can make the £250 a month contribution.'

'Oh, we've decided, have we?' Sam said sarcastically.

'This is our children's education we're talking about, Sam.'

'Yes, yes, OK. I'll go running in the street. Probably get knocked down by a car.'

'Well, then we'll have your life insurance and we won't have to worry about all this, will we?' Jackie asked brightly.

Sam sipped his pint.

'Two hundred quid it is, then. Jackie and I also talked a bit about assets the other day.'

'Yes, I gather she's very gung-ho on shares,' Sam said.

'Will you take this seriously?' Jackie snapped at him.

He shut up, and I had the floor.

Investing in Shares

Sounds scary, doesn't it? It isn't. It's actually quite simple. Let's say you're a fan of Boots the Chemist. You think the branches are well run and reasonably priced, you like their own-brand shampoo and you often buy their sandwiches for lunch. You think it's brilliant that the larger branches now stock cool brands like Benefit, and you think that the loyalty scheme is a good one. Whenever you go into a Boots store there are always plenty of people in there, particularly in the run-up to Christmas, when everyone is buying perfume and aftershave sets. On that basis you figure that the company must be doing good business, making a profit. And you would like to share in its good fortune. So you decide to buy a bit of the company, in the form of a share.

In order to purchase a share, you need a stockbroker. Do not be put off by this. You do not need to go to the City to engage an arrogant wideboy in a pinstriped suit. You can if you like, but it's no longer the only option. Your bank or building society will probably offer a sharedealing service, though it is unlikely to be the cheapest option.

Stockbrokers offer three different types of service:

Execution-only. You tell the broker what to do and he or she does it. That's it.

Advisory. In addition to buying and selling shares, the

broker will advise you on what you should be buying and selling, and when you should be doing it.

Discretionary. The broker manages your entire portfolio, buying and selling at his or her discretion. You say what you hope to achieve from your investment – growth, income, or a bit of both – and then let the broker get on with it. If you are opting for this sort of service, you will need to have a significant sum to invest. You cannot just turn up with £1,000 and expect the broker to do something with that. Most will ask for around £100,000, although a few will accept as little as £20,000.

'Right,' said Sam. 'So I guess we would be doing the execution-only thing. How much do you need to invest, then?'

'As much as you need to buy the shares you want to buy and to cover costs. TD Waterhouse, which is one of the larger telephone and online brokers, charges £11.95 for an online trade, or around £17.50 over the phone. If you trade often, you'll get a better rate.'

'OK,' Jackie said. She looked nervous. 'The thing is . . . I'm not really sure which companies I want to buy.'

'I know. And I'll bet you don't want to spend hours researching companies or monitoring their performance.'

'Not really, no,' she replied.

Buying a share on the basis that you like the company can be a good starting-point for investment. It makes sense that if you like the company's products, and other people like the company's products, then that company could make money in the future. But there's obviously more to it than that. There are remarkably few companies that jump out at you as brilliant investments, and there are quite a few one might have thought would be perfectly solid that have gone wrong.

If you are going to invest in individual shares there is no alternative to doing a lot of careful research. The Internet is a great source of information (though you should never trust the tips you get in investing chatrooms), as are the quality newspapers.

Investing directly in individual shares is tough. It requires nerves of steel and a lot of homework. If you're a beginner, you'd be better off sticking to collective investments – funds made up of lots of different shares which are selected for you, either by computer or by a fund manager.

START A CLUB

Many women come to the stock market via investment clubs as they find the collaborative approach more to their liking. They are able to talk through ideas with friends or colleagues before buying a share, and this gives them confidence. The other advantage of being in a club is that it gives you a little more purchasing power. If you have only £25 a month to put into shares that's not going to go very far. Band together with ten friends and you've got £250, which is more like it.

Investment clubs were hugely popular in the late 1990s, when the stock market was booming. In shakier times, there are fewer of them about, but if you are interested in the stock market and are a little nervous about going it alone, clubs can be a really good way to get started.

Ideally, a club should have around ten members – fewer and you lack purchasing power, more and meetings start to get unwieldy and difficult to organize. You'll need to organize a preliminary meeting at which you can discuss your aims (do you want to go for risky shares or are you looking for nice, steady earners?), monthly contributions and a joining fee. An initial fee is a good idea since it'll give you some initial purchasing power. You'll also need to elect a chair, treasurer and secretary – it sounds bureaucratic but you do need someone to run the club and make sure that the money and paperwork are taken care of.

Proshare, a not-for-profit organization that promotes share ownership, publishes an investment clubs manual that contains all the info you'll need on how to start a club, as well as the tax forms you'll need to fill in and so on.

Collective Investments

'That sounds much easier,' Jackie said, relieved.

It's also less risky. Investing in a collective investment – a unit trust, investment trust or OEIC – is another way of diversifying. If you buy shares in just one company and that company performs badly, then your investment loses value. If you buy shares in 100 companies, then it doesn't matter so much if one or two or three of them perform badly. But for a small investor to buy shares in 100 companies directly, they would need to have a huge amount of money to invest. If they have just £1,000, they couldn't possibly achieve that – unless they invested through a fund. Funds can take your £1,000 and invest it in 100 companies because they also have £1,000 or £2,000 or £10,000 contributions from hundreds of other investors.

Types of Fund

You can invest in a whole range of assets through an investment fund, including shares, bonds and even commercial property. There are hundreds of different funds available, and just to confuse matters further there are a few different types too.

In the old days, there were unit trusts and investment trusts. Now we have unit trusts, investment trusts and OEICS. Unit trusts and OEICS are essentially the same type of vehicle – the OEIC is just the modern version. But there are important differences between this type of fund and investment trusts that the investor should beware of.

OEICS and Unit Trusts

These are simply pooled funds of money. They are open-ended vehicles: this means that their size is not limited. The fund will expand every time a new investor puts money into it.

Investment Trusts

These are quoted companies, listed on the stock market. When you invest in an investment trust, you are actually buying shares in the trust. Investment trusts are closed-ended: there is a set number of shares in the company. As a result, the price of a share in an investment trust is influenced not just by the value of the assets it holds but also by investor demand. If there is great investor demand for shares, the price will rise above the value of the assets – the trust is then said to be trading at a premium. If it falls below the net asset value because lots of people are selling the shares, it is trading at a discount.

Now, while the differences between OEIC and investment trusts may seem fairly technical, they do have important implications for the investor.

Charges

Unit trusts and OEICS charge initial and annual fees. Initial charges may be as high as 5 per cent of the investment, while annual management charges tend to be around 0.5 to 1.5 per cent. Investment trusts do not levy these charges, although annual management costs of around 1 per cent are paid directly from the trust's income – so there is, effectively, an annual charge to the investor.

The level of charges is important. Remember the compound interest calculation. Well, just take a look at the impact of only the initial charge on a £1,000 lump sum investment over time. Assuming that charge is 5 per cent, it will reduce the value of the lump sum to £950. Now watch:

	£950 invested	£1,000 invested
over 10 years	£1,869	£1,967
over 20 years	£3,676	£3,870
over 30 years	£7,232	£7,612

(assuming 7 per cent growth p.a.)

Paying 5 per cent, or just £50, seems reasonable. But if you look at the final outcome, paying £380 is a lot less of a bargain. Investment trust companies tend to use this argument as a reason to buy their funds rather than unit trusts and OEICS.

Risk and Rewards

Unit trusts and OEICS are not permitted to borrow money, but investment trusts can. This is known as gearing. Its effect is to magnify market movements. If a fund is highly geared and the market surges upwards, the trust will see exceptional gains. But if the market falls, losses will be exacerbated too. Investing in a highly geared trust is therefore more risky than investing in a similar unit trust or an investment trust that does not borrow money.

'So which type is better?' Jackie asked.

'I was afraid you would ask that,' I replied. 'I don't think you can say that one type is necessarily better. Both have plus and minus points. When it comes to choosing a fund, the best way is perhaps to choose the area of investment you wish to target – say UK blue chips or European smaller companies – and then see what's on offer in that area.'

'Uh-huh.' Sam looked at Jackie sceptically. 'I hope you're following all this, Jacks,' he said. 'Because I'm getting confused.'

Jackie looked up from her notebook, on which she had been scribbling furiously.

'Well . . .' she began.

'Look,' I interrupted. 'We're covering a lot of ground, because I think it's better that you understand the options, but it really isn't that complicated. Let's recap. You need to put aside £250 a month. You're going to start by building up a cash fund in one of the accounts Jackie and I discussed. Then you're going to start investing in shares, not directly, but through a fund. Now we just need to choose a fund.'

Which Fund?

Ideally, you will want to build up a balanced investment portfolio, so you'll have a whole range of funds covering the entire risk spectrum. When you're starting out, you want your first investment to be fairly balanced all by itself. If you are simply looking for growth, rather than income, you might consider one of the large, generalist investment trusts, such as Foreign & Colonial, Scottish Mortgage or Witan. These are enormous trusts (F&C, for example, has gross assets of over £2 billion). Financial advisers often recommend these trusts to beginners because they invest all over the world, in hundreds of companies, so they are hugely diversified, both geographically and across different sectors and sizes of company.

Picking the right fund takes a bit of research. If you are not confident enough to do this yourself or if you simply haven't the time, it may be worth your while speaking to a financial adviser. However, you will find that some independent financial advisers' websites are extremely helpful when it comes to fund picking. One of the more comprehensive sites is Bestinvest (*www.bestinvest.co.uk*). You do not have to be a client to use the portfolio planner. Simply key in your aims, how much downside you are prepared to tolerate, your timescale and the sum you have to invest, and it will suggest both an asset allocation and the sorts of funds you might want to purchase. The site has fact sheets on all the funds, so you can do a bit of your own research too. The personal finance pages of the weekend newspapers can also point you in the right direction.

Here's an example. If I go to the Bestinvest website and tell them that I have £5,000 to invest, that I require between 2 and 4 per cent in income from my investments, that I am investing for between seven and ten years and that I can tolerate losses of up to 10 per cent, it will come back to me with an investment model – 'balanced cautious' – and a list of suitable investment funds. It tells me that I should consider Framlington UK Select Opportunities, Invesco Perpetual Corporate Bond, Invesco Perpetual European High Yield, Liontrust First Growth and New Star Sterling Bond. It will also give me detailed information on who manages each fund, how it has performed and so on.

Financial Advice

A website portfolio planner can give you a general idea of which fund you might want to pick, but if you need further reassurance, or if you have a large amount of money to invest, you might think about turning to an independent financial adviser (IFA). IFAs have rather a spivvy reputation, and if there's one thing us girls don't like it's a spiv. But in fact there are plenty of completely non-spivvy, helpful and for some people invaluable IFAs out there, so don't write them off.

You don't need an IFA if you're wondering which bank account to stash your £50 a month savings in. You don't even need an IFA if you've got £200 a month to invest in the stock market. But as your financial affairs become increasingly complex, particularly when it comes to tricky areas such as tax planning, life insurance and pensions, you may find a bit of financial advice extremely helpful. Talking to an IFA can also save you time, since they'll do all the tricky admin for you (and may even do your tax return for you), and hopefully it could make you richer, by helping you avoid poor investments and steering you towards the decent ones. A good IFA should be able to help you discover your own attitude to risk and help you define your investment goals.

So how do you find one, and what will you have to pay him (or her – female IFAs do exist, you know) when you track your IFA down? The best way of finding someone reliable is through personal recommendation, so ask around. If your friends aren't the type to know a good IFA, then your parents might, or their friends might. If no names come up that way, then you can do a search through a group called IFA Promotion, which, as its name suggests, is a group that promotes the use of IFAs. It can help you find some firms in your area.

Next, you need to do some interviews. Make appointments with a few advisers – most will offer you an initial consultation free of charge – as this will help you to get a feel for whether you can have a good working relationship with the adviser. It's no good going to someone you don't like, feel patronized by or don't think you can trust. You also need to ask some important questions:

- How much will you have to pay? Since December 2004, all IFAs have had to present you with a menu of ways in which you can pay for their services, with the basic choice being either that you pay them a fee or that they receive commission from financial services companies on the products they offer you. Many people prefer fees, since this way it is easier to see how much you're paying, and for what.
- What qualifications does the IFA have? All IFAs must have a Financial Planning Certificate (FPC), but this is the bare minimum. There is a whole host of more advanced qualifications, so find out which your adviser has. You should ascertain how long they've been in the business too.
- Does the firm specialize in any particular area? If you're twenty-two and wanting to invest an inheritance, then you don't really want to be talking to a firm that specializes in

helping people plan their retirements. Likewise, if most of the firm's clients are millionaires with four homes in four different countries and investment portfolios running into the hundreds of thousands, you might feel a little out of place if you're just wondering where to spend this year's ISA allowance.

Note that not all financial advisers are independent. There are now three types of adviser:

- Tied agents, who sell the products and services of just one company. These are the sales staff who work for banks and building societies. They'll be able to give you generic advice on products, and they can talk to you about the specific products that they offer, but they won't be able to tell you whether a Barclays fund is any better than a Lloyds one, for example.
- Multi-tied agents, who sell the products of a number of companies. They'll be able to compare a range of products, but only from a set list of firms, so you won't be getting a full picture of the market.
- IFAs, who should have no ties to any one firm. There is one small caveat to this last point, however, and that is that there is nothing stopping an IFA recommending products and services offered by companies that own more than 10 per cent of its stock. So you should find out who owns the firm too.

Tracker Funds

'What about trackers?' Jackie interjected, all of a sudden. Then to Sam, 'See, I know the lingo.' Then back to me,

'The other day, you kept talking about tracker funds. Those would be a good starting point for beginners like us, wouldn't they?' And back to Sam, 'Trackers are funds which track the performance of the stock market.'

'And how do they do that?' Sam asked her.

'They just do,' she snapped.

'Trackers,' I said, coming to Jackie's rescue, 'invest proportionately in all the companies in an index, so that they will match the performance of that index. So say, for example, that Marks & Spencer makes up 1 per cent of the FTSE 100, then the FTSE 100 tracker will invest 1 per cent of its money in the shares of Marks & Spencer.'

'Precisely,' Jackie agreed.

'Thank you. But the use of trackers is a hotly disputed topic. Some experts claim that you are better off opting for a fund that is actively managed – a fund where the manager uses his or her own discretion to pick shares – in order to get the best results. The other school claims that fund managers are an overpaid waste of space.

'Actively managed funds are more expensive than trackers, as you would expect, because you need to pay a fund manager plus a whole term of researchers and analysts who decide where to put your money, whereas with a tracker the work can be done by a computer.

'Now, while I'm not saying that all fund managers are an overpaid waste of space, I have to admit that the statistics appear to back up the claims of the pro-tracker lobby.'

Every year, a new slew of statistics purports to show just how rubbish the average fund manager is at doing his or her job. In 2004, WM Company, a firm of financial analysts, claimed that only eight managed UK equity funds had outperformed the FTSE All Share Index over a twenty-year period. That's eight out of forty-four. Not exactly a great strike rate. A different analysis, which included a much higher number of funds, showed that of 276 funds, sixty-one beat the index.

'Still not brilliant,' Sam said.

'No, it isn't, although of course if you'd picked one of the sixty-one, you'd be out on top, and even if you picked one out at random, without doing any research, you still had a one in 4.5 chance of beating the index. However, in a bull market, when the index is soaring, there does not seem to be much point in paying a fund manager 5 per cent when you could get perfectly good performance just by following the index higher.'

'But what about when we're not in a soaring bull market?' Jackie asked.

'Then things aren't so good, and that's just one of the few obvious problems with trackers. The aim of the shrewd investor should be to buy low and sell high. Trackers do not do that, because they have to reflect the composition of the index they are tracking. In many cases, buying a tracker does not give you a very good spread of investments. Just look at the FTSE 100. It's all oil companies, banks and pharmaceutical companies.'

'Christ, it's like investing in Satan himself,' Sam groaned, downing the rest of his pint.

'Yeah, not overly ethical. And the other point is – as Jackie mentioned – you don't want a tracker in a bear market, or even one where the market is just bumbling along, rising a little, falling a little, not really going anywhere in particular, because that's where your money will follow.

'In those sorts of markets – the more difficult markets – what you want is a brilliant fund manager who can pick outstanding shares. To use a revolting marketing phrase, you want a manager who adds value. The problem is, of course, that not all fund managers do add value. And in any case, trying to pick the ones that will is hugely difficult.'

'So you go for someone with a track record?' Jackie asked.

'That's probably the best way of doing it. Look for managers who have performed consistently well in their sector.'

'OK, but how do we find them?'

Again, doing your own research will help. If you read financial sections of the newspapers, you will see that certain names crop up. Most papers have a regular analysis of investment funds, giving a weekly analysis of a chosen fund or type of fund.

Websites such as Morningstar and Trustnet give you fund performance statistics. They will also tell you who manages the fund and how long he or she has been there, which will give you an idea of how the manager has done relative to others in his or her sector. Again, the Bestinvest site is very helpful, since it gives a biog of the manager on its fact sheet, as well as a graph focusing on the manager's performance.

Jackie was fiddling with her swizzle stick pensively.

'What's up?'

'It's just . . . I know we're being total sell-outs anyway, but I really don't want to invest in Satan. I'd rather not give my money to companies that wreck the environment and sell arms to dictators.'

'Oh, come on!' Sam exclaimed. 'Selling arms to dictators is a great British tradition.'

She shot him a withering look. 'I'm serious, Sam.'

'I know.' He smiled cheekily and squeezed her knee. 'And you know that I agree. So are any of these funds not the tools of blood-sucking capitalist pigs?'

Ethics

In fact, there are quite a few funds with an ethical bent. EIRIS – the Ethical Investment Research Service – publishes a guide to ethical funds that you can order over the phone or download from the Internet. In fact, EIRIS does not just cover investment funds. It has advice on all aspects of financial services, including where to find IFAs who specialize in ethical matters.

'It's ideal for sandal-wearing bunny-huggers such as yourselves,' I told them.

'Cheers. Jacks said earlier that they perform just as well as other funds. Is that true?' Sam asked me. 'I mean, I know performance isn't the only consideration, but we are trying to make some money here.'

The established view has always been if you invest ethically, you have to sacrifice performance, because ethical fund managers have a much more limited pool of shares in which to invest. However, that idea is increasingly being challenged by the performance figures, which demonstrate that if you pick the right funds, going green can pay dividends. Isis Stewardship Income, which is one of the most established investment funds in the UK (also one of the stricter funds – it holds no shares in banks, oil companies or pharmaceutical companies), returned 40 per cent over the five years to 2004, against a sector average of just 9 per cent. Between 1998 and 2004, tracker funds fell, along with the index, by 14 per cent. The average ethical fund lost no value.

'Well, I definitely think we should start with an ethical fund,' Jackie said firmly.

'What about that one you just mentioned?' Sam asked. 'Isis Stewardship Income? Would that be right for us?'

'Isis Stewardship Growth would be better suited to your purposes. You can buy it through a fund supermarket and within an ISA, so it would be a good starting point for you. What I'd suggest is that you begin by investing a lump sum, and then contribute by regular savings - a regular amount each month.'

Regular Savings

Investing by regular savings takes some of the stress out of investing in the stock market, because you need not worry too much about whether you are investing at the wrong time. In fact, worrying about whether your are investing at the right or wrong time is an entirely pointless exercise since the short-term movements of the market are impossible to predict. Having said that, almost everyone who invests does find themselves, for a while at least, worrying about the short-term movements of the market nevertheless. But you will find yourself much more worried about the state of the market on Tuesday if on Monday you invested a lump sum of £1,500 rather than if on Monday you had invested £150. When you invest by regular savings, it does not matter if you invest on one of the market's good or bad days; in fact, if you invest by regular savings over a period of ten years, the likelihood is that these things will even themselves out. Investing by regular savings means that you need not concern yourself too much with the day-to-day volatility of the stock market.

Saving for Baby

We decided to treat ourselves to dinner as a reward for working so hard and ending up with an actual decision, so we headed off to Limani on Regent's Park Road for some Greek food and a bottle of cheap red wine.

I thought that the money talk might have been over, but all of a sudden, through a mouthful of meze, Sam asked, 'What about those child trust fund things? Don't we have one of those, Jackie? Are they any good?'

I took a deep breath.

Child Trust Funds (CTFs) are a relatively new invention of the Labour government, offered to all children born on or after 1 September 2002. In order to qualify for a CTF, you must claim child benefit (something every parent is entitled to do). Once you have done so, you will be sent a voucher for £250, or £500 if you qualify for the full Child Tax Credit (for details on this, see Chapter 8). That voucher can then be given to a bank, building society or investment manager of the parents' choice, depending on whether they want the money to be held in a cash account or to be invested in the stock market or bonds.

The child's parents, grandparents or friends are welcome to contribute up to £1,200 a year to the fund tax-free, while the government has pledged to add an extra £250 (or £500, depending on family circumstances) when the child reaches their seventh birthday. However, the money cannot be touched, by the child or by anyone else, until the child reaches the age of eighteen, at which point it becomes theirs to spend as they please, whether that be on university tuition or a holiday in Ibiza.

Sam and Jackie had put Lila's CTF money into a cash account, a decision they were no longer happy about.

'I thought that it was a good idea to keep the money safe, but, having had all our conversations about risk and reward, I'm not sure any more,' Jackie said to me.

Her doubts were well founded. Many experts argue that, since the amounts involved are fairly small, it is pointless to leave CTF money in cash accounts. As one commentator put it, 'Parents should be aiming for the best possible returns on their child's money – £250 left in a cash account will be barely enough for a round of drinks when the child turns eighteen.'

Over long periods of time, the real value of cash is eroded by inflation, so parents should definitely think about putting their child's money into the stock market, for the early years at least. Once the child reaches the age of about fourteen or fifteen, parents can think about moving some money into cash accounts if they are worried about markets falling.

In fact, the default CTFs will do this automatically. These are 'lifestyled' funds, which take on more risk in the early years and gradually reduce the proportion of money in risky investments over the life of the fund.

Another problem for Jackie and Sam was that while Lila qualified for a fund, Roman did not, since he was born before the September 2002 cut-off date.

'We were thinking of taking out one of these baby bond things as an alternative,' Sam said. 'I saw one advertised in the papers.'

'I'd steer clear of anything specifically structured as a savings plan for children,' I told them. 'In general, they tend to be over-complicated, inflexible and expensive. You don't need a special savings plan for children – that's just a marketing ploy. Simply find a good savings account, or invest some money in the market.'

'Christ, it does get really bloody complicated, doesn't it? There must be a simpler, easier way, surely?' Sam looked at me imploringly. 'Some sort of get-rich-quick scheme. Perhaps we could become property magnates,' he said, a gleam in his eye.

'There are, as far as I can make out, two ways to get rich quick,' I replied. 'You could win the lottery – the odds of doing so are roughly 14 million to one – or you could marry a millionaire. Oh no, you can't. You're already married. Anyway, the odds of finding a willing millionaire are probably even longer.'

'I'm sure there are plenty of millionaires who'd want to marry me,' Jackie cut in.

'Don't leave me, darling,' Sam said, giving her leg a squeeze. 'I'll win the lottery soon. Promise.'

The non-existence of free lunches may be a cliché, but clichés become clichés for a reason. Any get-rich-quick scheme should be treated with the utmost scepticism. The other day I received a letter urging me to 'BECOME A PROPERTY MILLIONAIRE OVERNIGHT!' If it really were that easy to become a successful property magnate, wouldn't everyone be doing it? Here's another cliché: anything that looks too good to be true invariably is.

Scams

In recent years a couple of scams have specifically targeted women. The best-known are the Hearts and Women Empowering Women schemes. Both are pyramid schemes. What happens is this. You are invited to participate in the scheme, investing a set amount. In the Hearts case, it was £3,000. At the next meeting (usually a party where everyone stands around quaffing champagne and feeling empowered), you invite two friends, who must also contribute £3,000. When you pay in your cash (which is in fact a 'gift' to other women, who are already members of the scheme) you have your name entered on the bottom tier of the pyramid. In theory, once a further eight people (including your two invitees) have joined the scheme, you receive £24,000 as your reward.

It sounds fantastic – and it is, for those who join early on in the scheme – but within no time at all the figures start failing to stack. Take eight new members of the scheme. In order for them to get their money back, sixty-four new people will have to be recruited. And in order for the sixty-four to get their money back, 512 people need to be recruited. If they want their money back, a further 4,096 must join. And then you need 32,768. And then just over a quarter of a million. And so on. Some respectable journals – including the *Spectator* – have claimed that there is nothing wrong with this type of scheme. It's just good, clean fun, they say. It isn't. People can and do lose their money all the time, and there is absolutely no come-back, since the schemes are not regulated. Steer well clear.

Scandals

Some scams are obvious. But there are other ways to lose your shirt. Over the past twenty years there have been a series of financial scandals, all of them involving established, seemingly reputable businesses. Personal pension plans, endowment mortgages and split-capital investment trusts have all been the subject of mis-selling scandals. The latest has involved 'precipice bonds', a type of bond linked to the performance of stock market indices. There are no sure-fire ways to avoid getting caught up in this type of scandal, but there are some common-sense steps you can take to help ensure that your money stays safe.

1. Trust no one. It sounds harsh, but in the end you have to rely to some extent on your own research and judgement. Make sure you know what's going on with your money.
2. Be sceptical of claims made by salesmen. Never be afraid to ask questions.
3. Shun fashion. Just because everyone else is piling into buy-to-let doesn't mean you should. Over-hyped ideas quickly turn to bubbles, and those will always burst.
4. Never buy anything you don't understand. If a product seems very complicated, ask yourself why.
5. Do not assume that the government will bail you out if something goes wrong, but keep very careful records of your investments. Write down the important points made in conversations with advisers or salesmen, taking down names and dates. Even better – get something in writing. This will help immeasurably if you ever need to make a mis-selling claim.
6. Think of the worst-case scenario. Assume that economic and market conditions will change suddenly, rapidly, and for the worse.
7. Diversify, diversify, diversify.

5. Don't Ever Go Hungry: Planning for Retirement

Going hungry is not something I am in any danger of at the moment. I have spent the past few weeks being wined and dined to within an inch of my life. Mark really likes to eat. And drink. And shop. And stay in expensive hotels (we were at the Hotel Montalembert in Paris last weekend. To die for, as Nikki might say. She is *so* jealous). We're having a lot of fun, and I really like him, although I do feel that we seem to spend our entire lives consuming. Plus I'm having to run five times a week just to prevent myself putting on weight.

So this weekend, I'm taking a break – from Mark and from London. I'm off to Edinburgh, partly because it's so lovely in spring, but mostly to see my grandmother. My father phoned last week to say he's really concerned. She's had flu and is terribly frail. They're not sure she's going to be able to stay in her house much longer – and she's devastated. She's lived there for forty years and she loves her home.

I decided to take the train rather than flying, because it would give me a chance to think things over. Thinking about Gran having to face the tough choices that old age brings to us all had focused my mind on the whole pensions subject, so I'd come armed with a little light reading (much of it provided by Mark, who was starting to obsess just a little about my pensions provision or lack thereof) to help me sort things out in my mind. Mark has been steering me in the direction of a SIPP (a Self-invested Personal Pension), but these are quite complex and can be expensive, although they do allow you the freedom to control your own pension plan.

But I have to say that I was still not convinced that a conventional pension plan was the best way to go. So I decided to do some proper homework. I had four and a half hours to read up on the entire subject – from the most basic state retirement provision to pension plans for the wealthy – to see where I stood. Some of what I found was pretty frightening stuff, some of it was also really complicated and a lot of it just plain boring, but let's start out with the scary bit.

Say you would like an annual income of around £15,000 when you retire. After all, you'll have paid off your mortgage by then (hopefully), and there'll be no kids to feed and clothe, so that should be enough to provide for a fairly comfortable standard of living. So how much do you need to save in order to provide you with such a princely sum? Well, given standard assumptions (more on these later), if you're twenty-five, you need to be putting away around £105 a month. If you're thirty-five, you need to be saving around £205 a month. If you're forty-five, you need to save £400 a month. Scared yet?

No? Well, then, listen to this: 'The scale and implications of the pensions crisis are not understood. But I believe that it is up there with terrorism or global warming as a threat to much of what we value.' No, it's not some end-is-nigh nutter, but David Willetts, then Shadow Work and Pensions Secretary, speaking in 2004 about our failure to save for retirement.

Pension Poverty

Although my grandmother might find herself in a difficult position now, she's incredibly lucky compared with most women of pensionable age. My grandfather, who died six years ago, was an art dealer and made a pretty decent living. He left her with enough to live comfortably (although sadly not enough to be able to afford a full-time nurse). She still goes to the theatre, eats out when she feels like it and buys lovely, elegant clothes, as well as the odd jazz CD.

Her position is a world away from the average female pensioner in the UK. Women who have worked all their lives, those who do not have children or those married to wealthy men might enjoy a comfortable, even luxurious retirement. But these women represent a tiny minority. Those who have children, who have taken career breaks or worked part-time, and those on low incomes face a tougher old age. And you can forget all that rubbish about women taking their partners for a ride when they get divorced. It simply isn't true. In a tiny handful of cases, a few footballers' wives will get a large slice of their ex-husbands' assets. But they are a rarity. In general, divorced women who have had children find themselves at the very bottom of the pile when it comes to pension provision, and one in four single women pensioners lives in poverty.

The Fawcett Society, which campaigns to get a fair deal for women across a range of issues including pay and pensions, says that nearly half of women in the UK have a gross individual income of less than £100 a week. Could you live on that? I know I'd struggle. And the struggle will only become harder the older you get and the more help you need. Remember that even if you work until the age of sixty-five, you're likely to have a retirement of around fifteen years, because the average life expectancy of the British woman is now eighty. Fifteen years is a long time to live in poverty.

Despite all these scary statistics, one of the most difficult domestic issues facing UK policy-makers is how to persuade people to save more for their old age. We are repeatedly warned of the existence of a gaping black hole in the nation's finances, a 'savings gap' originally estimated to be £27 billion, but more recently inflated to £57 billion. To most people, though, these figures are utterly meaningless. And in any case, how does one plug a £57 billion hole?

A Fawcett Society poll found that if women were given an extra £100 a month, only 10 per cent would put it into a pension plan. A quarter would spend the money on their children or on clearing their existing debts. A survey carried out by Bradford & Bingley in 2003 found that the average British woman made saving for retirement a priority around the age of fifty-five, just five years before the female retirement age (or ten years away, for younger women). This is simply not good enough.

There are of course some people who simply do not have any money to set aside at the end of the month, but these are in the minority. The rest of us, if we are honest, could find something – even if it is just £50 a month – to save. So why aren't we saving? Part of the reason is that we would rather spend the money on ourselves or our kids, but there are other factors at work too. Many people find pensions confusing and complex. They *are* confusing and complex – there's no easy way around that one. Aware of pensions mis-selling scandals and stock market falls, people are worried about losing money. And for people in their twenties and thirties, it is difficult to get enthusiastic about pensions planning when they are struggling to pay off debts and scrape together a deposit for a home, since retirement seems such a long way off.

Let's just take a look at some of these objections to pensions. To anyone put off pensions by mis-selling scandals or the sheer complexity of the plans, I say this: these might be sufficient reasons to not invest in a pension plan, but they are not good reasons to neglect saving for your retirement at all. Read on and you'll discover why.

If you believe that at twenty-five you are too young to start saving for a pension, well, maybe so. Perhaps you are desperately trying to get on to the housing ladder, or simply trying to get rid of your student debts. I'm thirty-two and I still haven't started saving, so I don't have a lot of room to talk. But don't leave it too late. The earlier you start the better. Just take a look at a couple of examples.

Zoe is very conscientious and starts saving for retirement aged twenty-five, contributing £100 a month to her pension plan. When she turns thirty, she ups her contribution to £200 and at thirty-five she starts contributing £250 a month. She keeps up that contribution rate until she retires aged sixty-five. Assuming 7 per cent p.a. growth, she will end up with a final pension pot of £543,000. If, like most people, she takes 25 per cent of her pension as a lump sum and then purchases an annuity, which is a kind of insurance policy, she will end up with an annual income of just over £28,000. Very comfortable indeed.

Now take Chloe, who waits until the grand old age of thirty-five to start making contributions. Chloe puts £250 a month into her pension plan for her full working life, until she too retires at sixty-five. She has a much smaller pension pot, of just under £250,000. She will have an annual income of just under £13,000. Not quite in the comfort zone.

Ideally, you should be saving half your age as a percentage of your salary into your pension fund. So, if you are thirty-five, you should be putting 17.5 per cent of your earnings aside. If you are fifty, you should be saving a quarter of your salary.

But for many people – for most of us in fact – that simply isn't possible and the idea of putting £100 a month into a pension plan seems very far-fetched. However, I would point out two things. First, a retirement plan is not a luxury but a necessity. And second, even putting aside small amounts will help. Stakeholder pensions accept contributions of just £20 a month. If you were, from the age of twenty-five, to make £20 monthly contributions, you could still build up a final fund of £37,700 by the time you reach the age of sixty-five, and this would give you an annual pension in today's money of £2,829. Not a fortune, certainly, but this would give you £55 a week to add to your basic state pension.

State Pension

This is where it all gets both complicated and rather tedious. But it's also really important, so bear with me.

The basic state pension is £84.25 a week in 2006/7, or just £50.50 a week for someone who has qualified on the basis of their partner's National Insurance Contributions (NICs). The value of the state pension has gradually but steadily been eroded since, in 1980, the Conservative government decided to break the link between the state pension and earnings, pegging it instead to the rate of inflation. Despite protesting at the time, it has taken the Labour Government until 2006 to pledge to restore that link, and even then it is unlikely to take place before 2011. Today, the value of the state pension is a paltry 14 per cent of average earnings.

Everyone who has paid sufficient NICs qualifies for the basic state pension once they reach retirement age, which is sixty-five for all men and for women born on or after 5 March 1955. Women born before 6 April 1950 can retire at sixty. Women born between those two dates need to count the number of months or part-months by which their birth date falls after 5 April 1950 and add that number to sixty. For example, someone born on 6 June 1953 was born thirty-nine months after the cut-off date, so they can retire at sixty-three years and three months.

In order to qualify for the full basic state pension you need to pay NICs for nine out of every ten years of your working life. In other words, if you are to qualify for the full entitlement, you need to have an almost unbroken work record, from the age of twenty until you retire. Anyone with fewer than ten years' NICs has no state pension entitlement at all.

This is where most women lose out badly. Only half qualify for the full basic state pension. Of people without a full basic pension 91 per cent are women. They lack sufficient qualifying years, usually because they have taken time off work to raise children. Many will have made some contributions, so will qualify for a reduced pension. Those who have not made enough contributions to qualify for a pension in their own right have to rely on their husband's contribution record. They can draw the married women's pension when their husband retires, but, as we have seen, this is worth just £50.50 a week. If you are not married, you do not qualify for your partner's pension.

It seems unjust that women should be punished with a lower pension just because they are the ones who, more often than not, stay at home to raise children. And this government has admitted that women's pensions are 'a national scandal'. It is currently looking at reforming the system so that everyone would qualify for the same benefit, no matter how many years they have worked. As yet, this is just a proposal.

HOME RESPONSIBILITIES PROTECTION

Doesn't that sound quaint? HRP was introduced in 1978 to help address the problems facing women, or indeed men, who stay at home to look after their kids. It is a little-known and fairly complicated system, which means that it does not help as many people as it should.

HRP reduces the number of qualifying years you need to be eligible for a full basic state pension. Note that it covers full tax years only: if you have worked for only part of a tax year, then you cannot claim HRP for that year.

You qualify for HRP if you are receiving child benefit as the 'main payee' for a child under the age of sixteen; if you are on income support and are not claiming Jobseeker's Allowance because you are staying at home to care for someone, rather than actively seeking work; or if, for at least thirty-five hours a week, you look after someone who is ill or disabled, and who is receiving the requisite allowances from the benefits agency (Disability Allowance or Constant Attendance Allowance).

S2P

You can supplement your basic state pension with the state second pension, also known as S2P. In order to receive this additional pension, you must make Class 1 NICs, unless you are looking after a small child, or are a carer.

S2P is earnings-related, so the more you earn, the more you get. Rates change every year, based on a complicated formula worked out by the Department for Work and Pensions. S2P is new: it replaced the old State Earnings-related Pension Scheme (SERPS) in 2002. In general, it is more generous to those on lower incomes than SERPS was.

For the purposes of S2P, if you earn up to £11,200 a year, you are treated as though you earn £11,200. The same is true if you are not working but are looking after a child under the age of six, or if you qualify for a carer's allowance because you are looking after someone who is ill or disabled.

Contracting out

OK, now it gets really complicated. You can opt to 'contract out' of the additional state pension, in which case a part of your NICs (known as the National Insurance rebate) is paid into either your occupational scheme or your private pension plan. This can be as much as £2,000 a year, depending on your age and your salary.

It sounds good, but it is notoriously difficult to figure out whether or not contracting out is a good idea. There is no guarantee that, should you contract out, you will end up with a larger pension income than you would have received if you had stayed in S2P. Indeed, *Which?*, the magazine of the Consumers' Association, found one fifty-year-old woman who had contracted out of SERPS (S2P's predecessor) to end up with a private pension of £817. If she had remained in SERPS she would have received £2,029.

But then again, your additional state pension income is not guaranteed either. Its payment is subject to the whim of the government of the day. Many financial experts say they do not trust the state to keep its promises, so would encourage contracting out. But you must take advice before making a decision either way.

The best way to figure out how much your state pension will be, including S2P, is to ask for a pension forecast from the government. You need to get hold of a form BR19 from your local social security office to order one. But suffice to say that the state is not going to keep you in the lap of luxury. The likelihood is that state pension provision is likely to get worse, rather than better, over the course of our lifetimes. We are now expected to make our own provisions for old age. Relying on the state will increasingly be regarded as a last resort.

So what are our options? Those who work for a firm that offers an occupational pension scheme would be advised to sign up to that. The rest of us must content ourselves with private pensions. Or we can go alternative, choosing not to invest in a pension plan but to make other investments in the hope that they will keep us in our dotage.

Pay Less Tax with a Pension

You don't have to take out a pension plan. It is not compulsory, although some people believe that it should be. You could just dream up your own investment strategy, following some of the principles outlined in the previous chapter. You could save up a cash fund or buy shares or even property as part of your own, unofficial pension plan.

But there are a couple of important advantages to saving within a pension plan. One is that you are not able to touch the money until you retire, so no matter how tempted you are to dip into your funds to pay for a holiday in Barbados or a new conservatory, you will not be allowed to do so. The second is that you get generous tax breaks. You get full tax relief on your pension contributions, which means that if you are a basic-rate taxpayer, for every 78p that you put into your pension fund, the government contributes an extra 22p, taking you up to £1. If you are a higher-rate taxpayer, you get an even better deal: for every 60p, the government adds 40p. No income tax is charged on your pension fund, nor is there any Capital Gain Tax on your pension investments.

A-Day: The New Pensions Regime

The most radical changes to UK pensions in a century took place on A-Day: 6 April 2006. Pensions simplification, as the changes are known, abolished the eight different sets of rules which governed how much you could put into a pension and how much you could take out, replacing them with one set of rules for everyone and for every type of pension scheme. So if you have an occupational scheme or a private pension, the rules are now exactly the same.

Contributions. Everyone can contribute up to £215,000 a year, or 100 per cent of their salary if that is the lower figure, to their pension plan. There is also a lifetime limit on the size of your pension fund, set at £1.5 million in 2006/7. If you have more than this in your pension fund when you come to retire, the extra is taxed heavily, at 55 per cent.

Tax-free cash. When you draw your pension, you can take 25 per cent of its value as a tax-free lump sum.

Trivial pensions. If your pension scheme is very small, less than 1 per cent of the lifetime limit (i.e. £15,000 in 2006/7), you are entitled to take the whole lot as a cash sum, a

quarter of which is tax-free and the rest taxed at the basic rate. You will not have to purchase an annuity.
SIPPS. You will be allowed to hold residential property funds within a self-invested personal plan, though you will not be able to invest directly in residential property through a SIPP.

Occupational Schemes

Around half of the working population are members of occupational schemes, and with good reason. They tend to be good value, although sadly they are no longer quite as generous as they used to be. Occupational schemes are great because your employer will make contributions on your behalf. Moreover, most occupational schemes offer a whole package of benefits, including a pension if you have to retire early because of ill-health, a pension for your partner should you die and life insurance should you die before retirement. So if your employer offers you a scheme, you should definitely check it out. There are two main types of occupational pension scheme.

Final-salary

Also known as defined benefit schemes, these are by far the most generous and attractive schemes. They are also almost impossible to come by these days unless you work in the public sector, since firms have calculated that they are too expensive and risky to run.

In a final-salary scheme, the pension you will get on retirement is defined as a proportion of your salary. The percentage of pay which you contribute to the scheme will vary to ensure that you are saving enough to provide for that proportion. The advantages of this type of pension are that you know how much you will retire on and that your employer takes the investment risk. If the pension fund's investments perform badly, it is the employer, not you, who bears the rising cost as a consequence. There are disadvantages for people who move jobs very frequently, since those who leave such schemes early tend to be penalized disproportionately.

Money-purchase

These are also known as defined-contribution schemes and are now far more common than final-salary pension schemes. They work in much the same way as a personal pension, although your employer will still make contributions on your behalf.

Contributions are kept in an individual pot and it is up to you to choose where you would like to invest the money, although there will usually be a 'default' option if you do not want to make the choice. Unlike with a final-salary scheme, if you have a money-purchase pension there are no guarantees as to what you will get when you do in fact retire, and the investment risk is borne by you rather than by the employer. There are no guarantees with this sort of scheme, so if the fund performs badly, you get a smaller pension.

What Happens If You Switch Jobs?

The rules of different schemes may vary but in general, if you have been a member of the pension scheme for more than two years, you can either leave the pension where it is or transfer your money to a new occupational or private pension plan. If you leave the money behind, it must be increased in line with inflation up to a maximum of 5 per cent annually. If you have been in the scheme for less than two years, you can usually take a refund of your contributions and have your pension cancelled.

How Much Should You Pay into Your Scheme?

You can contribute up to £215,000 a year, or 100 per cent of your salary, whichever is the lower.

IS YOUR MONEY SAFE?

The money paid into a personal pension is not 'safe' in the sense that the value of shares can go down as well as up, so if your personal pension is invested in shares and the stock market falls, you could lose money. What fewer people realize is that the money paid into occupational schemes is not 'safe' either.

The employees of Turner & Newall (T&N), an asbestos manufacturer, made contributions to their occupational pension scheme throughout their working lives, safe in the knowledge that they would get a decent pension income once they retired. But they didn't. T&N is owned by a US firm, Federal Mogul, which was forced to file for bankruptcy as a result of a number of asbestos-related claims. All of a sudden 40,000 current and former employees faced a terrible injustice: they were not going to get the pensions they had saved for all those years. Those who had already retired were told they could see future payments frozen, while some employees who had yet to retire might receive less than 40 per cent of the pension they thought they would be paid.

Daylight robbery? Damn right. But the employees of T&N

are not the only ones to have suffered catastrophic losses thanks to their pension funds being wound up. In February 2005, the Pensions Action Group held protests in central London and at the Labour Party Conference on behalf of the 65,000 people who have lost some or all of their occupational pensions because their schemes had been closed. In most cases, these were people in their fifties or sixties who had spent their whole lives contributing to a pension only to see their contributions used to pay the pensions of other people – namely those in the scheme who have already retired.

The case of occupational schemes is being addressed. The government has resolved to set up a Pension Protection Fund (PPF) which would compensate workers if their company pension scheme is wound up. However, this will not help people whose pension funds have already been wound up.

Even your state pension is not 100 per cent guaranteed. If the government changes the law, it could reduce your pension benefits, and it can do so retrospectively. However, eroding pension rights is politically extremely sensitive so few governments undertake this lightly.

Pensions for Everyone: Stakeholders and Private Pension Plans

If your company does not offer a pension scheme, or if, like many women, you work part-time and do not qualify, you can still purchase a personal pension to save for your retirement. A personal pension is just a savings plan sold by banks, building societies and insurance companies. You can open one at any age up to seventy-five, and you can draw your pension at any time between the ages of fifty and seventy-five. The self-employed, even the unemployed, are entitled to a pension plan too. You can even start a pension plan for your children!

Stakeholder pensions were introduced in 2001 and were designed to cater for people who have relatively low earnings (between £11,200 and £26,500) and who are not in an occupational scheme. But, provided you do not have an occupational pension, anyone can take out a stakeholder, whether you earn £1 million or nothing at all. These are available from banks and insurance companies, like any other type of personal pension, but, unlike other personal pensions, they are also available through your employer. Any firm that has more than five employees and does not offer another type of occupational scheme must offer you a stakeholder pension, although your employer is not required to make contributions on your behalf.

The advantages of a stakeholder are that they are cheap, flexible and portable. Annual charges are capped at 1 per cent of the value of your fund and no other fees are permitted. You can contribute as little as £20 a month to a stakeholder pension and can vary your contributions whenever you like. If you are going through a particularly difficult stage money-wise, you can cease contributions altogether without incurring a penalty. You can switch your pension fund from one management company to another without paying any charges.

Where Is the Money Invested?

If you choose an ordinary personal pension – stakeholder or otherwise – you will be given a choice of the type of fund in which you would like to invest your money. You might choose an actively managed fund, a tracker, equities or bonds, or, most likely, a mixture of equities and bonds. Once you have made your broad choice, the bank or insurance company will deal with the details of investing your fund. The question then is how to choose which fund manager to entrust with the all-important management of your pension contributions.

There are three main factors to consider. The first is fund choice. The range of funds on offer from the investment manager is important in order for you to be able to get a good spread of investments. Remember that for most people this is a fairly long-term investment – you may be saving for thirty years or more – so you do not want to be restricted in your choice of investment area.

The second thing to consider is the level of charges. Although these may seem trivial, over a long period of time, a small difference in charges can have a significant impact. For example, imagine that one fund manager charges an average annual charge of 2 per cent, while another charges just 0.8 per cent. Over thirty-five years, assuming contributions of £200 a month and an average annual return of 7 per cent, the more expensive fund would grow to £226,000, while the cheaper one would return £299,000.

The final factor is investment performance. Clearly you want to be able to pick a fund group which is going to manage your pension fund well and there is no simple way to do this. Either you will have to do your own research, looking at how various groups have performed, how long their managers have been around and how consistent their performance has been, or you could get an IFA to do the legwork for you. Since pensions are such a complex area, this can be one of the times when getting advice from a good IFA really pays off.

Self-invested Personal Pensions (SIPPs)

If a personal pension plan is a CD player, then a SIPP is an iPod. Instead of being restricted to the handful of funds offered by your particular fund manager, you can choose any one of the thousands on offer. You can also hold individual shares within your SIPP, as well as commercial property and residential property funds, though the Government backtracked on its original pledge to allow savers to invest directly in residential property.

SIPPS have traditionally been marketed at wealthier savers, because they used to be fairly expensive to set up and run, but there are now plenty of low-cost SIPPS on offer should you want to manage your own pension fund.

Drawing Your Pension

To sum up, pensions are difficult to understand and come in a bewildering range of shapes and sizes, but you do get very generous incentives, in the form of juicy tax breaks, to invest. However, pension plans come with strings attached. You might think, on retirement, that the money would be yours to do with as you see fit. It is your money, after all, earned with your sweat and toil, saved up over the course of your working life. But you would be mistaken!

Annuities

As we've seen, you can choose to retire at any time between the ages of fifty and seventy-five. Once you do, you will have to draw your pension. Everyone is now able to take 25 per cent of their pension fund as a tax-free lump sum. With the remainder of your money, you must buy an annuity from an insurance company. This must be done before you reach the age of seventy-five. The only exception is if you choose an alternatively secured pension (see below) or have a very small pension fund (less than £15,000 in the 2006/7 tax year), in which case you can take your pension without purchasing an annuity.

Annuities work in much the same way as a mortgage, except backwards. You give an insurance company a lump sum – your pension fund – and in return it pays you an income for the rest of your life. There are various different types of annuity:

Level annuities. These pay a set level of income every year. This is the simplest form of annuity and it offers you no protection against inflation, which is a distant disadvantage. The purchasing power of £1,000 diminishes to £776 over ten years, assuming 2.5 per cent inflation, or to just £599 assuming 5 per cent.

Joint-life annuities. These are usually purchased by married couples. The annuity will continue to pay out until both partners have died.

Index-linked annuities. These pay a rising amount over time in order to help counter the effects of inflation. The drawback is, of course, that you will receive a lower income when you first buy your index-linked annuity than you would if you had bought a level annuity.

Escalating annuities. These rise by a fixed percentage each year, say by 2 or 5 per cent. Again, your initial payments will be lower than they would had you bought a level annuity.
Investment annuities. With these the amount of income you receive will depend on the performance of certain investments. This is obviously a riskier type of product than level or index-linked annuities.
Guaranteed-period annuities. These promise to pay an income for a fixed period of up to ten years, whether or not the purchaser survives for that length of time.
Impaired-life annuities. These are for people who have medical conditions that are likely to shorten the course of their lives and pay higher rates than conventional annuities.

Smoking Is Good for You: Annuity Rates

When you purchase an annuity, what you are doing, in essence, is taking out an insurance policy against living too long. The longer you live, the better value that insurance policy will turn out to be. So people with medical conditions get better annuity rates because they are expected to die sooner, and therefore the insurer expects to have to pay out for a shorter period of time. This is the real kick in the teeth about annuities. If you live for twenty years after you purchase the annuity, you will get a good deal and the insurer will lose out, but if you die the day after you purchase it, in most cases the insurer keeps the lion's share of your entire pension fund, which could be hundreds of thousands of pounds.

When an insurer sells you an annuity, it is making a risk calculation. The shorter it believes your life will be, the higher the rate it is prepared to offer you. This is the one time in your life you will be rewarded for being a smoker – because they are more likely to die from any number of nasty diseases, smokers get better annuity rates than health freaks. But this is also one of the many times in your life that you will be penalized for being a woman. At present, women are paid lower annuity rates than men because we live longer than they do.

Most people purchase their annuity from the insurance company with which they held their pension fund. But you don't have to do this and in the vast majority of cases you should not. You should instead pursue the open-market option, and you can significantly increase your income by doing so. Annuity rates can vary by as much as 30 per cent, so it's important to shop around. For example, a woman aged sixty with a pension pot of £100,000 could get an annual income of £5,628 from Axa Sun Life, but £6,244 from Norwich Union. That's a difference of more than £50 a month.

What Happens If You Die Shortly after Taking out an Annuity?

This depends on the kind of annuity you have. If you have a single-life annuity, the payments will simply cease. If you have a joint-life annuity, then your spouse will receive benefits until he dies. Alternatively, if you take out a guaranteed annuity, income will be paid for the guaranteed period.

Annuities: Everybody Hates 'em, the Government Doesn't Care

Annuities are unpopular. People do not like the fact that they are compelled to spend their money, which they have spent a lifetime saving, on a product from an insurance company. And they do not like the fact that, once they have chosen their annuity, there is no going back. You cannot cancel an annuity or switch to an alternative provider. If you marry after you have purchased an annuity, you cannot name your new spouse as a beneficiary.

People dislike annuities because they are seen as bad value. Certainly, they look poorer value today than they have in the past. Annuity rates are based on long-term gilt (government bond) rates and gilt rates are in turn linked to interest rates. Since interest rates are now relatively low, and since we are living longer than ever, annuities look particularly bad value for money. In 1990, the average annuity rate was around 10 per cent. Today, they're hovering around the 5 per cent mark. In other words, in 1990 your £100,000 pension pot would buy you an income of £10,000, whereas today it'll get you around half that. That is because, back in 1990, the base rate of interest was more than 13 per cent. It is now below 5 per cent.

Despite their unpopularity, policy-makers seem determined not to abolish the compulsory purchase of annuities (although there are some ways around it: see below). They are concerned that, left to their own devices, people would either spend their pension funds too quickly or make poor or rash investment choices, and the state would then have to bail them out when everything went wrong.

Avoiding Annuities: Unsecured and Alternatively Secured Pensions

If you do not wish to purchase an annuity when you retire, you can either avoid or delay by choosing an Unsecured or Alternatively Secured Pension (UP or ASP). If you chose an UP (this used to be called income drawdown), you delay purchasing an annuity to the age of seventy-five. Your money can remain invested and you are restricted to taking no more than 120 per cent of the annual income you would get if you had a single-life, level annuity. The risk is that if your investments perform poorly, you could lose some of your pension fund and end up in an even worse position when you do purchase an annuity at seventy-five.

If you choose an ASP, you do not have to buy an annuity at all. However, you are entitled to take no more than 70 per cent of the annual income payable from a single-life level annuity at seventy-five. The advantage of an ASP is that you may be able to leave your pension fund to your children or other relatives. These are complex areas and anyone facing such choices really needs to take independent advice.

DRAWING YOUR STATE PENSION

It's quite simple actually. A few months before your sixtieth birthday (for younger women, it will be your sixty-fifth), you will be sent a pack inviting you to claim your pension. If you don't receive one, get in touch to find out why. As soon as you get your pack, put in your claim to ensure you will receive your payments on time. This is very important, because if you make a late claim, it will be backdated only three months. And remember that you don't actually have to have retired to claim your state pension.

I glanced out of the window and noticed that we were already approaching Newcastle. How time flies when you're sifting through pensions literature . . . My head hurt and I was exhausted. A couple of things kept running through my mind. One was that I wished I worked for a generous employer with a well-funded company scheme. The other was that the simplification rules have made pensions more flexible and more attractive. But then . . . the whole annuity situation dissuaded me. It just doesn't seem fair that after a lifetime of slog and saving, someone else gets to tell you how to spend your cash.

I was just mulling over this injustice when the phone rang. It was Susannah.

'How are you?' I asked her.

'I've got a current account!' she said, all excited.

'Excellent. Well done. So you're feeling a bit more positive?'

'Well, sort of,' she said. 'I'd feel a lot more positive if I actually had some money to pay into my spanking-new current account, but fingers crossed I will soon.'

'Really?' I asked, surprised. 'Are you expecting a settlement already?'

'Oh, God, no! We're still miles off. We're still waiting for a court date. No, I mean I think I may have a job!'

'That's fantastic, Susannah! Well done!' I gushed, all of a sudden realizing that I probably sounded a tad patronizing.

'Oh, I wouldn't get too excited,' she said, sounding a little sheepish. 'It's not terribly glamorous. I've applied for a part-time job in an art supplies place in the village. They know me well as I buy all my stuff from them, so they don't seem to mind the fact that I'm ancient.'

'You are not –'

'And speaking of ancient,' she interrupted, 'I have yet another thing to ask you. I was lying in bed last night, just thinking about how things might get a bit better if I at least had some money, when it struck me. I'm not going to get a pension, am I? I've never made any contributions.'

'Funny you should mention pensions. I'm just this minute doing some research. And the news is not all terrible, actually.'

'Oh, thank God. I was just picturing myself as a bag lady.'

'I don't think it's going to come to that. I can tell you how the system works in very general terms, Susannah, but it is absolutely essential that you speak to a specialist independent pensions adviser to discuss how best to approach pensions during the settlement. It is a really complicated area, particularly as Ed's probably got quite significant benefits accrued and you don't have anything at all.'

Pensions and Divorce

Pensions are treated just like any other asset when you divorce, so precisely who gets what will depend on the circumstances of the couple involved and on the decision of the court. Neither party's basic state pension is up for grabs. This is untouchable. However, divorced women who have not worked can still qualify for a basic state pension based on their ex-husband's contributions in the years that they were married. All other pension arrangements, including the state second pension (S2P) or SERPS, as it used to be known, are fair game.

When the court is deciding how to divide up assets, it will take into account the pension rights of both parties, particularly the contributions made and benefits accrued during the marriage. Take two scenarios. In one, a man makes pension contributions for fifteen years, then he marries. He continues to make contributions throughout their marriage, but this lasts only five years. In the second, the man makes contributions to a pension plan for three years before he marries. His marriage lasts for twenty-five years before it breaks down. The wife in the second scenario would stand a much greater chance of getting a 50–50 split of pension rights than would the wife in the first.

When it comes to dividing up pension rights on divorce, there are three main ways of doing this.

Pension Sharing

This is relatively new. Introduced in 2000, pension sharing allows a part of the pension to be transferred from one party to another. Sharing can work in two ways. Either the spouse can become a member of the pension scheme, but this is unpopular with administrators, or the pension can be transferred externally, either added on to an existing pension plan or as a completely new one. Pension sharing has the advantage of allowing a clean break between the former partners if they so desire, there is no need for contact when benefits are actually drawn and it can happen soon after the divorce.

Earmarking Order (also known as an attachment order)

There is no pension transfer, but when the benefits are paid out it is as per the court's instructions. This can be problematic. For example, if the court has ordered that the man should pay 25 per cent of his tax-free lump sum to his ex-wife, he could get around that by not taking a lump sum. Or if she is entitled to a share of the income from an annuity, he could delay buying the annuity for as long as possible in order to avoid giving her a share of his income.

Offsetting Agreement

If the pension is very small – say, a fund of just £5,000–£10,000 – the courts could simply decide to give the spouse an extra slice of the couple's current assets – say, a slightly higher percentage of the proceeds from the sale of the house – and leave the pension untouched.

Sounding mighty relieved, Susannah thanked me for my help and said she'd ring her lawyer straight away. I went back to my reading, but I was finding it hard to shake the conviction that I really didn't want a pension plan at all.

Pension Rejection

Many people decide that, despite the generous tax breaks, pensions and annuities are too complex and too inflexible for their liking. This is a perfectly reasonable standpoint. Although in most cases it makes sense to take advantage of occupational schemes (where your employer will be making contributions on your behalf), nowhere is it written that you must have a pension plan. After all, although you receive tax relief upfront when you contribute to a pension, you must buy an annuity at some point, and the income from this is taxable.

You can choose to fund your retirement by alternative means, but you will of course miss out on the initial tax relief, which means that you may have to put aside larger sums to begin with. And you will be able to do whatever you like with your money. If it has not been held within a pension plan, no one can force you to buy an annuity – although no one is stopping you either. You have total flexibility.

I arrived in Edinburgh feeling as though I had read *War and Peace* twice. I hopped in a taxi and was at my grandmother's house within fifteen minutes. She greeted me at the door looking as tired as I felt.

'You look wonderful,' she said to me with a warm smile, welcoming me into the hallway.

'You look tired, Gran,' I said, giving her a kiss on the cheek.

'I'm old,' she replied. 'I'm always tired. Tell me about your new boyfriend.'

'Bloody hell! Let me put my bag down at least,' I said, laughing. 'Who told you anyway?'

'I have my sources,' she said with a grin. 'Anyway, I'm glad you got rid of the last one.'

'You and everybody else,' I said, rolling my eyes.

My weekend with Gran was wonderful. She looked pretty awful – she admitted that she'd recently had a nasty bout of flu – and she seemed to be struggling to move about more than the last time I'd seen her, at Christmas, but she was very cheerful and seemingly determined to remain in the house. I tried, as delicately as I could, to broach the subject of her having to move ('if the worst came to the worst') but she wasn't having any of it. In fact, despite being eighty-nine and ill, she was talking about going on an art holiday to Tuscany next summer.

LONG-TERM CARE

Many people face the unpleasant prospect of having to move out of their homes in old age as a result of their deteriorating health. Statistics show that around one in three 65-year-old women will need long-term care – women are more likely to need care because of their longer lifespans.

Moving from one's own home is not just distressing, it can be very expensive. Laing & Buisson, a firm of health sector analysts, says residential homes cost around £18,000 a year, while nursing homes cost around £26,000. The state will not usually provide you with much assistance if you have assets of more than £20,000, and that means anyone who owns their own home.

In some cases, elderly people may sell their home in order to pay for care, but many people do not want to sell the house, either because they hope to be able to move back into the property should their health improve or because they wish to leave it to their children or grandchildren.

Care funding takes two main forms: pre-funded policies, which are either investment or insurance policies that can be used in the event that you need care, or immediate-need policies, which work in the same way as annuities. The market for pre-funded policies is very small: demand for the policies is low since so few of us ever plan for the eventuality of having to move into a home. If you purchase an immediate-needs policy, an income will be paid direct to the care home, gross of tax, for the life of the individual concerned. Alternatively, you could use the income from a conventional annuity to pay for care, in which case the income is paid to you, rather than the home, but it is taxed.

Options at this stage of life are complex and many conventional independent financial advisers may not be able to help. You need to seek out specialist advice: bodies such as Age Concern or Help the Aged will be able to point you in the right direction.

On the way back home I tried not to feel too depressed about Gran's health and her options. If the worst did come to the worst, surely between myself and my parents we would find a way to help her remain in the house? I had no idea what employing a full-time nurse would cost, but I suspected it would be frighteningly expensive. I resolved to look into it, and perhaps to consider persuading Gran to let us take some of the equity out of the Edinburgh property in order to help her remain there. It was worth considering.

It is easy to get depressed or worried about retirement prospects, but it's worth remembering that while we may face great difficulties as we grow old in Great Britain today, we face a lot more fun too. Fifty-five years ago, a specialist travel agency aimed at the over-fifties called Saga was established. It had one sole destination: Folkestone. Today, it takes pensioners to the beaches of Thailand and the jungles of Latin America on a regular basis. A mere 8 per cent of its business is in the UK.

I got back to London late on Sunday night and went straight to bed, ignoring the persistent blink of the answer phone, and did not listen to my messages until I'd got back from my run on Monday morning. It was all the usual suspects: Susannah, saying that she would ring me on the mobile; Nikki, wanting to know what 'lush joint' I was staying in this weekend; Mum, wanting to know how Gran was and reminding me that Dad was 'still going on about that pension thing'; Michael, 'just to say hi' (a likely story); and Kate, sounding breathlessly excited, banging on about some 'amazing flat near Magdalen roundabout' that she and Al had set their sights on. Nothing from Mark. Yes, I know he knew I was away, but still. All I'd had from him all weekend was a paltry text message.

I ignored all the messages and began putting my pension plan into action. The initial phase was twofold: to set up a cash account, into which I would pay money destined for the deposit on my buy-to-let, and to use this year's ISA allowance by investing in some fairly aggressive funds. I already own a small portfolio of more run-of-the-mill, core holdings, so I can afford to be a little adventurous.

I made my applications online and was feeling extremely smug about the good start I'd made to my pensions provision when the phone rang.

'How was it, then?' It was Mark.

'OK . . .'

'Just OK?'

'Well, she's not well. She looks really frail. I mean, she still seems incredibly up, you know, talking about holidays in Tuscany and what have you, but I don't think she's going to be doing much jet-setting any time soon.'

'Well, she's – how old is she?' he asked.

'Eighty-nine.'

'That's a pretty good run, then, isn't it?'

A good run? We're talking about my grandmother, not a bloody car. I asked how his weekend had been.

'Pretty dull. I had to work most of the time. I missed you.' And then in the next sentence, 'Did you think any more about that pension stuff we talked about?'

'You're such a romantic.'

He laughed.

'Actually I did, and I decided against it.'

A moment's silence.

'You decided against what?'

'A pension plan. I'm going to save, obviously, but I'm going to do it outside the pension plan. I just feel more comfortable doing it that way, and I like the flexibility.'

'Do you enjoy paying tax?' he asked irritably. 'We talked about this . . .'

'I know we did, and of course I don't like paying tax. I read through the stuff you gave me and I understand the issues . . .'

'Are you sure you understood?'

'Yes, I bloody understood,' I said, getting quite annoyed myself. 'And I've made a decision. I'm going to save, and invest, and possibly buy some property . . .'

'But with a SIPP . . .' he started.

'Yes, I know. Look, I have to get on. I've got a deadline,' I lied, keen to put an end to this discussion.

'OK. Fine. Do it your way. I'm glad your gran's on the mend.'

But she isn't, I thought to myself as I hung up. You would know that if you were actually listening to me.

6. First-time Blues: Buying Your Own Home

I rang Kate immediately after my tetchy conversation with Mark, but she wasn't at home and her mobile was turned off. At work, no doubt. My next move was to call her mother, to give her the latest update, and to have a chat with Dad, who was much more understanding about my decision than Mark had been. Still slightly annoyed by how patronizing he had been, I rang Nikki for a good bitch. She was on great form.

'Three down, seven to go!' she chirruped, without so much as a hello and how are you.

'I'm sorry?'

'I've finished paying off another credit card!' she crowed gleefully. 'God, I never thought paying the cards off could be as satisfying as loading them up!'

'That's brilliant news, Nik. I'm so pleased for you.'

'Well, I'm very pleased with myself. But enough about how fabulous I am. Where were you at the weekend? St Tropez? I was going to ring you on the mobile but I know how tetchy you can be. Plus, I didn't want to interrupt anything . . .'

'I wasn't with Mark,' I told her. 'I was up in Edinburgh with Gran.'

'Oh, God, of course you were. You told me that. Sorry. How is she?'

I told her, and she actually listened, which was gratifying. I also told her that Mark had been a bit of a git when I spoke to him that morning. She made all the right noises about how he was indeed a git and should have been more understanding, but she also pointed out that he was only trying to help with the pensions planning, and he did have a very demanding job after all, so perhaps he was a little stressed, and perhaps I should be a bit more understanding. Perhaps. I put all thoughts of him aside, and spent the day writing about mortgage repayment protection insurance.

Kate's call that evening was a welcome distraction from work.

'We've found such a lovely flat! We are so excited!' she cooed at me. Then, 'How's Mark?'

I said fine and didn't tell her what had happened that morning, as I knew it would only irritate her, that she would think I was being difficult and unreasonable. Maybe I was being difficult and unreasonable.

'Never mind him, tell me about this place you've seen.'

'Well, it's kind of small. It isn't exactly what we were looking for, because we were thinking, y'know, long term, we should get a three-bed place with a garden in the eventuality that we do one day have kids. But bollocks to that! Because we've been looking and frankly, for the money we've got, it's just impossible. We'd have to move such a long way out, and to such nasty bits of outer Oxford . . . But if we're just going for a one-bedroom flat . . . the choice is much better!'

'Just one bedroom?' I asked dubiously. 'Is that going to be enough room?'

'Well, with the two of us working every hour God sends, it actually is enough. So long as we have a fairly decent amount of storage space. OK, so we won't be able to have people over so much, but at least we'll be in there. No longer renting. We'll have somewhere of our own. I don't care where property prices are going, I really want that.'

*

Kate and Alex are in the position that many young (and not so young) people find themselves today: desperate to get on the property ladder, unsure as to which way prices are headed, nervous about staying out of the market, terrified of what it will cost to get into it. And terror is a rational enough response, when you take a good hard look at where property prices were ten to fifteen years ago and where they are now, and – most scary of all – when you try to guess where they will be in five or ten years' time.

Lies, Damned Lies

House price statistics are, like any stats, notoriously unreliable. However, if you look at Land Registry figures – and these show the average prices of residential property sales – you will see that the average house price in England and Wales in the early part of 1995 was a little over £66,000. By the end of 2004, average prices across the country had almost trebled, rising to £188,000. In Greater London, average price leapt from £95,000 to £287,000.

For the first-time buyer, life has become very hard indeed. Moneynet, a mortgage website, said that in July 2005 the average value of a home purchased by a first-time buyer was £198,000, with the average mortgage taken out by a first-timer around £134,000. If you don't know much about mortgages, I'll put that in perspective. The monthly repayments on a loan of that size would be around £820, assuming a mortgage rate of 5.5 per cent, and you would need to be earning around £38,000 in order to qualify for the loan.

But property purchase is a frightening prospect not just because house prices are so high, but because everyone is terrified of how far they might fall. Most commentators believe that the UK will see a much slower housing market over the next few years. The most pessimistic among them say prices could fall by anything up to 20 per cent. For newcomers to the property market, a 20 per cent fall in property values could be catastrophic. For those who have borrowed close to or all of the value of their property, a fall of this magnitude would leave them in serious negative equity, where the value of the property is less than the value of the loan secured on it. This is a nasty situation to be in, since if you were forced to sell your property, you would still end up owing the bank money, even after you handed back the proceeds of the sale.

ARE WE HEADING FOR A CRASH?

At the time of writing, it is the received wisdom that house prices in many parts of the country will fall. Indeed, we have already seen falls in many areas, although in some places prices have actually bounced back, particularly at the top end of the market in London. However, there is no agreement on whether they will slip back gently or fall off a cliff. No one knows whether we will face a crash the likes of which we last saw in the late 1980s and early 1990s, when, at the end of a period of just over two years, prices had fallen by 20 per cent, leaving hundreds of thousands of people in negative equity. Tens of thousands lost their homes. Could we face a similar crisis in the near future?

It's unlikely. House price pessimists say that the housing market is fundamentally overvalued. First-time buyers have been priced out of the market, undermining the basis of the housing market's strength. And price-to-income ratios are now higher than they were in the 1980s, when they hit around five times income. They are now closer to 5.5 times average income. Moreover, overall debt burdens are substantially higher than they were in the 1980s. We have a great deal more outstanding on personal loans and credit cards than we used to.

Against that, there is the fact that interest rates are still less than a third the level they were in 1990. Fewer houses are being built in the UK today than at any time since the Second World War, yet we have net immigration into the country and, more importantly, a greater number of households. High divorce rates and low marriage rates mean there are a great many more single households than there used to be. Bridget Jones does have her uses.

Anyone buying a home to live in rather than as an investment should not worry too much about the direction of the housing market, so long as you know that the price is right for your circumstances. If you are purchasing a home to live in, your prime concern should be whether you can afford the mortgage repayments.

'Can you?' I asked Kate.

'Well . . . it's a bit out of our price range,' she admitted.

'Aren't they always? What's the damage?'

'One eighty.'

'And your upper limit was?'

'More like one sixty.'

'That's quite a way out of your price range, Kate.'

'I know, but I really want it,' she said, not for the first time, nor the last in that conversation.

Get the Figures Right

If you want to buy a home, the first thing to do is to figure out your price range. In the old days, banks and building societies used to lend you no more than three times your income, or 2.5 times joint income. But as house prices have risen, income multiples have been stretched. Today, the basic multiples are around 3.5 times single income or 2.75 times joint income. In some cases, these income multiples can be stretched. Four times single income and three times joint are becoming more widely available, while some lenders will push the boundaries even further. NatWest, for example, has a special loan for professional applicants that allows you to borrow up to five times your income. But you need to think very carefully about borrowing such large amounts. Let's say you earn £30,000 and you borrow four times your income – that's £120,000. If you take out a competitive mortgage charging 4.74 per cent, your monthly mortgage repayments will be £683. That's around a third of your take-home pay. Borrowing such a large amount leaves you very vulnerable to interest rate rises if you have a variable-rate loan, since your costs will rise along with rates.

It has become increasingly popular among lenders to consider not just income but affordability. In other words, they will take into consideration not just your income but your other financial commitments, such as personal loans and credit cards, as well as your monthly spending on other items.

However, when you are doing your initial sums, it is probably a good idea to think conservatively, taking the standard multiples of 3.5 and 2.75. So if you earn £30,000, you could usually borrow up to £105,000. If you earn £30,000 and your partner earns £25,000, you would usually be able to borrow up to £151,250.

Traditionally, home buyers would have a deposit of at least 10 per cent of the purchase price in addition to this. If you have money for a deposit, all the better, but if you do not, it is now possible to borrow 100 per cent of the value of the home.

Remember that in addition to the price of the property itself, there are other costs to take into account, including legal, valuation and mortgage arrangement fees, which can add up to £1,000 or more, as well as structural surveys, which can cost hundreds of pounds. And then there is stamp duty, a tax levied as a percentage of the purchase price of the property.

Stamp duty rates for 2006/7

On properties with a value up to £125,000	no tax to pay
£125,001–£250,000	1%
£250,001–£500,000	3%
More than £500,000	4%

So if your property costs £180,000, you are looking at paying £1,800 in stamp duty.

Kate and Alex had set their sights on a place with an asking price of £180,000. But with a joint income of £52,000 and a deposit of £10,000, they should really have been looking at places between £150,000 and £160,000.

'Oh, no!' Kate howled at me. 'We're not going to have enough!'

I could sense I was in for an evening of melodrama. Home purchase is a very emotional issue.

'Hold your horses, Katie,' I said in my calmest voice. 'There are still other options and – in any case – you may not want to offer the asking price. In fact, you almost certainly don't want to offer the asking price. In this market, you may be able to knock a bit off.'

How to Get on to the Housing Ladder If You Actually Cannot Afford It

Get Your Parents to Help

If your parents own their own home and have done so for quite some time, the likelihood is that they've done rather well out of property. Many parents find themselves in a position where they can remortgage their home, withdrawing a slice of the equity which can then be lent (or given) to their children to help out with a deposit.

You do need to be a little bit careful with this. If your parents give you the money, then there are no complications unless they die within seven years, in which case their gift to you would form part of their estate and there would be an Inheritance Tax bill to pay on the money. If they loan the money to you on the understanding that you will pay it back within a certain time, then officially you should inform your lender that you have borrowed a part of the deposit. Not to do so would constitute mortgage fraud.

If your parents do not wish to remortgage, or if they simply do not have the money to give you, they could act as guarantors on your home loan, which would enable you to borrow a larger sum. For example, say you earn £20,000 and you want to buy a property which costs £110,000. Usually, a bank will lend you £70,000 or £80,000 at the very most, leaving you up to £40,000 short. This is where your parents can step in. They can agree to guarantee the remainder of the loan, though you would still have to find a way to meet the repayments. In some cases, your parents will have to agree to guarantee the entire debt, not just the slice that you cannot cover. You should take advice before you proceed down this route.

Offsetting

A handful of loans, including some offered by Woolwich and Newcastle Building Society, allow you to offset your mortgage debt with your parents' savings, which would mean that you would not have to pay interest on that portion of the loan, and that your parents would receive no interest on that portion of their savings. For more on how offset works, see page 169.

Buy with Friends

This is a tricky one. It seems to make perfect sense. You're all living together anyway, and the four of you have far greater purchasing power than any individual on his or her own. But you do not necessarily have four times the purchasing power. Traditionally, banks and building societies have offered 2.5 times your joint incomes, although these days, if you go through a broker, you may be able to borrow up to four times joint income. This could be an enormous amount, so you need to be very careful – take legal advice before you make any firm commitments.

You should also ask a lawyer to draw up an agreement specifying what will happen should one person want to sell out or leave the house. At twenty-five you may feel that you're happy to live with your girlfriends for ever, but it's amazing how quickly a move-in-with-me proposal from the man of the moment can put an end to all that girlie bliss. If you don't want to end up losing friends, be very careful about buying together.

Shared Ownership

Shared ownership schemes, which are usually run by housing associations and not-for-profit organizations, allow you to buy a part-share in a property if you cannot afford the full purchase price. You will usually be able to buy between 25 and 75 per cent. You must then pay a subsidized rent on the remaining share of the property, and have the option to purchase that share at a later date, once you can afford it.

Housing associations usually, though not always, prioritize buyers who are living in council housing or who are on local authority waiting lists. However, if you find yourself priced out of the market in your area, you may be eligible, so it's worth finding out about local schemes.

Key-worker Schemes

If you work in one of the 'key' fields identified by the government, you may be eligible for help with purchasing your property under the Key Worker Living Scheme. Public-sector workers such as nurses, teachers, police officers and social workers are among those who may qualify, although in order to be eligible, your sector must have serious recruitment problems and your maximum household income should be no more than £60,000.

To find out whether you are eligible, you need to contact the zone agent covering the area where you work (not the area in which you live). The zone agent will be a registered social landlord, usually a housing association, who markets housing schemes for local key workers. You'll need to check out the Office of the Deputy Prime Minister's website (*www.odpm.gov.uk*) to find your local zone agent.

Get a Mortgage Agreed in Principle

A mortgage is a loan secured against a particular property, so you cannot actually get a mortgage until you've found the home you wish to purchase. However, you can ask a lender if, all other things being equal, they will lend you a certain amount. It is important to do this before you have found your dream home, since having a loan agreement in principle will speed up the purchase process considerably, lessening the likelihood of your being gazumped.

So the next thing you need to do, once you have figured out the finances for yourself, is make sure that, in reality, a mortgage lender will see things the same way. Most lenders will give you a yes or no answer on a loan fairly quickly, since all they need to do is to carry out a standard credit check. They do not require to see proof of income or any other documentation, as they would when you apply for your actual mortgage.

'Oh, my God!' Kate wailed down the line at me. 'Why didn't anyone tell me about the mortgage in principle thing? Why didn't you tell me?'

'Well, I didn't actually know you'd begun house hunting in earnest,' I said. 'Look, it's not the end of the world. But if you're serious about making an offer, then you need to do that straight away.'

'But who do I get an agreement in principle from? Shall I just go to my bank?'

'No!' I said, rather too fiercely. 'Whatever you do, don't just go to the bank.'

Choosing Your Mortgage

Not so long ago, mortgages came in two basic types: fixed and variable. But, like most areas of personal finance, home loans have become a great deal more complicated over the past decade or so. In addition to fixed- and variable-rate loans, you can now have trackers, capped mortgages, discounted deals, cashback mortgages, self-certified loans and current-account mortgages. There are hundreds of different deals on the market, and it is highly unlikely that your bank will offer you the very best deal available.

One way of choosing is to go through a mortgage broker. Brokers know their way around the market, so they will be able to identify good deals. Some brokers charge fees, which may be worth paying if your situation is particularly complex, or you have specific problems in getting lenders to offer you a loan (perhaps you have an unusual property, or have had financial difficulties in the past). Using a broker can be a good idea – they often have exclusive deals that you will not be able to find elsewhere – and paying a fee should not be a deterrent, considering that buying a home is probably the largest purchase you will make in your life. However, so long as you do your homework and are sure that you understand the concepts involved, there is no reason why you should not be able to source a perfectly good deal all by yourself. First, you need to understand how different types of deals work, and which would be best suited to your needs.

Variable Rate

As the name suggests, the rate on your loan will vary, and its level is entirely at the discretion of the lender. The level of mortgage rates is determined by prevailing interest rates, but just because the interest rate falls does not mean that your mortgage rate will fall. Variable-rate loans are not pegged to interest rates, so if your lender is being greedy, it can widen its margins at your expense.

The attraction of variable-rate loans is that they are fully flexible: you can switch to a different type of loan at any time without penalty. The disadvantage is that you cannot be sure what your monthly mortgage repayment will be next month or next year.

Fixed Rate

Fixed-rate loans have a set term – usually one to five years, though you can have fixes going up to twenty-five years – during which time the rate (and therefore your repayments) will not change. The advantage of this type of loan is that you know where you stand – and this can be very comforting for buyers who have borrowed large amounts relative to their income and cannot really afford to see their monthly repayments creep higher.

The disadvantage is that interest rates could move against you. Say, for example, that the base rate of interest is 4.75 per cent and you take out a four-year deal charging 5.15 per cent. Six months later the base rate falls to 4.5 per cent and six months after that to 4 per cent. While your rate – and your repayments – stay the same, someone with a variable-rate loan would see their repayments tumble by £40 a month, assuming a loan of £100,000. Of course, if interest rates move in your favour, then you find yourself with a cheap deal. So before you choose a fixed-rate deal, you need to think about whether rates are likely to move, when and by how much.

If you take out a fixed-rate deal and interest rates do move against you, you could of course switch to another loan. But in most cases there is a fee – known as a redemption penalty – for switching from a fixed-rate loan during the time in which the fix applies. Some loans even have extended redemption penalties, which apply even after the term of the fix is over. These deals, although very cheap initially, are best avoided, since you can end up being tied into an uncompetitive rate for years.

Trackers

Like variable-rate mortgages, trackers move with interest rates, although, unlike variable-rate loans, these must follow interest rate movements by a specified amount. For example, you might have a tracker loan pegged at 0.5 percentage points above base rate.

Capped Mortgages

A cap aims to combine the best features of variable- and fixed-rate loans, while avoiding the worst features of both. With a capped loan, rates will vary, but a ceiling or cap is put on how high the loan rate can rise. For example, you may have a three-year loan capped at 5.75 per cent. This gives you peace of mind, in that you know that your repayments cannot rise above a certain level, but you also know that, should rates fall, you should see some benefits (though again, there is no guarantee that your lender will lower your mortgage rate in line with interest rates). Once again, there are usually redemption penalties during the lifetime of the cap.

Discounted Deals

These are variable-rate loans, but with a discount from the standard variable rate for a certain period, which can be anything from three months to several years. You may have to pay a redemption penalty if you wish to switch during the discounted period.

Current-Account and Offset Mortgages

These allow you to set your mortgage debt against your current account and savings. To take a simple example, say I have a £100,000 mortgage, savings of £20,000 and a current account balance of £5,000. With a current-account mortgage, I would pay interest not on my full mortgage debt, but on £100,000 – £20,000 – £5,000 = £75,000. Assuming a mortgage rate of 5 per cent, I would be paying monthly interest of £438 rather than £584. However, since I would not be earning any interest on my savings or my current account, the net saving is not quite as great as it at first appears.

Moreover, the rates you can get on current-account and offset loans are not usually the most competitive in the market. In general, you have to pay a little over the odds for current-account loans, so brokers argue that offset deals only really become worthwhile if you have at least 10 per cent, and preferably 20 per cent, of the value of your mortgage in a linked savings account.

If you have a mortgage of £100,000 and savings of just £1,000, the total saving you will make by linking the two is just £3,305 (assuming a rate of 5.95 per cent). You could have saved a great deal more than that by seeking out competitive rates. However, if you have savings of £10,000, you will save almost £28,000 in interest payments over the term of a twenty-five-year loan. Now it is starting to look interesting. And if you have £20,000 in savings, your interest bill is cut by £47,000. Which means that you will probably be able to repay your mortgage loan before its full term of twenty-five years. So for those with large cash savings, an offset plan is certainly worth thinking about.

Cashback Mortgages

As the name suggests, a cashback loan offers you a cash sum on completion of your loan deal. This may be just a token amount of around £250, but it may be a more significant sum. Some deals offer 6 or 7 per cent of the total value of the loans as cashback, usually with an upper limit imposed, but this could be as high as £30,000.

Cashback deals are very tempting to first-time buyers who may need to buy furniture or white goods, or simply to provide an emergency fund, just in case. However, look at the deals carefully, since the rates are not always competitive, and you will usually need to repay the cashback if you remortgage within a certain period.

Self-certification Loans

These were originally designed to help the self-employed find mortgage loans, although these days they can usually get standard mortgages from most lenders. And many full-time employees choose to go self-certified for one reason or another.

When you apply for a self-certification loan you state your income, but you do not have to offer proof of it in the form of a payslip or accounts. In most cases you do have to provide a statement of your income certified by an accountant, however. Self-certified loans are obviously useful for the self-employed, but they are also used by many employees, since you can take into account sources of income other than simply your annual salary. If you usually get a bonus, for example, this can be taken into account.

Recently there have been fears that many employees are applying for self-certification loans as a means of increasing the sums of money they can borrow, since it is easier to exaggerate your annual income if you do not have to provide documentary evidence. In fact, some brokers have even been accused of encouraging borrowers to exaggerate their earnings. Lying about your earnings is stupid for two reasons: first, because you are highly likely to fall into difficulties if interest rates should rise, and secondly, because mortgage fraud is a crime.

Repayment Methods

In addition to there being a host of different types of mortgage, there are also two ways in which you can repay your loan. One is to repay both a slice of the capital and the interest on it each month. The other is simply to repay the interest, so that at the end of the loan term, the full amount borrowed is still outstanding and would need to be repaid in one payment. Paying interest only can look very tempting, because it reduces your monthly repayments significantly. However, if you pay the interest only, then once you come to the end of the term of your loan, which is usually twenty-five years, you will still owe the bank the capital – the original amount you borrowed from them to buy the house. So if you borrow on an interest-only basis, you need to be saving up for the capital repayment somewhere else, in an investment fund or cash account, or most commonly in an endowment policy.

The Endowment Scandal

Endowment mortgages were hugely popular in the 1980s, when interest rates were high. Salesmen aggressively marketed endowment policies – a type of investment vehicle – because they could earn large commissions on the sale, promising customers the earth. Many people took out endowments having been told that they would definitely grow at a sufficient rate to pay off the mortgage – some were even promised surpluses. However, the majority of endowments failed to grow fast enough. A recent report said that 80 per cent of endowments would not meet their targets – that is, they wouldn't grow fast enough to be able to pay off the capital owed at the end of the mortgage term. There were lots of reasons for this: insurance companies which sold endowments set premiums too low in an attempt to make their policies more attractive, while poor investment performance meant the funds did not grow fast enough. As a result, millions of homeowners were left with a shortfall on their mortgages. Many will qualify for compensation. However, the endowment scandal clearly demonstrates the dangers of opting for interest-only loans.

Tips for Choosing the Right Mortgage

Don't be dazzled by attention-grabbing headline rates. Ask the lender (or your broker) to calculate what the loan is going to cost you over a given period – say, seven years, since this is the length of time most people stick with one loan.

Do consider other costs and incentives. Most fixed, capped and discounted loans will have arrangement fees, which can be as much as £600, or even higher if you are looking at taking out a very large loan. On many mortgage deals, lenders offer discounted valuation and legal fees, which can be worth considering, particularly if you are remortgaging and borrowing only a relatively small amount.

I pointed Kate in the right direction, told her to talk it over with Al and ring me the next day. I hung up, made dinner, poured myself a large glass of wine and settled down in front of *Nip/Tuck*, but something was bugging me. I rang Kate again.

'How many times have you seen this place, Kate?' I asked.

'Once. But we don't need to see it again. We really love it.'

'Go back,' I said. 'Arrange another viewing and go back. Do it at rush hour, to see how bad the traffic noise is, because – Magdalen roundabout? It's fairly noisy. Or in the evening, to find out how noisy the neighbours are.'

'Well . . .'

'How many other places have you seen?'

'A couple,' she said, 'and they were bloody awful.'

'Just a couple?'

'We've made up our minds!'

'OK. But go back and see the place again. Please. And don't tell the agent you're in love with it. They'll use that against you at a later date. Be interested, but a little bit cool. OK?'

She promised to do so, and I went back to scenes of blood, gore and perfect breasts.

FREEHOLD OR LEASEHOLD?

If you buy a house, you will usually buy the freehold. That means that once you've paid off the mortgage (or immediately if you pay cash), you own the property and the land on which it stands lock, stock and barrel. However, if you buy a flat, you will usually find that you are buying the leasehold. The lease runs for a certain number of years – usually around ninety-nine, but they can be as long as 999 – during which time you have to pay ground rent (which is often a token amount) to the freeholder. The terms of leases vary enormously, but in most cases the freeholder is responsible for the maintenance of the building itself, so if the roof leaks, for example, it is up to the freeholder to fix it. The leaseholder is, however, responsible for the maintenance of her own flat.

It is a bizarre quirk of the property system in England and Wales that ownership of the property reverts to the freeholder once the lease has run out. For this reason, you are not advised to purchase a property with a lease of less than sixty years. In practice, you do not have to hand over the property to the freeholder once the lease runs out but can opt to extend it. However, this can be very expensive. Alternatively, if you and the other owner-occupiers in a block of flats can come to an agreement, you can opt to buy the freehold.

A couple of days after our initial conversation about the flat, Kate rang back to tell me they had been to visit it again and that yes, there was a little traffic noise, but not so much that they couldn't live with it. In any case, they could always buy double-glazing.

'Did you think any more about mortgages?' I asked her.

'We've spoken to Al's parents and they're prepared to be guarantors. They've completely paid off their mortgage, so they shouldn't have any problems. And we found a deal that's specifically geared to professionals, so being a doctor pays off for once. It's with Newcastle Building Society.

We get a fixed rate for five years, which also helps, since we'll know exactly what we have to pay for the immediate future.'

'That sounds good,' I said. 'Well, so long as Al's parents know exactly what they're getting themselves into, I think you should go ahead and apply.'

'And if they say yes, then what happens?'

'Then you make an offer.'

Making an Offer

Before you make an offer, you need to find out how realistic the asking price is. This will depend on a whole host of things, including the prices of similar properties in the area, how long the house has been on the market, the condition it is in and the way the housing market is going. The house may be perfect, but if you are negotiating in a buyer's market, don't make life easy for the seller. Listen to the estate agent's advice, but don't take what they say for granted. They work for the seller, not for you.

Kate and Alex made their application the following morning and rang the agent with their offer. They had decided to go for exactly 10 per cent below the asking price, offering £162,000. The offer was rejected. Al was the one to receive the bad news. He decided not to tell Kate straight away, as she was working in A&E and he didn't want to be responsible for loss of life or limb. So I found out before she did.

'She's going to be so upset,' he said. He sounded genuinely afraid.

'Oh, don't be ridiculous!' I scoffed at him. 'You hardly ever get your first offer accepted. Just nudge it up a little.

And don't be disheartened if they say no to that offer too. It's all cat and mouse stuff now.'

The sellers did reject their new offer, of £165,000, but a week later Kate and Alex's third offer, of £170,000, was accepted. I was just getting ready to go out to dinner with Mark when she rang, full of optimism, her head buzzing with design ideas.

'I'm thinking of painting the hallway a kind of dark red,' she told me. 'And we'll do the bathroom in green. Not like avocado green, but sort of bottle green. It sounds gloomy, but actually, with the right tiles, I think it'll look amazing.'

'Mm-hmm,' I agreed distractedly, glowering at the contents of my wardrobe, which were scattered over my bed. 'Sounds great. You know, I really don't have anything to wear. I'm not just saying that. I actually don't.'

'Of course you do! Don't be ridiculous. Wear that red top I like. It's not like he'll notice anyway.'

'Oh, thanks so much,' I replied grumpily. 'And I wore the red thing last time we went out.'

'Well, wear that black wraparound thing, then. And I didn't mean that he specifically wouldn't notice you. I just mean men, not noticing stuff.'

'Well, he does actually. We were sitting around watching TV on Sunday and there was something on – I don't even remember what – but this girl was wearing this great little jacket and I started going on about how I'd really like one, and he says "Yeah, well, you do need to expand your wardrobe."'

'What?!' she shrieked. 'You what? He told *you* to buy new clothes?'

'Yeah, all right, Kate, I can hear you.'

'What a cheek!' she yelled, ignoring me. 'I hope you told

him to piss off. What was he wearing at that moment in time anyway? A rugby shirt? A nice cable knit sweater his mum gave him for Christmas?'

'I . . . can't remember. Anyway, I was kind of annoyed, but I don't think he meant to be mean. He's just one of those guys who expect a girl to turn up in a new frock every time they go out.'

'Well, that's bloody ridiculous.'

There was a short silence.

'But what do you think about green for the bathroom?'

'Kate, I hate to spoil your *Wallpaper** moment, but I think you might be getting a little ahead of yourself. You're not moving in just yet.'

'I know, there's a survey and then the conveyancing. But that shouldn't take long, should it?'

'Kate, there are lawyers involved. It takes ages.'

Surveys

Once you have found the place you want to buy, and once your offer has been accepted, you need to get a survey done. In fact, you could have a survey done before you make your offer, but they can cost hundreds of pounds, so you need to be serious about the place. There are three different types of survey.

Basic Valuation

This is carried out by the lender for the purposes of the mortgage, and a copy will be sent to you, which seems fair since you foot the bill of between £150 and £300. These valuations are, well, pretty basic. Their purpose is solely to establish whether the property is mortgageable. So you must have your own, more detailed survey carried out.

Homebuyer's Report

This is the survey carried out by most buyers and is perfectly appropriate for conventional houses and flats that are in reasonably good condition. You can commission your own surveyor to carry out the report, or ask your lender to arrange it on your behalf. You can expect to pay up to £450 for the survey, which will cover the general condition of the house, recommendations for repair and maintenance, any major defects you should be aware of and legal issues such as rights of way.

Full Structural Survey

A full survey can cost anything up to £1,000, but if you can afford it, you should get one done. If you are buying a property which is more than three storeys in height, which is in any way unusual (with a thatched roof, for example) or which is more than 100 years old, you must get a full survey done. It will make for daunting reading, since the surveyor will note down every last detail and defect in the property, but it will give you a very clear idea of how much work the property may need, which in turn will indicate how much you may need to spend on the house at a later date.

Surveys do not, however, tell you whether you should buy the house or not. If you have concerns, you may want to discuss them with an architect or a builder before you go ahead.

Conveyancing

This is the process by which the title to the property is transferred from one person to another. It sounds simple enough, but in fact it can take months to complete. Your solicitor will need to check the legality of various contracts, carry out local searches and prepare the contract for sale. You can do the conveyancing yourself, if you do not want to pay a solicitor to do it for you (it will set you back at least £300), but it involves a considerable amount of work even if you know the law, and for a legal novice it is a mammoth task. It is also a very important one. Get it wrong and you could end up paying a couple of hundred grand for a garden shed, not a three-bed semi with garden and shed. If you do decide to do the conveyancing yourself, contact the Land Registry for the requisite forms.

BUYING PROPERTY IN SCOTLAND

There are some key differences you should be aware of if you are planning to purchase a property in Scotland rather than England or Wales. For starters, once you've purchased the property – it's yours. There is no equivalent of the leasehold system. House purchase is usually quicker in Scotland, and the system leaves less room for gazumping, but in some ways it is more nerve-racking for the seller. There are differences in the purchase process too:

- The mortgage is arranged before you make an offer.
- A survey is also carried out before making an offer.
- The seller sets a price above which offers will be accepted. If there is more than one bidder, the seller's solicitor will set

a deadline by which sealed bids must be made. It's a bit like playing poker – you will usually only get one chance to bid.

- Once an offer has been accepted, the solicitors complete the 'missives'. This is a bit like exchanging contracts in England and Wales, only in Scotland once both parties have agreed to the offer (which happens quite early in the process), you are legally bound to continue with the sale, and may be liable for the other party's costs if you decide to pull out.

It was turning out to be a gloriously warm spring and I was depressed as hell. I had mountains of work to do, the roof of my flat had started to leak (and I am the bloody freeholder, so I have to pay for it to be repaired), I had put on four pounds since February and Mark was not exactly turning out to be the man of my dreams. He was nice. Polite, good-looking, hard-working, occasionally a little insensitive, a tad arrogant and sometimes really quite dull. But for some reason I couldn't quite bring myself to break it off. I'd only just finished breaking up with someone. Surely I deserved a break from breaking up? After all, he wasn't a monster. It struck me that not being a monster wasn't perhaps sufficient to make him eligible for boyfriend status. But I still didn't do anything about it.

One particularly lovely Saturday morning in May, I decided to invite Mel out to lunch to have a good moan. I took her to the Oxo Tower, since it was such a nice day, and had just launched into an oh-why-is-my-life-so-rubbish? whinge when I caught sight of Michael approaching from the other end of the restaurant.

'Oh, my God! Look who's here!' I cried out.

Mel turned round. 'Oh, shit, I forgot,' she mumbled through a mouthful of salad. 'He rang just as I was leaving the house and I said he could join us for dessert. Sorry, Tasha. Hope you don't mind.'

'Of course I don't,' I said, and I really didn't, although I sensed my audience was about to go from sympathetic to scathing.

'You're early,' Mel said, standing up to give him a kiss. 'We haven't even got to the main course yet.'

'Sorry,' he said, grinning, 'but I was starving, so I thought I'd crash.'

As I'd anticipated, Mel listened kindly to my complaints. Michael did not.

'Correct me if I'm wrong,' he started out, 'but I believe it was a mere three months ago that you came to my flat to cry on my shoulder about the last bloke . . .'

'When did you go to Michael's flat?' Mel asked me.

'A while back,' I replied. 'We bumped into each other in town and he made me cottage pie.'

'Oh,' Mel said. She looked vaguely put out.

'As I was saying,' Michael went on, 'you were moaning about the last one, and I said your problem was that you always went for safe, boring blokes, and you told me that I was talking complete crap, and now here we are and you're with another safe, boring bloke and you're bloody miserable.'

I didn't really have a riposte to that, as he appeared to be correct, so I just glared at him.

Mel was gazing thoughtfully at her glass of wine. I decided to change the subject.

'Are you still planning to sell the flat, Mike?'

He was, but he was torn between using an estate agent ('evil, weaselly little bastards') and doing the work himself.

Estate Agents

Estate agents have a dreadful reputation. A good reason for this may be that although there are plenty of reputable agents out there, there are also plenty of cowboys. Not surprising really, considering that estate agents need no formal qualifications, do not need to belong to any recognized professional body and don't need to give any firm evidence to support the price tags that they slap on houses. But just because agents are not required to be members of recognized professional bodies does not mean that there are not plenty of agents who are. Any agent which is a member of the National Association of Estate Agents (NAEA), for example, has to adhere to its code of conduct and is likely to have had extensive training. If agents are also members of the Royal Institution of Chartered Surveyors (RICS), they will have some professional qualifications.

Once you have identified several agencies that have membership of the NAEA or RICS, invite them to value your home. Valuations are free, so you should ask at least three or four estate agents. Valuations can vary quite significantly. Don't necessarily go for the agent who gives you the highest, since this may just be a desperate bid for your business. Remember that putting an unrealistically high price on your home can be disastrous: you will end up having to accept a lower price, but in the meantime your home will have been sitting on the market for months, and this will lead buyers to believe that there is something fundamentally wrong with the place.

How Many Agents?

Given their unpopularity, you might have thought that one agent was enough, but this is not necessarily so. You can ask one, two or many agents to sell your property.

Sole Agency

This is where you instruct one agent to sell your house. For the term of your contract with that agent, you are not permitted to engage another agent, and if someone just wanders in off the street and asks you to buy your home, you will still have to pay commission to that agent, despite the fact they had nothing to do with the sale. The advantages of sole agency are that it is cheaper and your agent should work hard to make the sale; the drawback is that you are restricted to the client base of one agent.

Joint Sole Agency

This is where you instruct two agents to work together to sell your property. The agents should be a good pairing – perhaps one is local and the other national. This tends to be a more expensive arrangement, but of course you will have two agents trying to sell your home, so hopefully it should be seen by a wider range of prospective buyers.

Multiple Agency

This is where you instruct a number of agencies to sell your home, each of which is working independently of the others. The possible drawback with multiple agency is that the individual estate agents may not work that hard to sell your place because they are not guaranteed commission on the sale.

How Much Does an Agent Cost?

This is negotiable. In general, agents charge between 2 and 3.5 per cent (plus VAT, which is 17.5 per cent of the fee), but competition from online property sites has pushed commissions lower, so some agents ask as little as 1 per cent. Contract terms are also negotiable. Most agents will ask for three months to sell your house, but you should try to talk them down to six to eight weeks. That way, you can walk away if you're not happy with the job they're doing.

Once you've engaged an agent, check them out. Walk past their window to see if your property is prominently displayed. Are there photos of your place on their website? Make sure they're working for the money.

Engaging an agent is expensive. Let's take Michael's place, which is worth around £250,000. If he engages an agent charging 2.5 per cent, he'll end up paying a little over £7,300, including VAT. So say you want to save yourself seven grand, what are the alternatives?

Private Sales

You can of course sell privately. The problem with private sales is twofold: first, you have to do your own marketing, which can be tricky, and second, you have to do the viewings yourself. Valuation is not a problem, since you can always invite a load of estate agents round to do the valuation for you and then not engage any of them! Or you could pay a surveyor to do a valuation if you really wanted to, but it seems a little pointless.

Marketing your property is much easier than it used to be. You can use the traditional methods: classified ads, little cards in shop windows, a 'For Sale' sign outside your property, but now you have the added reach that the Internet offers. Online sales sites are hugely popular, and although many charge a fee, it will still be significantly less than what you would pay an estate agent.

The second problem is that of arranging viewings. Inviting a stranger into your home is not always a good idea – particularly for women on their own – so you may want to ask someone else to be present when you are showing your house.

Auction

Around 30,000 houses are sold by auction every year. The advantages for the seller are that you get an immediate exchange of contracts – there is no waiting about for mortgage applications to be approved or searches to be completed – and that you know the minimum price you will receive for the property – your reserve price – assuming of course that it does sell. If you do sell your property at auction, the sale counts as an exchange of contracts and the buyer must pay a 10 per cent deposit, with the remainder of the funds to follow within twenty-eight days.

Selling by auction is, however, not a great deal cheaper than selling through an agent. You will need to pay an initial fee of around £250 to have your property included in the auction house's catalogue, and once your property is sold, you will have to pay a commission of between 1.75 and 2.5 per cent.

When picking auction houses, take a good look at their

catalogues. If you are trying to flog an ultra-hip urban-industrial space in Shoreditch and their books are full of quaint country cottages, you can be sure that you've not yet found your match.

WHAT ABOUT BUYING AT AUCTION?

Not for the faint-hearted, this. The pros of buying at auction are that you can do the deal quickly and that you may find a bargain. The cons are that you are rushed into making a huge decision under pressure, so it may not be a wise one. And of course you might be outbid.

If you do fancy buying at auction, the key thing is to be prepared. Get hold of a load of auction catalogues and see what's available. Go to a few auctions at which you do not plan to bid, just to get a feel for the whole process. If you do spot a property in one of the catalogues that you fancy bidding on, arrange a viewing. If you think it makes the grade, and if you're really serious about bidding for it, get a valuation and survey done.

Obviously if you do not win the bidding, you will have wasted money on the valuation and survey, but it would be foolish in the extreme to buy a property without knowing whether it is structurally sound or what it's really worth. Don't take the guide prices in the auction catalogue too seriously. Most properties will sell for well in excess of that.

Remember that you will have to put down a 10 per cent deposit on the day of the auction if you are successful and that you will need to get a mortgage arranged fast, so it makes sense to get an agreement in principle before the day.

On the day of the auction, make sure you get there in plenty of time. Check the addendum to see whether your property has been sold or withdrawn. Don't open the bidding, if you can help it. You want to keep your cards close to your chest. Be assertive – wave your arms around if you want to make a bid. Don't be afraid that if you scratch your nose you will have inadvertently put a £1 million bid on a property.

Michael took a long slug of red wine and sighed. 'It might just be simpler to go with an agent. I really can't be bothered with showing people around myself. Although it might be a good way to meet women,' he added with a sly little smile.

Mel cuffed him over the back of the head. Affectionately, I thought. I gave her a look. She blushed.

'Have you made up your mind about where you want to move to?' she asked Michael, turning away from me.

'Southwark. London Bridge. Around here even. I've been looking, and I'll be able to get a pretty decent two-bed place for what I'll make on my flat plus last year's bonus and a huge mortgage. I'm really looking forward to having some space. And maybe a view of the river. Chicks love a view.'

Mel rolled her eyes.

'But I need to sell my place first. Actually, Mel, I was thinking you might come around and, you know, Laurence Llewellyn-Bowen it up a bit. You're good at that sort of thing.'

'It'll cost you,' she quipped.

Michael hailed the wine waiter right on cue.

Michael had to dash off after lunch, but Mel and I decided to wander along the river to the Tate Modern for a bit of post-prandial culture. I was in no mood (after several glasses of wine) to stand on ceremony.

'So what is going on with you and Michael?' I asked her.

'Nothing,' she said quickly, gazing out across the Thames and quite pointedly not looking at me.

'You are a terrible, terrible liar,' I told her. 'There was all this . . . atmosphere at lunch. Have you two been . . . ?'

'No,' she said with a sigh. Then, 'OK, yes, but please don't tell anyone. Especially not Kate. Everyone thinks he's such a shit –'

'He is a shit.'

'Yes, I know he is.' She sighed again.

I put my arm around her. 'But he's also lovely,' I conceded. 'It's just . . . remember last time?'

'No, I don't. I've completely forgotten the seven months I spent sitting on the sofa in my pyjamas, sobbing uncontrollably,' she said sarcastically. 'Of course I bloody remember. It was bloody awful. But then . . . I don't know. We've just been getting on so well, and I like him so much, and . . .' Another big sigh. 'After Amy and Ade's party –'

'That was months ago!' I cried. 'I can't believe you've not said anything. Does Nikki know? Does Amy know?'

'No. No one knows, because there's nothing to know. It's not . . . a relationship. It's just a thing.'

'Mm-hmm. And you're happy with that?'

She sat down on a bench in front of the museum and started to cry.

I spent Sunday hibernating, reading the papers, ignoring the phone. Mark rang twice. The sound of his voice irritated me. Michael rang too, but I couldn't trust myself to speak to him without yelling at him for making my friend unhappy. I rang Mel a couple of times, but she wasn't picking up either. So I sat in my living room, gazing bitterly out at the glorious sunshine, listening to the twin soundtrack of the kids on the estate next door yelling obscenities at each other and my downstairs neighbours' drum and bass, and felt a desperate need to escape. I needed somewhere to flee to. A cottage in the country. The French countryside, preferably. Couldn't that be my pension plan? A stone cottage set among vineyards and olive groves in the heart of the Luberon?

The fact that I didn't have any spare capital would be a problem, but not an insurmountable one. I could always remortgage. Like everyone else who bought property in the 1990s, I had seen my flat appreciate considerably in value, so that although I hadn't paid off a great deal of my original mortgage loan, in theory I now owned a significant share of the equity in my home. That equity could be tapped and used to do more than just fix the roof and retile the bathroom; it could be invested elsewhere.

All the Rage: Remortgaging

In 2003, 45 per cent of all the money lent by banks and building societies was in the form of remortgages. That's right: almost half the money lent was not to buy a property, but simply a renegotiation of the debt outstanding on an existing property. The remortgaging boom has been fuelled by a whole host of factors: increased competition (and therefore better deals) in the mortgage market, greater consumer awareness of the choice out there and of course the sharp increase in house prices. Because people are not just remortgaging in order to get better deals. Many have been remortgaging in order to tap into the growing equity in their homes.

Taking equity out of your home may or may not be a good idea, depending on circumstances, but remortgaging to cut costs is almost always a good idea. Many people will take out a discounted or a fixed-rate mortgage when they first get their loan, but after a few years, once the fix or cap or discount has run out, they find themselves switched on to the bank's standard variable rate (SVR). This is rarely competitive. Yet many people don't bother to switch away. They are deterred by the expense and hassle involved in remortgaging. And, unlike switching bank accounts, switching mortgage lender is time-consuming and expensive. But it is also worthwhile.

Clear Cut Mortgages, a broker, said in 2004 that British homeowners wasted a total of just over £8 billion every year by failing to switch away from uncompetitive SVRs to cheaper deals. The monthly repayments on a £100,000 home loan charging the average SVR of 6.75 per cent are £690. The repayments on the same loan switched to a good discounted rate – say, a two-year deal charging 4.49 per cent – would be £555. That's a difference of £140 a month, or £1,680 a year.

Remember that remortgaging is not free. You need to pay for a valuation, which costs a few hundred pounds, solicitors' fees and possibly an arrangement fee for your new loan, so you should budget for as much as £1,000 to spend on the remortgaging process. As we have seen in the example above, however, that money can be recouped in the first year of your remortgage. Some lenders will offer you incentives to remortgage. Tesco Mortgages, for example, has a three-year discounted deal which offers free valuation and legal fees. The arrangement fee is £399, but that will be your only cost. Fees-free deals are well worth considering, so long as the rate is right. Unless you have a very small mortgage, the rate should always be the most important consideration.

Remortgaging costs will be higher if you are switching out of a deal that carries redemption penalties. A typical redemption penalty will be several months' interest, although it may be calculated as a percentage of the loan. Clydesdale Bank has a three-year fix, for example, which charges 3 per cent of the total amount repaid if you switch during the first two years, or 2 per cent if you switch in year three. Assuming you have a £100,000 loan and you switch during year two, you will have to repay £2,000 to the lender in fees.

Not everyone remortgages to cut costs. If you have paid off a significant chunk of your original mortgage, or if your house has risen in price, you can remortgage in order to raise funds from your property. I was thinking, for example, of remortgaging in order to pay to fix my roof and to raise some money to put down as a deposit on a new property – preferably one in a picturesque part of France.

Buying Property Abroad

The property purchase process will vary enormously depending on where you want to buy a home, so you will need to seek out specialist advice appropriate to your chosen country. The most common destinations for UK buyers are Spain, France and Italy, but we are becoming more adventurous, looking east to recent EU entrants such as the Czech Republic, and west to Florida. It is absolutely essential to take advice before you initiate the purchase process.

Most people decide they want to buy a property abroad in September. They'll have just come back from two fabulous weeks in a farmhouse in Provence / villa in Umbria / apartment with pool in Marbella (delete as appropriate) and they'll have decided that they absolutely cannot bear the British food / countryside / people any longer and they simply must have a place to which they can escape a few times a year (or in some cases permanently).

We've all felt like that – who wouldn't after two weeks in the Mediterranean sun, drinking reasonably priced red wine and eating cheese from the local market, hundreds of miles from the Northern Line? But rushing into things is very foolish. Think about where you want to buy. Do you have even the most basic grasp of the local language? Will the local people be pleased to see another British family snapping up a property in the area, pushing house prices further out of their children's reach?

Gauging the local temperature is hugely important if you're planning to live in your new home. Try to find out whether you'll be welcome or whether the locals have had enough of the British. And find out what extra expenses will be incurred if you decide to buy a place abroad. Property prices might seem dirt cheap on the Continent, but you'll find a range of other fees which you wouldn't encounter over here. Estate agent fees, for example, which are payable by the buyer, can be as much as 10 per cent of the purchase price, while notary fees and the purchase tax can add a further 10 per cent. In France, stamp duty is just under 5 per cent, while in Spain, a property transfer tax of 7 per cent is charged on all but newly built homes.

Wherever you decide to buy, a few common-sense general rules apply:

- Don't sign contracts you don't understand. If the contract is written in a foreign language, use a lawyer who speaks both that language and your own fluently. Don't take any risks. You wouldn't be the first buyer to shell out hundreds of thousands of pounds, only to find that the property does not really belong to you, since it never really belonged to the person who sold it to you.
- Get an independent valuation, just the way you would in

the UK. Properties may look idyllic, but they could be in a far worse state of repair than they appear.

- Make sure that you are not taking on someone else's debt when you purchase the property.
- If you're buying a property that is still being built, make sure that the necessary planning permission has been agreed.
- Open a bank account in the local currency and set up standing orders to pay bills and local taxes.
- Get tax advice from accountants based in both the UK and the country in which you are purchasing to make sure that you do not fall foul of the authorities.

What's Italian for 'Mortgage'?

There are three main ways in which you can finance the purchase of property abroad. First, if you own property in the UK and if you have paid off most of your mortgage, you can remortgage your UK property and use the funds to buy a property abroad. Bear in mind, however, that if you cannot meet your repayments, it is your UK home that would be directly at risk.

Second, you could borrow in the UK, but secure the loan against the foreign property. And third, you can borrow the money in the country in which your property is located.

In addition to choosing how to borrow, you need to decide what to borrow: euros, pounds or dollars. It makes sense to borrow in the currency in which you are earning, so if you are planning to move to France and will be earning a living there, then you should probably borrow in euros. If you're just looking to purchase a holiday home, then you would be better off borrowing in pounds.

Plenty of UK lenders, including Barclays and Abbey, offer mortgages on foreign properties. However, you would probably be wise to consult a specialist overseas mortgage broker, such as Conti Financial Services or Savills Private Finance, to advise you on how best to raise the money to purchase a home abroad.

On Monday morning, I sprang out of bed, all excited at my new idea of foreign property purchase. After spending a couple of hours trawling the Internet, looking at what was on offer, I was feeling a little less enthusiastic. French property prices just aren't what they used to be! Time was you could buy a chateau for around the same price as a three-bed semi in Croydon. No more. Prices in the most desirable parts of France (desirable to us Brits, that is), such as Provence and the Dordogne, have risen significantly over the past decade, as more and more attractive stone farmhouses have been snapped up by Peter Mayle types seeking the perfect bolthole in the French countryside.

So perhaps I had been a little foolish, a little naive, to think that I would be able to afford a second home abroad (because believe me, if France is too expensive, then just wait until you see the prices in Italy). Perhaps, if I really wanted a place to escape to, I should be looking closer to home. A closer inspection of my options was probably a good idea.

The doorbell rang, interrupting my musings. I opened the door to discover a man delivering a bouquet of long-stemmed Oriental orchids. They were from Mark, just because he was thinking of me. I was hit by a wave of guilt. He was so sweet! How could I be so hateful and nasty? He wasn't dull at all. Nor was he insensitive. I called him straight away to say thank you. He was in a meeting, needless to say, but I left a very affectionate message on his voice mail.

Maybe I didn't have to leave the country after all! Perhaps all I needed was somewhere to escape London every now and again. OK, I would have to let it out for most of the year if I was going to cover costs, but I could save myself a few weekends, couldn't I? The Cotswolds were well beyond my means, but I could look at Yorkshire or Wales. It could count as part of my pension planning.

The Buy-to-let Boom

A decade ago, owning a rental property was strictly for the professionals. But it has become a much more mainstream occupation and for many people an important way of supplementing income and planning for retirement. Datamonitor, a market research firm, says that in 1999 the buy-to-let mortgage market was worth £3.1 billion. By 2004, it had grown to almost £20 billion. Growth has been fuelled by the property boom, and by the relatively poor performance of other investment vehicles over the past few years.

However, investment in property is risky, and the current market is a difficult one. You should ignore the ridiculous advertisements in tube carriages or on the radio, promising to turn you into a property magnate in no time at all – you should not expect rapid capital growth. Instead, you should be looking at the rental income you will be able to earn on a property and hope that, over time, steady capital growth will prove a bonus.

If you are genuinely interested in buy-to-let, you will of course want to buy at an opportune time, but you should not be overly concerned by short-term fluctuations in the property market. The fact that property prices are falling is not necessarily terrible news for buy-to-let landlords, since a paucity of buyers in the property market tends to mean that demand for rented accommodation will rise, and this will boost landlords' rental incomes. Professional landlords tend to use dips in the market as buying opportunities, in much the same way that experts in the City see stock market falls as the ideal time to buy shares.

Make Sure the Figures Stack

Getting your sums right is the key to successful buy-to-let investment. The first thing to ask is, can you afford it? You will have to put down a deposit of at least 15 per cent, while some lenders will ask for anything from 20 to 50 per cent of the purchase price as a deposit. Your monthly rental income should be at least 25 per cent higher than your monthly mortgage repayments, and ideally you should aim to earn 30 per cent or more above your mortgage repayments. Remember that the mortgage is not your only outgoing. There will be maintenance and insurance and you will have to pay income tax on the rent. Moreover, you cannot assume that the property will be rented out continuously, so you will need to take into account void periods.

Buy-to-let Mortgages

There is a much greater choice available for buy-to-let landlords today. A decade ago, loans were expensive and inflexible. Today, you have a range of variable and fixed-rate options with rates only slightly higher than those offered on residential mortgages. However, fees do tend to be higher – around £600 is not unusual – and you do of course have to put down a larger deposit. Buy-to-let loans are available from all the usual lenders, or through a broker. It is important to find a reputable broker, however, since, unlike the rest of the mortgage market, buy-to-let loans are not regulated by the Financial Services Authority. Paragon Mortgages, which specializes in buy-to-let, is the largest provider of residential mortgages to landlords and is a good place to go if you need advice.

Having done the sums, I could see that I wouldn't be escaping to my very own country cottage any time soon. I would need to save up for a few years yet – I didn't want to have to borrow too much, given that I was not entirely sure that house prices would hold up. I had to admit that Mark, who was stridently opposed to the buy-to-let idea, might have a point on this one, and that caution was probably the order of the day.

Gazumped!

One Thursday evening, while I was in the midst of my pre-going-out-with-Mark ritual of glowering hatefully at my wardrobe, the phone rang. I answered, but couldn't make out who it was for a while, so hysterical was the sobbing. As it turned out, it wasn't Nikki mid-crisis this time, but Kate.

The worst had happened. There had been a couple of hitches getting the mortgage arranged and another buyer had come in with a better offer. Significantly better, the estate agent had told Kate, who was heartbroken. Not only had they lost the property they had set their hearts on, but they had already spent several hundred pounds on surveys and legal fees. Suddenly finding herself back at square one was more than she could bear. To make matters worse, Al was in Leeds on business.

'I couldn't come down to London, could I, Tash?' she sobbed. 'I'm off tomorrow and Saturday and I just can't bear sitting here by myself, thinking about it.'

'Of course you can,' I said. 'Get on the train right now. Do you want to go out or shall we just phone for a take-away and get drunk?'

'Take-away,' she snivelled.

'I'm so sorry, Katie. It's awful.'

'It's evil is what it is!' she cried. 'It shouldn't be allowed!'

Unfortunately, gazumping is a risk of the property purchase process in the UK, slow and laborious as it is. Estate agents are legally bound to pass on all offers to their clients, so should a higher offer come in, even after yours has been accepted, the seller could reject your offer in favour of the higher one. Under English law, you cannot be sure that the property is yours until contracts have been exchanged, and that, as we have seen, can take months.

There is no sure way to guard against being gazumped, but there are steps you can take to try to make sure that it doesn't happen to you. One is to get a mortgage agreed in principle, as this tends to speed the process up; another is to ask for the property to be taken off the market once your offer has been accepted. However, even if the seller agrees to take the property off the market, there is nothing to stop someone who had viewed the house at an earlier stage from making an offer.

You can ask the sellers if they will agree to a lock-in agreement. This means that you agree to exchange contracts within a certain time period, and both of you put down a deposit – usually around 2 per cent of the property purchase price – as security, so that if one party pulls out of the sale, they forfeit their deposit. You will need to get a solicitor to draw up a water-tight lock-in agreement.

It struck me immediately I put down the phone that I was in fact supposed to be meeting Mark in two hours' time and I suspected that he would be less than impressed with me for cancelling at such short notice. My suspicions were correct. He was extremely pissed off. Why, he asked, did I have to drop everything and go running every time one of my bloody friends had a bloody crisis? I reminded him that Kate and Al were his friends too, and that he was welcome to come and hang out on the sofa with us. He harrumphed and said he couldn't let Toby down (Toby being a school-friend of Mark's with whom we were due to have dinner). I said I was sure they'd have a better time just the two of them anyway, and he didn't deny it. Secretly a little relieved (Toby was brought up on a farm and is a touch too Country-side Alliance for my tastes), I nipped down to Threshers to stock up for Kate's visit.

I regretted the wine the following morning when I woke to realize that I had a deadline for a national newspaper that afternoon and had to write 800 words with a pounding hangover. However, the subject of my article was, as luck would have it, equity release, a topic I'd been intending to look into anyway, as I thought it might be an ideal way for Gran to remain in her own home with a full-time nurse.

You're Living in a Goldmine: Equity Release

The equity in your home is the difference between your mortgage and what the home is actually worth. It's the cash value (to you) were the house to be sold. One way of withdrawing money from your home is through equity-release plans, which are available to the over-sixties.

There are various ways of doing this, and it can be a useful tool for older homeowners who wish to supplement their income. However, it is not suitable for everyone and it is very important that you are aware of all the potential pitfalls before you proceed.

There are two main types of equity release:

Lifetime mortgages. These work like any other type of mortgage – you borrow against the value of your home – with the important exception that you do not pay any interest on the loan. It rolls over until the homeowner dies or goes into long-term care, at which point the house can be sold to pay off the loan.

Reversion plans. With a reversion plan, you sell all or part of your home, at a below-market rate, in return for an income, but you retain the right to live in your home for the rest of your life. It will become the property of the lender once you die.

Both types of scheme have their disadvantages. With a lifetime mortgage, the interest rolls up quickly, so if you live for a long time, your estate could have an enormous debt to pay once you die. With a reversion plan, you could be selling your home, or a chunk of it at least, at a discount of 50 per cent, which does not seem like very good value.

Many advisers do not like equity-release plans, seeing them as a last-resort form of borrowing. However, they do have their uses. In addition to providing older people with an income to supplement their pension, they can be used to reduce an Inheritance Tax liability.

Inheritance Tax is payable on any assets you have over and above the threshold, which is £285,000 in the 2006/7 tax year. So if your home is worth £300,000, your estate will have to pay tax at 40 per cent on £15,000 once you die: a bill of £6,000. Now £6,000, I'm sure you'll agree, is a lot of money to give to HM Revenue & Customs. For that reason, some people use equity release to reduce the value of the property a little so that it falls below the IHT threshold. In other words, you can try to spend the money before you die rather than letting the Revenue get their hands on it.

While I knew that my grandmother would not want to contemplate the idea of the house no longer being in the family, I thought we could at least mortgage a part of it to help pay for her care. I suggested it to Dad, who was keen, but he said he would need to broach the subject delicately. I left it in his capable hands.

7. Holidays in Hell: Travel and Other Insurances

Three weeks later, I was on my way to Italy on holiday. A couple of days after the row over me cancelling our dinner date, Mark rang, not to say sorry, but to say I was forgiven (ha!) and that he had booked ten days off in mid-June. How did I feel about a few days on the Amalfi coast? Honestly, I felt a little apprehensive about going anywhere with Mark, but I decided what the hell, I hadn't had a holiday all year, I deserved it.

We arrived in Naples at midday. It must have been about thirty-five degrees in the shade, humid as hell, and the airport was complete chaos. I was doing my level best to stay cheery, but Mark had lost his temper at least three times before we finally collected our bags (why had I packed two, he wanted to know?), found the right car hire desk, located the car (why had I booked the very smallest car available?) and – worst of all – negotiated our way on to the coast road which heads west around the Bay of Naples towards Sorrento. So I'm not the world's greatest navigator! I was starting to develop a sinking feeling about this holiday (had my initial instinct been right after all?), but I was determined to reserve judgement until we had reached the hotel and were sitting, gin and tonics in hand, on the terrace. He did, after all, have a very stressful job and he hadn't had a holiday for some time. Perhaps it would just take him a while to get into it.

The drive was a little stressful too – you don't want to

meet an Italian bus doing sixty going around a corner on one of those narrow roads, believe me – but when we reached Ravello, my spirits lifted. A small village perched on a clifftop above Amalfi, there are breathtaking views along one of the most beautiful stretches of coastline on the Med.

And the hotel! Needless to say, Mark had insisted that we stay at the best (and most expensive) place in town, for a couple of nights at least. So we'd booked into the Palazzo Sasso, an extraordinary twelfth-century villa surrounded by manicured gardens, views over the bay and a fantastic pool. It was also quite terrifyingly expensive, but Mark was determined that we should just spend a few days there before moving to a more modest place down in Amalfi. I told him that was the wrong way round – we should do the cheap place first. He looked annoyed and said that he'd booked the only dates available.

We checked in and explored our room, which was small considering the cost, and with mountain rather than sea views, but it was still stunning. I took a long shower, slipped my new Liu-Jo sundress over my bikini and made my way down to the pool. Mark was already there, sipping a beer and reading *The Economist*.

'This is so amazing,' I said, bending down to give him a kiss.

'It certainly is,' he grinned, looking immediately more relaxed than I had seen him in weeks, or perhaps ever.

I sat down on the lounger next to him. 'Thank you so much for arranging for us to come here,' I said.

He pulled me closer and kissed me again. 'My pleasure,' he smiled, and went back to his *Economist*.

Our first two days in Italy were fine. Just fine. The hotel was amazing, Ravello is beautiful, the food was sublime and we got on well. But it was fine. And I think that if you are staying in what must be one of the most romantic places on earth, with someone with whom you've been in a relationship for less than six months, you're hoping for better than fine. So now I knew, and I was pretty sure he did too. But neither of us was going to have the talk now, here, so early in our holiday. We'd just get on fine, have a nice time and not ruin a holiday in the sun. Then someone would say something on the last night maybe. So we lay by the pool, read our books, sipped cocktails, went for walks and secretly wished we were there with someone else. Well I did, anyway.

And if I was vaguely disappointed by the way things had turned out, that paled into insignificance when early on the third day of our holiday I received a phone call from my father. I knew the second I heard his voice that it must be bad news, and it was. Gran had slipped and fallen the evening before, shattering her hip. She had managed, after a while, to call an ambulance, but died in hospital in the early hours of the morning of heart failure. I got out of bed, shut myself in the bathroom and cried. Neither Dad nor I had said anything about it, but I knew we were both thinking the same thing – if we'd organized to have someone with her, someone looking after her full-time, she might have got help earlier. She might have been OK. She wouldn't have lain there, in terrible pain, all alone, trying to get to the phone.

That afternoon, I started to make arrangements to return to London.

'There's a flight back to Heathrow tomorrow at midday,' I told Mark, who looked nonplussed.

'You're going back to London?' he asked.

'Yes, of course I am. They're holding the funeral in Edinburgh on Friday, so if I get back tomorrow afternoon I can catch the train up on Thursday,' I said.

'Right,' he said. 'OK.' He turned his back to me.

'What did you think? That I'd just carry on with my holiday?'

'No . . . of course not. I'm sorry. But –'

'But what?' I snapped.

'Nothing.'

He stared out of the window for a few minutes and then said quietly, 'There's no sense in me going back, is there?' I couldn't believe it. No sense, no, and no feeling either.

'No, there isn't,' I said, and went out for a walk.

We drove to the airport the following day in total silence. He dropped me at the departures entrance (I insisted he did not come in) and it was with great relief that I entered the air-conditioned airport building alone. I checked in, bought the papers, sat in a corner of the departure lounge and cried as softly and discreetly as I could until we were called to board.

I settled into my seat next to a middle-aged businessman, who took one look at my blotchy face and asked, 'Disastrous holiday?'

'You could say that.'

'Fight with the boyfriend?'

'Death in the family actually.'

'Oh, sorry.' He looked suitably chastened. 'You been on the Amalfi coast, then?'

'Yes. It's lovely.'

'It is. Expensive, though. Hope you had travel insurance.'

I put on my headphones.

*

The insurance issue had been playing on Mark's mind too the night before as we ate dinner, in rather stony silence, at a little restaurant in the town square.

'It's an Easyjet flight, Mark. It cost nothing,' I said, when he asked.

'No, but the hotel . . .'

'What about the hotel? You're staying, so we're not cancelling anything.'

'But we've paid for two people . . .'

'Yes, I have insurance!' I snapped at him. 'For God's sake! I'll sort it out when I get back, all right?'

'Will they pay out?'

'I'd imagine so, yes. Can we talk about something other than money now?' I asked.

He looked really hurt.

I think that, in his way, he was trying to be helpful. It was just that travel insurance was the last thing I'd wanted to think about. Now, sitting on the runway, a middle-aged bloke had brought it up again and for some reason it made me want to laugh. Yes, I had insurance! Marvellous! Everything would be OK now!

Travel Insurance

Actually, travel insurance is no laughing matter. Three years ago, Nikki went skiing for the first time with her then boyfriend, Evil Tom. Evil Tom had planned the holiday as an elaborate apology for sleeping with one of Nikki's work colleagues, the latest in a string of betrayals. It says a lot about ET that his apology involved taking Nikki plus a group of his closest friends (all accomplished skiers) halfway up a

French mountain and then leaving Nik to fend for herself while he and his mates did black runs and got drunk. Nikki spent the first couple of days on the nursery slopes and was pleased to discover that she was a natural, or so her instructor said. She relayed this information to ET over après ski that evening, and he, convinced that the ski instructor had actually been making a pass at her and determined to separate her from the instructor while at the same time proving to her that she wasn't really all that when it comes to serious slope action, suggested that she go with him and the rest of the boys the following day. He promised they would take care of her, which of course they didn't.

She fell and broke her wrist, had to be stretchered off the slope, put in an ambulance, taken to hospital and patched up. All this was bad enough (bloody painful, apparently), but it was made a great deal worse by the fact that she hadn't bought any insurance before she left. So one bloody painful wrist and an £800 medical bill. Ouch.

Millions of people travel uninsured every year. Most have no idea what medical treatment abroad costs. Few people realize that bringing someone home from Europe on an air ambulance costs around £9,000, and that if you have to be brought back from the States it costs £27,000. Ouch indeed.

Go Multi-trip

In 2003, more than 80 per cent of the travel insurance policies bought were for single trips. But buying single-trip insurance policies makes sense only if you travel no more than twice a year (and I'm not just talking about proper, two-weeks-in-the-Caribbean type holidays – you can lose all your belongings just as easily on a weekend jaunt to Barcelona).

A single girl buying a single-trip insurance policy for two weeks in Spain can pay as little as £10 if she shops around for the cheapest policy. But she would pay just £30 for a year's cover (in Europe), which would allow her to take as many trips as she pleases, so long as no single trip lasts for more than thirty-one days. She would pay upwards of £40 for a multi-trip policy covering the globe.

In addition to multi-trip policies offering good value for money, purchasing one policy saves you the hassle of thinking about travel cover every time you go away. This way, you can buy your insurance once a year, like car or home contents insurance. And then, when your boyfriend decides to whisk you away on a surprise trip to Paris for your birthday, you don't have to worry when you lose your Tiffany earrings in the Jardin des Tuileries. Or something.

Send the Travel Agent Packing

Under no circumstances should you purchase travel insurance from a travel agent. They earn huge commissions for selling it and it can be as much as three or four times what you would pay if you shopped around. A family of four buying insurance from Lunn Poly would pay nearly £160. If they bought their insurance from Sainsbury's Bank, it would cost them just under £40. Some agents will try to bully you into buying their cover by refusing to book your holiday unless you do so. If they do this, you should really take your business elsewhere, but if you want the holiday, you can sign a form saying you will make your own insurance arrangements. Another trick is to offer you a discount on the holiday if you take the agent's insurance: this is illegal. If an agent tries it, report them to the Office of Fair Trading. Although you should not buy travel insurance from your travel agent, you should buy it from someone when, if not before, you make your booking. Otherwise you will not be covered if you need to cancel your trip.

You've Bought Insurance, but Are You Covered?

There's no short cut here: you actually need to take a look at the fine print on your travel policy. I know it sounds tedious (and believe me, it is), but it will be worth it if you need to make a claim.

There are a few obvious things to look out for:

- *Winter sports.* You will probably have to specify that you want winter sports cover when you buy your policy as it is not generally included. Make sure that your insurer covers snowboarding, as well as skiing, if snowboarding is your thing.
- *Dangerous sports.* Anyone planning on bungee jumping, abseiling, paragliding, white water rafting or any other foolish pursuit needs to check with the insurer that it is covered. You may have to phone the company to get a firm yes or no on the precise activity you have in mind. Remember that something you deem run of the mill (like riding a motorbike) can be classed as a dangerous sport by some insurers.
- *Pre-existing medical conditions.* Insurers will not pay out if you fall ill or need to cancel your holiday as a result of a chronic condition, such as diabetes or cancer, which you had prior to buying insurance. If you do have a chronic condition, make sure that you mention it to the company when you purchase the policy.
- *Personal possessions.* The limit for baggage cover can be as low as £500, with just £50 for individual items, which is not much good if you're packing your digital camera, Gucci shoes and Missoni bikini.

- *Excesses.* Many insurance policies have excesses on personal belongings or cancellation. Check how much they are, and whether they apply per person or for the whole family. For example, a £50 excess does not seem so bad for a cancelled trip, but if each member of a family of four has to pay the excess, the policy looks poor value.
- *Terrorism.* You are not usually covered for acts of terrorism, although if, for example, you are planning to travel to a country which is then targeted by terrorists, and if the Foreign Office recommends that you should not travel there, then the travel agent or airline will usually offer you an alternative holiday. Before you travel to any country that has problems, whether with terrorists, bandits, high crime or civil unrest, check the Foreign & Commonwealth Office website. If the FCO recommends that you do not travel to a place and you go anyway, your travel insurance will be invalid. You can now buy specialist cover to protect you against acts of terrorism, as well as things like air rage, if you're particularly paranoid.

Once You're There

Look after your stuff. The insurer won't pay out if you leave your digital camera and mobile phone on the beach when you go for a swim. Some insurers insist that you keep valuables in the main hotel safe (not even the safe in your room will do). And look after yourself. If you 'deliberately expose yourself to unnecessary danger', by running with the bulls in Pamplona, for example, your insurer is highly unlikely to pay out if you are injured. You are not covered if you injure yourself while drunk or on drugs either, so watch yourself when you're dancing on that podium at Manumission.

If you are the victim of crime while on holiday, you must

report the incident to the police within twenty-four hours. Without a police report, the insurance company will not pay out.

I was back in Clapham by seven on Wednesday evening. I couldn't face unpacking, or even speaking to my parents. Not just yet. I knew Dad would hold it together, but Mum and I would be hopeless once we started talking. I needed to know about arrangements for the funeral, about flowers and speeches and train tickets to Edinburgh, but I just couldn't face it. So I ran a bath, poured myself a large Jack Daniel's and had a good cry. Again.

Then I rang Nikki.

'I'm getting in a taxi now,' she said. 'I'll be with you in half an hour.' That's what she's like.

An hour later, she received an exasperated call from Andrew. 'Where the hell are you?' he demanded to know. She explained. He was very understanding, but wanted to point out that she really should have turned off the stove before she left, as the flame had blown out and the flat was filling with gas. That's what she's like.

Home Insurance

When Nikki finally got up the courage to leave Evil Tom a couple of years ago, she moved into her current flat in West Hampstead. She'd been there about a week, it was a Saturday afternoon and she had planned a night out with the girls. She was running herself a bath, had put on some tunes, lit all the candles and so on, when the phone rang. It was ET, of course, calling her to tell her what a terrible mistake she was making and how she would never be happy again. They argued, as you do, for around an hour, until

Nikki's bathroom floor collapsed, dumping the contents of the bathroom not so neatly into the kitchen. Had she bought home insurance? Had she hell.

'Do you know what the worst part of the whole bloody thing was?' she asked me later that evening. 'Bloody Tom. He bloody knew that I wouldn't be covered. It was the first thing he said to me: "You aren't insured, are you?" I could just imagine him smirking down the phone. If I'd had a gun, I would have gone round to his place and shot him.'

When you think about it, it is quite likely that things will go wrong soon after you move into the place. You're getting things connected, like washing machines, you're excited and distracted, you're having house-warming parties . . . So it really is important to buy contents cover as soon as you move in.

How much your home insurance costs depends on a huge range of factors. Your postcode is important, since if you live in a high-crime area, you'll have to pay more. It will also depend on the level of cover you require. You will pay more if you want accidental damage cover as well as 'all risks' insurance, which covers certain items, such as cameras or binoculars, which are taken outside the home. Your mobile phone will not generally be covered under an all-risks policy.

Shop around for cover, because there is a huge difference in the premiums on offer. Just do a quick search on an insurance-broking site, such as Insuresupermarket. I was given quotes ranging from around £13 to £43 a month. But don't just go for the cheapest quote – you'll need to take a look at the cover they're offering. Some insurers, for example, offer 'new for old', which means that if your ten-year-old carpet is ruined by flooding, they will buy you a new one; some will cover items left in the garden; some offer cover for bicycles. On the subject of gardens, if you have impressive items of statuary adorning your lawn, or a small shoal of Koi carp in the fish pond, you will need to take specialist cover.

Your premiums will also depend on the value of your home contents, of course. And this is where many of us get home insurance badly wrong. More Than, the insurer owned by Royal & Sun Alliance, produces a home contents index which tracks the average value of the contents of the British home. Its findings make for interesting reading. It says that the contents of the typical home are worth £44,500, yet around half of homeowners thought their contents were worth less than £20,000, and more than two-thirds thought their contents were worth less than £30,000.

The value of our homes is riding rapidly, thanks to the enormous quantity of gadgetry we have all built up. Most kids now own PlayStations, most adults now own iPods and virtually everyone has a computer, plus at least three TVs. Your wardrobe can be worth a bit too. How many pairs of shoes do you own that cost £50 or more? Costs can add up pretty quickly, so before you buy insurance, walk around your home, noting down the estimated value of the contents of each room. And remember to raise your level of cover each year as you acquire more and more stuff. Just think about all the possessions you have acquired over the past twelve months – the clothes and CDs and DVDs and jewellery . . . It all adds up.

It often makes sense to buy cover online – some insurers will offer discounts of up to 15 per cent if you buy over the Internet. Another trick is to pay annually, rather than monthly – some insurers charge as much as 30 per cent APR for the pleasure of taking your premiums each month.

Once again, you need to read the small print of the policies to make sure that you will be able to claim should the worst happen. Some policies require you to have approved locks on doors and windows; others stipulate that you must keep certain valuables under lock and key. And, like travel cover, there will be maximum limits on individual items.

Buildings Insurance

Unlike home contents insurance, buildings cover is not optional if you have a mortgage on your property. Buildings insurance covers the actual bricks and mortar and is based not on how much the property is worth but on how much it would take to rebuild. It covers you against fire and flood, and in some cases subsidence. For those who live in flats, buildings cover may be collective and is usually arranged (though not paid for) by the freeholder. For everyone else, it may make sense to buy your buildings and home contents cover together.

Nikki arrived clutching two bottles of red wine, her face streaked with tears. She'd been very fond of my grandmother, and the feeling had been mutual. Gran loved the way Nikki always came to Edinburgh with four pairs of shoes and two handbags, even if it was just for the weekend. 'She is so glamorous!' Gran always said to me, peering at the scuffed boots which I, no doubt, had been wearing for days.

'I can't believe it,' Nikki said softly, giving me a hug. 'I just can't believe it.'

We sat on the sofa for a while, and I cried a lot. She poured the wine and held my hand for ages, occasionally passing me the box of Kleenex.

After a while, when I was calmer, she asked, 'Would you like me to drive you to Edinburgh? I can borrow Andrew's car. Or is Mark going to take you?'

I laughed, only slightly bitterly. 'Mark's in Italy, Nik.'

She looked shocked. 'He didn't come back with you?'

I shook my head.

'Bastard.'

'Oh, I don't know. He didn't know her, and things aren't . . . Well, it was pretty much over anyway, it was just that neither of us had bothered to say it yet.'

'I'm so sorry.'

'Oh, I don't care about that at all. He could not be further from my thoughts. Well, until we started talking about him anyway.'

'So shall I drive you?'

'That's OK, Nik. I've already bought the train ticket. Besides . . .' I gave her a wry smile.

'There's nothing wrong with my driving!' she spluttered indignantly, knowing exactly what I was going to say.

Motor Insurance

There is plenty wrong with her driving actually. I've lost count of how many accidents she's had. All of them have been minor, thankfully, but she does not instil the greatest of confidence behind the wheel. She gets really annoyed if I say anything about it, though, since I don't own a car and never have done. In fact I only got my driver's licence two years ago. In any case, I'm really pleased that I don't own a car, because cars are horrendously expensive to run. Including the cost of car finance, depreciation, servicing, tax and insurance, running a car costs more than £400 a month. And that excludes parking tickets or speeding fines. Given how spectacularly pricey the whole business is, you may as well save as much money on car insurance as you can.

Car insurance has always been one of those very rare areas of life in which women actually get a better deal than men. I always find myself in trouble for saying that this is because women are better drivers. Irate letters arrive from Jeremy Clarkson types insisting that women are not better drivers, they just cause many fewer serious accidents than men do. (If you ask me, that makes us better drivers, but there's little point in arguing with these people.)

Gender is not the only factor that influences premiums. The cost of your car insurance is determined by where you live, where your car is parked, your age, your occupation, whether or not someone else will be driving the car, whether or not you use the car for work, your claims history, whether or not you have any driving convictions, the kind of car you drive, the security on the car and your annual mileage.

Clearly, there are various factors that you cannot change – such as your age – and some that you are not about to change just in order to get cheaper car insurance – such as where you live and your occupation. But there are steps you can take to make sure you're as low a risk as possible, such as fitting an alarm and/or an immobilizer if you've got an older model. Taking a slightly higher voluntary excess than the standard £100 will also lower premiums, as will limiting your mileage. If you're very young, adding an older driver to your policy may cut your premiums. If you're a car lover and drive a fast, flash motor, you might want to take an advanced driving test to demonstrate to the insurer that you're not some girl racer.

Norwich Union now offers 'pay-as-you-go' car insurance for drivers aged 18–21, which, it claims, could lower young drivers' premiums by as much as 30 per cent. It works like this: you have an in-car 'black box' installed for a one-off fee of £199. It then calculates how many miles you drive and at what times. You will pay more for driving between peak hours.

Another other obvious way to cut costs is to shop around. Insurers do not reward loyalty, so there is little point in sticking with your current company if you can get a better deal elsewhere. If you have Internet access, shopping around is fairly simple. If not, you may as well set aside an entire day to ring round and make calls. It is worth your while asking a friend with Internet access, or even going to an Internet café, to search on sites such as *www.insuresupermarket.com* or *www.confused.com* for the best quotes. You'll need your driver's licence and registration document to hand before you start shopping.

You will also need to decide what level of cover you want to buy. Third-party insurance is the lowest level of cover, the absolute minimum you must have. This covers you for damage and injuries that you, or your passenger, cause to another person or their property in an accident, but it does not cover you or your car. Third party, fire and theft cover gives you the same level of cover plus insurance against your car being stolen or damaged by fire. Comprehensive insurance covers you for all this, plus the damage to your own car in the event of an accident. Note that the difference in premiums between third party, fire and theft and comprehensive cover is often quite small, so it is worth getting quotes for both.

Nikki helped me pack, and I rehearsed the reading that Dad had asked me to give at the funeral. Every time I started it, I began to cry, so that by the fifth time it was actually almost funny, in a weird way, and Nikki and I were half-laughing and half-crying like a couple of lunatics. I decided it would be better to leave the reading to the train, when I could consider it in a mood of quiet contemplation.

'You will you be able to come up for the funeral, Nik? You can stay at the house with us.'

'Of course I will! Of course. Since you don't need me to drive, I'll fly on Thursday night. I'm horribly busy at work.'

'Thank you.'

She had an odd smile on her face.

'What is it?'

'Nothing,' she said, shaking her head. 'It's . . .'

'What?'

'I was just thinking about the last funeral we went to.'

I was blank for a second, then we both said, 'Elvis!'

Pet Insurance

Amy used to own a Pomeranian called Elvis. He's dead now. He was very overweight and he developed heart disease. I'm not joking. No one jokes about Elvis now that he's gone, and he was no laughing matter when he was alive either. He must have bitten just about everyone Amy knows at one point or another. Lucky none of us are litigious, because she never got him insured. I can't imagine why, because he was a sickly little bastard. He must have cost her thousands in vets' bills before he finally gave up the ghost about a year ago. Amy held an elaborate funeral in her back garden, which was only slightly marred by Michael, Mel and Nikki sniggering uncontrollably in the back row. Amy still hasn't bought another pet. She says he was irreplaceable. Too right.

Anyone who owns a pet knows that vets' bills are high, but most of us drastically underestimate just how expensive a pet's illnesses can be. If your cat breaks its leg, the cost of treatment is likely to be around £900; treating a dog with a broken leg costs upwards of £1,200. Diabetic dogs cost around £800 a year to treat, while the cost of a hip-replacement operation is around £1,500.

Your pets can cost you in other ways too, by biting strangers, damaging property or causing accidents. Dog owners have to fork out millions of pounds in compensation every year to drivers who've been involved in accidents as a result of a dog running out into the road. And a surprisingly high number of pets – around half a million – go missing or are stolen every year.

Despite the high cost of owning a pet, only around a quarter of pet owners have insurance. This is not really so surprising, since much of it is worthless. Market research shows that insurers turn down just over 1,000 claims a month. Just under half of policies impose a twelve-month limit on treatment, so that if your pet develops a chronic condition, the insurer will cover vets' bills only for the first year of treatment. Moreover, many people find that once they have made a claim, their premiums suddenly shoot through the roof.

Having said that, any pet is likely to become ill at least a couple of times during its life, particularly if it lives to a ripe old age. And insurance can be bought quite cheaply. For example, monthly premiums for a boxer under eight years of age living in south London start at just under £7 a month, while for a Burmese cat under eight years of age they are just over £4 a month. The majority of insurers will not cover cats and dogs over eight, though a few do, including Sainsbury's and Animal Friends.

As ever, you need to look at what is excluded: most policies won't pay out for pre-existing conditions, flea control, vaccinations, spaying or castration. Note that pet insurance policies are just for pets: if your dog is a working dog – a guard dog, for example – you cannot insure him or her under a standard pet policy.

Standard pet insurance policies cover dogs, cats and rabbits. If you want to insure other animals, birds or reptiles, you may need to go to a specialist insurer and will certainly be looking at much higher premiums than you would if you were insuring a Border collie. Exotic Direct covers all manner of pets, including birds of prey and reptiles.

Talking of reptiles, I was just boarding the train to Edinburgh on Thursday morning when Mark rang. I didn't pick up. I was feeling wretched and just couldn't face talking to him. I didn't really want to talk to anyone, but I felt I ought to leave the phone on in case my parents rang. I was dreading the next few days. The funeral was the following morning. I was still terrified about the reading – it would be awful if I just sobbed through the whole thing. Then we would need to spend the next few days sorting out Gran's things. I couldn't bear the thought of being in the house without her. It just made my heart ache.

All in all, I planned on being away for around ten days – the will was due to be read on Tuesday, and Mum, Dad and I had to be there – then we'd probably need at least a few more days to get things sorted out. Since I was due to be on holiday anyway, there were no work commitments to cancel.

It was a stiflingly hot day and the train was crowded with people, most of them taking long weekends, I guessed. Quite a number were travelling with children, which irritated me no end. Yes, I'm one of those people who believe there should be no-children carriages on trains. I was glowering at one particularly chirpy little blonde creature who was singing the same nursery rhyme (or Britney Spears song, I couldn't really tell) over and over again when she looked across at me. I must have seemed like the hateful bitch monster from hell, because she stopped singing immediately and grabbed her father's hand, a look of fear passing across her face. Her father put his arm around her and she looked up at him with the sweetest expression you could imagine, and I felt more wretched than ever.

How empty my life was and what a terrible person I must be – some old witch frightening children on trains! I was gripped by a monstrous self-pity, as I wondered bitterly who would shed tears at my funeral if I were to be snatched away? Well, all my family and friends, I suppose, but it wasn't like having a child, someone who relied on you completely, someone who counted on you every single day, who was completely yours.

Mournfully, I recalled a conversation with Jackie and Sam when Jacks was first pregnant with Roman, when they asked me to be godmother. I was touched, but at the same time completely terrified by the idea. To deflect attention from my own fears, I started babbling on about how they would have to take out life insurance now. They both looked highly sceptical, but I was insistent. There are plenty of types of insurance, like pet or travel, that you can neglect in the vain hope that nothing will ever go wrong, but you cannot take risks with life insurance once you have a family.

Life Insurance

This is not a fun subject, I'm warning you now, but it is one that you need to address if you have a family, or even if you just have a partner and a mortgage. More than a third of people with dependent children have no life cover and less than a third rank it as a priority. This is very foolish. Life cover should rank high on your financial to-do list – after paying off debts, perhaps, but before making any serious stock market investments.

If you do need to buy life cover, you have two options:

- *Term assurance.* This covers you for a set period, which is usually the length of time you have until you retire, but can be for the term of a mortgage, or any other term you pick. If you buy level-term assurance, the premiums and cover remain the same for the length of the policy; decreasing-term assurance means that the level of cover decreases over the life of the policy.
- *Whole-of-life insurance.* This covers you, as the name of the policy suggests, for the whole of your life. Premiums are also payable throughout your lifetime.

How Much Do You Need?

How much life cover you purchase may well depend on how much you can afford, but how much you need is another matter entirely. This depends on whether you are married or in a long-term relationship, whether you have a mortgage to pay, whether you have children, and whether or not they are in private education, whether you wish to be able to pay for them to go to university . . . and so on. Plus you need to take into account how much you earn: if you weren't around, what earnings would the family lose?

Just because you're not in paid employment does not mean that you shouldn't bother with life insurance. Don't do yourself down: full-time mothers are worth a huge amount financially, despite the fact that they don't get paid for what they do. It's estimated that full-time mothers do around £400 worth of work each week, putting in as many as sixty-four hours a week – that's twenty-seven more than permitted under the European

Working Time Directive. So if you, as a full-time mum, were not around to do the work, someone else would need to be hired to do it – at a cost of more than £21,000 a year. So stay-at-home mothers need life cover just as much as mums in full-time employment do.

In general, single people without dependants do not need life insurance. However, if you have a mortgage, and if you would like to leave your home to someone else in the event of your death, you could take out life insurance to cover the mortgage. If you do not have any insurance, your home would be repossessed by the lender in the event of your death. If you died without life insurance and had other debts, your estate would be pursued for any money you owe.

A good rule of thumb when calculating how much insurance you need is five times joint income if you just have a mortgage to pay, ten times joint income if you have a mortgage and one child, and fifteen times joint income if you have a mortgage plus two or more kids. Obviously, if you are a single parent, you will have to work on a multiple of your income alone, and you can scale down the sum insured as your mortgage reduces.

It is not as expensive as you might think. Say you're a single mum with one child, earning the national average wage of around £25,000 a year. You ought to get ten times your income in life insurance – £250,000. Assuming that you are thirty-five years old and a non-smoker, your life insurance premiums could be as little as £20 a month, but you do need to shop around in order to get the best rates. Life insurance premiums vary enormously. For example, a non-smoking thirty-year-old woman would pay £10.50 a month to insure herself for £250,000 if she went to Sainsbury's Bank, but £26.68 if she went to Cornhill Direct.

Remember that life insurance is really death insurance: you are covering your family in the event of your death. As such, its cost is influenced by the risk of your dying. The greater the risk, the higher your premiums will be, so your age, gender, general health, whether or not you smoke and your occupation are all taken into account. So, for example, a man aged thirty will pay around £8.50 for £100,000 of life insurance, while a woman the same age will pay about £1 less, because women tend to live longer than men do.

Buying insurance when you are still relatively young is well worth it, because premiums rise steeply as you get older: a woman of forty would pay £10.70 for £100,000 of life cover, while her fifty-year-old sister pays £16.58. Quitting smoking will also help you cut costs, reducing your premiums by around £50 a year. In order to qualify for non-smokers' rates, you must have been tobacco-free for at least twelve months when you apply for cover. Don't be tempted to lie about this. The insurer may not find out, but if they do, your cover will be invalidated and you'll just have been wasting money.

Couples may want to consider buying joint life insurance, since it can work out cheaper than buying individual policies. However, the difference is less exaggerated than it used to be, so do your sums carefully. Note that you do not have to be married in order to buy a joint life policy, although there must be a 'provable financial interest' between the two of you when you buy the policy. So if you have a mortgage together, if one person is reliant on the other partner or if you have children, you could purchase joint life insurance.

If you bought life insurance several years ago, it is probably worth switching your cover now, as premiums did fall quite significantly in the late 1990s and early 2000s, although they are now on the rise again. The main reason for the dip in premiums was that in the 1980s insurers were expecting the AIDS virus to have a devastating impact on populations, and so the costs of life insurance went up sharply. The epidemic they had expected did not materialize in the West – in fact life expectancy has just continued to lengthen every year. However, a number of factors, including tougher regulation of the insurance industry, mean that premiums are now set to rise. So buy now!

Critical-illness Cover

And the depression just keeps on coming. Critical-illness insurance is designed to cover you if you should fall seriously ill. When you make a claim, the insurer pays out a lump sum, which you could then invest to provide you with an income to meet basic expenses, to pay for nursing care and to cover the cost of any adjustments needed to your home, for example, if you are no longer fully mobile.

This is a horrible subject, I know, which is probably one of the reasons why so many people don't take out critical-illness cover. Less than a quarter of women do. If you don't have critical-illness cover, you need not feel too guilty. It's not like shirking on your pension contributions or life insurance policy. It isn't absolutely essential. Before you buy critical-illness cover, make sure you have enough life insurance, and possibly an income-protection policy, and take advice. This is a complex area, and it is very easy to be persuaded to buy something unsuitable.

Critical-illness policies tend to be very specific about what they will cover and what they will not. Most policies cover seven core conditions: cancer, coronary artery bypass surgery, heart attack, major organ transplant, stroke, kidney failure and multiple sclerosis. Some will also cover a range of other illnesses, including blindness, coma, deafness and Parkinson's disease. However, the number of conditions covered varies hugely from policy to policy, so it is very important to take a good look at the fine print before you go ahead.

Some insurers will cover you against 'total and permanent disability' (snappily known as TPD), which means that you are covered if you are unable to work due to an accident, or after an illness, whether or not that illness is named in the policy.

Another point to look out for is whether the policy will pay out if you are unable to do your own job or only if you cannot do any job at all. This is hugely important. Imagine you are a surgeon and suffer an illness that renders you unable to practise surgery, but which does not disable you so much that you could not do another job – say, working on a checkout at the supermarket, or working in a call centre. If you had an 'any job' policy, the insurer would not pay out, because you would still be able to work.

Income Protection

As I discussed with Jackie a little while ago, it is very important to have emergency savings, preferably up to six months' salary, stashed in a savings account. This money could be used to cover your mortgage – your most pressing outgoing – should you lose your job, or fall ill and be unable to work.

It is important to make your own arrangements, because assistance from the state is extremely limited. The government will help pay your mortgage, but it will pay only the interest, not the capital repayments, on the first £100,000 of your mortgage. Moreover, if you took out your mortgage after 2 October 1995, you get no help for nine months. If you took it out before that date, you have to wait just eight weeks. This is completely arbitrary, it just happens to be the date selected to introduce the rule change.

There is an alternative to making savings and to relying on the state: income-protection insurance policies. There are two main types of policy: mortgage-payment-protection insurance (MPPI) and accident, sickness and unemployment insurance (ASU). As the name suggests, MPPI covers your mortgage payments only, whereas with ASU you are insuring your entire income. The policies work in much the same way, although if you claim on an ASU policy the money is paid to you, whereas with MPPI the money is paid directly to your lender.

You need to be very careful when purchasing these policies. Don't give into the hard sell from your mortgage lender, as its policy is likely to be around a third more expensive than policies on offer from brokers.

Make sure that the cover is suitable for you. Many policies don't cover the self-employed or those on short-term contracts; nor will you be covered if you lose your job within six months of being employed, or if you knew when you bought the policy that redundancies were on the cards. Many policies insist that you have been with your employer for two years before you make a claim. And don't assume that the insurance salesman will make this clear to you when you buy! All they're interested in is making the sale. The Financial Ombudsman Service, which deals with insurance mis-selling, says it sees around 1,000 cases a year where self-employed workers have been sold insurance for which they are not eligible.

Note that many policies pay out for twelve months only, so if your employer offers a generous sick-pay scheme, it may not be worth your while buying this sort of insurance – you'd be better off stashing the equivalent of the premiums in a 'just in case of emergencies' savings account. There is usually a 30- to 60-day deferral period after you claim before the insurer will begin paying out.

Protection for Loans and Cards

In addition to buying insurance to cover mortgage repayments, you can also buy payment-protection insurance to cover other loan interest repayments. Payment protection is almost always fairly pricey, particularly if you buy direct from the lender. For example, say you borrow £5,000 over three years with an APR of 7.9 per cent. If you choose to borrow without the insurance safety net, your loan will cost you a total of £5,609. If you choose payment-protection insurance, you will pay just over £1,000 more for your loan. An alternative is to purchase insurance from an independent broker, since this is likely to be slightly cheaper, or to simply build up a decent amount of cash in savings to cover you should you lose your job. This last option is slightly riskier, although of course if you don't lose your job you still have your money in savings.

Are You an Uninsurable Risk?

Not everyone finds it easy to get insurance. Around 80,000 people are turned down for life, critical-illness or income-protection insurance every year because they have an existing or past medical condition, for example. Anyone with a history of circulatory problems, cancer, Crohn's disease or even diabetes may be rejected when they apply for insurance. In the vast majority of cases, you will be declined life insurance if you have tested positive for HIV or have AIDS.

However, just because you have been turned down by a mainstream insurer does not mean you are uninsurable. In many cases, independent brokers may be able to find you cover, although you will have to pay over the odds for it.

The problem of the 'uninsurables' is likely to become greater as genetic testing for various diseases becomes widespread. At present, you can buy up to £500,000 worth of life insurance and £300,000 of critical-illness cover without having to disclose the results of any genetic tests you might have had. If you want a higher level of insurance, you need disclose only the results of tests approved by the government's Genetics and Insurance Committee. At the moment there is only one – the test for Huntington's disease. However, this situation could change when the moratorium on genetic testing and insurance expires in 2006.

It used to be the case that gay men were charged higher life insurance premiums than everyone else because they were perceived to be at greater risk of contracting HIV/AIDS. However, this should no longer be the case, although gay men will typically have to undergo a more rigorous application process (including a medical and HIV test) than a married man would have to do.

Ill-health is not the only reason why people struggle to get insurance. Anyone who does a dangerous job, from cleaning windows to working in the police force, may also find it difficult to get income-protection insurance. Insurers tend to divide professions into four classes, with class one offering the cheapest cover and class four the most expensive. Insurers will take into account how much physical work people have to do every day, whether or not they come into contact with any hazardous substances, whether they work at great height (scaffolders, for example) or great depth (divers), whether they drive long distances and whether they are subject to high levels of stress.

It is worth noting that not all insurers draw the same conclusions about the professions. For example, some say that stockbroking is a high-risk profession, because of the levels of stress involved, while others deem it a standard, low-risk, white-collar occupation. Some now rank teaching as high risk because of stress levels. Some workers in particularly dangerous jobs might find it difficult to get affordable insurance, or even an insurer to cover them at all.

There are specialist insurers who are prepared to help. EqualityNow, a disability income-protection policy offered by Goodfellows, for example, does not load premiums on the basis of occupation. Moreover, it claims that it will not refuse to insure anyone – be they a stuntman or a soldier.

Private Health Insurance

The National Health Service is a source of much national pride, despite its many failings. This may be one of the reasons why the sale of private medical insurance has never really taken off here. Those who have it usually do so thanks to their employer. The main advantage of holding private health insurance is that you can have non-emergency treatment without the wait. If you need urgent treatment, either in an emergency or because you are seriously ill, you are likely to receive NHS treatment whether or not you have private insurance.

There are other reasons why private health insurance isn't popular. It's quite expensive – cover starts at around £25 a month – and there are plenty of conditions it does not cover. These include treatment for any chronic or terminal illness, HIV or AIDS, treatment relating to pregnancy and childbirth, any self-inflicted injuries, conditions relating to drug or alcohol abuse, cosmetic surgery, eye tests, dental treatment and vaccinations. That's a lot of exclusions.

Many people are put off the idea of purchasing private health insurance by the idea that they will need to take a rigorous medical examination in order to qualify. You don't. You will be asked to fill in a form giving details of your medical history, and the insurer may write to your doctor for further information, but that's it. In some cases, you may not even be asked about your medical history, but the insurer will offer a moratorium. This means that you will not be covered for any medical condition from which you have suffered over a given period, usually the past two or five years.

If you are keen to purchase medical insurance but find it too expensive, there are ways to lower your premiums. You could pay an excess, or agree to pay for part of your medical treatment if and when it is needed. Your premiums will also be lower if you agree to receive treatment at a specified hospital, or if you agree to receive NHS treatment when it is available within six to twelve weeks.

My parents met me at the station and we took a taxi back to my grandmother's house. As I had predicted, I could hardly bear to go inside. I just wanted to see her standing there in her kitchen, making the tea and chatting away about the book she was reading, or the latest album she had bought. My mum and I tried desperately not to go to pieces for my father's sake, but we failed. So as usual he was the strong one, comforting us, despite the fact that it was he who had lost his mother.

But after a while, Mum and I got around to making something to eat, and Dad opened a bottle of wine, and then another, and the three of us sat around the kitchen table reminiscing until the small hours.

8. Death and Taxes: Benefits and Taxes

The funeral service was beautiful. The wake was surprisingly festive given the high proportion of octogenarians present. The weekend that followed was horribly quiet. Nikki stayed the night at Gran's house with us on Friday, which made things a little easier, but after she left it was just the three of us – my parents and I – padding around among Gran's treasured things, feeling like intruders in her home, not wanting to touch anything and yet knowing that we had to sort everything out. It was horrible, but Dad was great, and Mum and I tried our hardest not to be too pathetic.

Another shock was to follow when, sometime later, we visited Gran's solicitor, a Mr Greaves, for the reading of the will. My parents and I sat in stunned silence as it was revealed that my grandmother had been considerably wealthier than any of us had imagined, with investments and savings running to around £200,000, in addition to her home. Gran had left around £30,000 to various charities, but the rest of the cash and investments were split between my parents and me, and we were to share the house.

We left the solicitor's office in a state of mild and collective amazement.

'Why didn't she tell us?' I asked Dad. 'We could have done something. She could easily have afforded to have a nurse. We talked about money when I was here before. Why didn't she tell me?'

'I suspect,' Mum said, 'that she wanted to leave you

something. You know what she was like. She felt it was important that some of your grandfather's money should be passed on . . .'

'I know, but so much . . . It's just . . . we could have . . .'

'I know,' said Dad, who looked terrible.

I was sure that he would take this to heart. This was his failure. He should have known, he should have insisted that they get her financial affairs sorted out, he should have taken control of everything. But at the same time we were all aware that she would never have allowed that.

Somehow we got through it. My friends rallied round, calling often. I was feeling pretty low and resolved to throw myself into my work.

I did have something else to occupy my mind – an inheritance of £29,000. This unexpected windfall, albeit from an unhappy source, had turned my mind once again to thoughts of buying a property somewhere. I knew that Gran would have loved the idea of me using her money to buy myself a bolthole in the country, either here or abroad. I resolved to start looking seriously again.

Inheritance Tax

My inheritance was smaller than it should have been. Not that I was complaining, but the size of the Inheritance Tax (IHT) bill was galling. HM Revenue & Customs (HMRC) says that 96 per cent of all estates have no IHT to pay, since they fall beneath the threshold, which is also known as the 'nil-rate band', which is £285,000 in the 2006/7 tax year. For IHT purposes, your estate is made up of everything you own, your share of anything you own jointly, any assets held in trust from which you receive an income and any gifts from which you still enjoy a benefit. For example, if you give your house to your children, but continue to live in it with them, then the house is still treated as yours for IHT purposes. Gifts you have given within seven years of your death are also included as part of your estate (these are known as Potentially Exempt Transfers, or PETs).

Some gifts are always exempt from IHT. These include all gifts between spouses, wedding gifts of up to £5,000 to children, of £2,500 to grandchildren and of £1,000 to anyone else, as well as all other gifts up to a value of £3,000 per tax year. Anything you leave to registered UK charities is also exempt.

IHT is payable at a rate of 40 per cent on that part of your estate above the threshold of £285,000, so in my case it worked like this:

Estate	
Home	£310,000
Other assets	£200,000
Total	£510,000
Less gifts to charity	£30,000
Value of estate for IHT purposes	£480,000
Less nil-rate band	£285,000
Taxable estate	£195,000
Tax due: 40% × £195,000	£78,000

Reducing Your IHT Bill

Seeing £78,000 of my grandmother's money go to the taxman was a bitter pill to swallow, but swallow it we had to. Like so many people, Gran had never thought of herself as particularly wealthy, so the idea of having to pay IHT probably never crossed her mind. Certainly she had never mentioned it to me.

More than a billion pounds could be paid to our chosen heirs each year if we planned properly to avoid paying too much IHT. The problem is that many people regard IHT as a concern of the rich, but the rise in house prices has meant this is no longer the case. In fact, if you are a homeowner and you live in the south-east of England, your estate is highly likely to face an IHT liability, since the average value of homes in the region is now just under £230,000. Some people simply don't care very much, since IHT is only paid after your death, so it isn't really you who has to worry about it. But if you would like to save as much of your money as possible for your dependants, rather than HMRC, there are ways of keeping your money out of its reach. You need to consult an accountant or financial planner about how best to do this, since the issues are complex and drawing up trusts is not something you can do yourself. However, there are various methods of shielding your money from HMRC. You can either spend it, give it away or insure against your IHT liability.

Spending It

There is a new breed of older people referred to as 'skiers'. They live in beautiful homes, take four or five holidays a year – usually in exotic locations – eat out often, go to the theatre and the opera whenever a show takes their fancy. They are

Spending the Kids' Inheritance. And why shouldn't they? They've worked hard all their lives to earn their money, so why should they live a miserly existence in their retirement just to enable them to leave the money to their kids?

Most people do want to leave something to their progeny, but if your kids are already doing quite well for themselves, thank you very much, then it makes sense to at least spend the money that will take your estate over the nil-rate band.

Giving It Away

As noted above, there are certain amounts that you can give away without any IHT implications. However, provided that you are likely to live at least another seven years, you can give away as much as you like since this money is then treated as a PET.

There may be circumstances in which you would like to give some money away – perhaps you are approaching the age when you would like the IHT clock to start ticking – but you do not want the stated beneficiary to have access to it immediately. For example, perhaps you are a seventy-year-old with a thirteen-year-old granddaughter. Your estate is worth more than the £285,000 nil-rate band and you would like to gift £50,000 to your grandchild. But you don't want her to have access to the money now. The way to get around this problem is to use trusts.

Now, although a trust may sound like something only Tara Palmer-Tomkinson would have, they are a very useful tool even for those of modest means. In simple terms, a trust is a written arrangement whereby an appointed person (the trustee) is given assets to hold and manage for the benefit of those named in the trust deeds (the beneficiaries). So in this case, you would appoint a trustee – usually an investment manager or bank – to manage the money until the beneficiary – your granddaughter – reaches the age of twenty-one, say, or until you die, whichever is the later event.

There are various types of trust and they have many advantages. For one thing, not only is the money held within them exempt from tax but so is any growth achieved. So if the trustee invests the money well and it grows to £70,000, there is no tax to pay on the extra £20,000 either. Moreover, trusts can be flexible. You might name your granddaughter as the default beneficiary but have on the subs bench, so to speak, other potential beneficiaries. These people do not have to be named; they can just be described. So, for example, if you think that more grandchildren may be on the way in a few years' time (perhaps another of your children has recently married), then they could be listed as potential beneficiaries and added to the default list at a later date.

Another way of using a trust, which is very useful for married couples, is to set up a discretionary will trust of the nil-rate band. This sounds complicated, but it could save you more than £100,000, so it really is important if you are married. It works by making use of both nil-rate bands, yours and your husband's.

The first thing you would need to do is to change the way in which you legally hold the property to become tenants in common rather than joint tenants. When one spouse dies, instead of the entire house transferring into the name of the surviving spouse, their half share can be transferred into a discretionary will trust, with the surviving spouse remaining in the house, free to live there until he or she passes away. When he or she dies, his or her half-share of the property, along with the half-share in the trust, can be passed to their children or other dependants free of IHT, since both nil-rates bands have been used.

The use of discretionary will trusts works for married couples and for couples with a civil partnership, but unfortunately not for cohabitees.

Insure against It

Gifts given out of income are also exempt from IHT, and a good use for your income could be to pay the premiums of a whole-of-life insurance policy, the benefits of which can be written into trust. This is quite complicated, but basically what happens is that you calculate what you think your IHT liability might be, and then set up a life policy for this amount. When you die, the policy pays out, into a trust which is set up on your death. That money can then be used to pay your IHT bill, which means that your family don't have to worry about it, and the entire process is speeded up.

Facing up to the Grim Reaper

Another way to limit your IHT liability is to write a will. If you die intestate, the state is likely to end up taking a large chunk of your assets, and in some cases could actually take the whole lot. That's one good reason for writing a will. Another is that, should you die intestate, your family could face an administrative nightmare – tracking down your assets, getting probate and so on – at a time when they least need the extra hassle. Yet another is that by writing a will, you ensure the people you want to inherit your worldly wealth actually get it. This is particularly important if you are not married: if you simply live with your partner, then they could get nothing if you die intestate.

However, it is hardly surprising that so many people fail to write a will. Confronting one's own mortality is not exactly a barrel of laughs. However, it is essential that you draw up a will if you have considerable assets and whenever your personal circumstances change dramatically: for example, when you marry, or divorce, or have a child. Writing a will need not be expensive. The Law Society says that a relatively straightforward will, for a fairly simple estate, should cost you no more than £200. Most people will get their family solicitor to draw up a will for them. If you don't have one, ask friends if they know someone good, or alternatively contact the Law Society for a list of solicitors in your area.

You could always do it yourself. Online will-writing sites, such as *www.bequest.co.uk*, *www.willwriters.co.uk* and *www.willwrite.co.uk*, will take you through the process and issue you with a written document within two weeks, for as little as £50. If you choose to go it alone, you'll need to do quite a bit of preparation. Start by thinking about what you want to achieve (for example, do you need to provide for anyone?), then draw up a list of all your assets as well as any debts you might have. Next, you need to draw up a list of beneficiaries, which will probably include your family, possibly some friends and charities, but could even include pets. Try to be as clear as possible when naming beneficiaries – give the full name as well as the person's relationship to you.

THE LAWS OF INTESTACY: OR WHO GETS WHAT

If you die without writing a will, the following rules apply:

- If you are married, your spouse will inherit your entire estate, so long as it is worth less than £200,000. If you are married and your estate is worth more than £200,000, your spouse inherits the first £125,000 plus a life interest in half the remainder, while the rest goes to your children. If you have no children, your spouse gets £200,000 and a life interest in half the remainder, while the rest goes to your parents. If you have no parents, the rest goes to your brothers and sisters. If you were an only child, then your spouse gets the lot.

- If you are not married but you do have children, your estate is shared equally between them. If you do not have children, the money goes to your parents, then to your siblings, then to your grandparents, then to your aunts and uncles and, if you have no family, the state takes the lot.

Musing over what to do with my inheritance took up only so much of my time. I spent much of the summer moping, despite my friends' best efforts to get me out and force me to have a good time. Mel and I went out quite a bit, sometimes with Susannah in tow. The three of us would invariably drink far too much and spend most of the evening complaining bitterly about how useless men are and how much better we all were without them. Then Susannah would start to cry. However, there was some good to come out of the 'three witches' get-togethers, as Michael had taken to calling them: Susannah and Mel were seriously thinking about going into business together. Mel had been working at the same graphic design company for years now, mostly designing food labels, a job which she found lacking in soul. Susannah, meanwhile, was eking out a pittance while juggling two jobs – one in the art supplies shop and another teaching fine art classes at an adult education centre. She was finding life a struggle on her measly income.

But they'd had an idea. Both were very creative. Susannah

was a brilliant seamstress and quite a talented artist. She'd been making hand-painted bags and tops for years – she'd give things to friends for birthdays and they'd ask her to make things for other friends and so on. But she'd never thought about actually selling any, despite their huge popularity among her friends, her friends' daughters and so on. Mel also has an eye for the accessory – she used to make handbags quite beautifully when we were at college, but she gave it up after she left, simply not having the time. They'd had an idea: Mel would construct her lovely bone-handled silk bags and Susannah would hand-paint them.

They thought that if they could produce, market and sell their stuff efficiently, they might just be able to make a living out of it. But both were total business novices and weren't exactly sure where to start. They were savvy enough to know not to quit their day jobs until they knew whether the business was a goer or not, but they just weren't quite sure how to do that. I promised that I'd speak to some contacts on the small-business side of things and get back to them. I also – foolishly as it turns out – suggested that Mel should maybe talk to Michael, since he knew quite a bit about getting investors interested in new projects, having worked for a venture capitalist firm for a few years.

'No bloody way,' Mel said firmly.

'Oh,' I said. 'You two are not talking, then?'

'They're all bastards,' she and Susannah chorused in reply.

Michael hadn't said anything to me about the pair of them not talking, but then I had been avoiding the subject of his new on-off thing with Mel whenever we spoke. But I did know that he'd accepted an offer on his flat and was waiting to hear from the sellers of 'an exceptionally spacious, warehouse-style, two-bedroom Victorian school conversion' within a five-minute walk of London Bridge. He had tried a low-ball offer so that there would be room for negotiation, he told me at dinner one night. Despite my reluctance to talk about it, the conversation did turn, inevitably, to what was going on in Mel's life.

'She's not talking to me,' he said mournfully.

'I know,' I replied.

I didn't ask why. He told me anyway. Apparently, there had been another girl and Mel had found out.

'For God's sake, Michael!' I hissed at him, really pissed off. 'You should just leave her alone now. You should just stay the hell away.'

He didn't say anything for a bit, just stared at his plate. Then, without looking at me, he said, 'I think I'm in love with her.'

Michael was depressed, I was depressed, Mel was heart-broken and Kate was going slowly mad in Oxfordshire. She rang every other day with another tale of an awful property she and Alex had visited. Among the horrors she encountered were rising damp, dry rot, kitchens encrusted with decades' ('I mean it! Decades!') worth of dirt, bathrooms encrusted with far worse, and rats, both dead and alive. I spent a couple of weekends with her in Oxford, with her spoiling me horribly, despite the fact that she really couldn't afford it, because she and Al felt so bad about fixing me up with Mark.

'He wasn't that bad, Kate,' I kept saying. 'We just weren't that well suited.'

And then she would eff and blind about what a total bastard he was for not coming back with me from Italy.

*

It was not Kate but Nikki who managed to drag me out of my depression. One Saturday morning, she turned up on my doorstep, clutching a load of forms and looking perplexed.

'I have to fill in a self-assessment form!' she complained loudly as I opened the door.

'Uh-huh,' I muttered at her, standing aside to let her in. It was kind of early for Nikki, particularly on a Saturday.

'Well, why?'

'I don't bloody know, do I?' I snapped at her, pushing my decidedly greasy hair out of my face. I could tell that she was about to snap back when she stopped and just peered at me, wrinkling her nose slightly.

'You look terrible,' she said. 'Just awful.'

'Gee, thanks. I've got a stinking hangover.'

'Go somewhere exciting last night, did you?' she asked with a grin.

I shrugged, not wanting to admit that in fact I'd actually sat alone on my sofa and got through one and a half bottles of gut-rottingly awful white wine from the newsagent's while watching episodes of *Friends* on DVD.

'You want coffee?' I asked her.

'No, I don't actually,' she said, casting a disapproving eye over my kitchen, which was in rather dire need of a clean, I had to admit. 'When's your cleaner coming?' she asked.

'She went back to Brazil,' I said mournfully. Nikki shot me a look. 'In July,' I admitted.

'Right.' Nikki had her determined face on. 'Enough's enough. We're cleaning this house, then we're going to Bliss. I don't care about the cost. You can pay. You've got plenty of money. Go on!' she yelled at me. 'Get in the shower! Actually, don't bother with a shower, you're about to get dirtier anyway.' She hung her leopard-print coat on the rack in the hallway and delved into the cupboard under the sink, re-emerging wearing a fetching pair of pink Marigolds. 'Let's get on with it.'

Several hours later, the pair of us were at a new spa in town, reclining in white fluffy robes post-hot salt scrubs, knocking back fresh-fruit smoothies. I hadn't felt so good in months.

'This is great,' I murmured to Nikki. 'Thank you so much.'

'No, thank you.' She grinned. 'You paid for it.'

'So I did.'

There was silence for a few moments as we sipped our smoothies.

'I've forgotten why you came round,' I said. 'It wasn't to clean my house, was it? Although thanks for helping with that.'

'Any time,' she said with a smile. After a second she added hastily, 'You know of course that I don't mean that. Get a cleaner.' We sipped again. 'Tax,' she said.

'Huh?'

'I came round because for some reason I've been sent a tax form. I thought only self-employed people had to fill in self-assessment forms.'

'Oh, that's right. No, they can send them to anyone. They've probably sent it because you fall into a higher tax bracket.'

'Can I just ignore it?' she asked plaintively. 'Cos I've already paid my tax.'

'No, you can't. They'll fine you. Once you've been sent a form, you have to fill it in. There's no escape.'

'Damn,' she muttered, slurping the last of her smoothie. She swung her long legs over the side of her lounger. 'You want another one of those?'

'Mmmm,' I said, my eyes closed, so relaxed that I couldn't be bothered to form words.

'If I get you one will you help me with my tax form?'

I just smiled.

Tax Doesn't Need to Be Taxing

Well, yes it does, actually. That's the point. But self-assessment doesn't have to be the horror that everyone makes it out to be. For some people it can be very tricky, and those people might want to think about hiring an accountant, but for people like Nikki – higher-rate taxpayers whose tax is deducted from their wages and who have no assets to speak of – and even for many self-employed people, it's really not that difficult. The important thing is to be well organized.

There are two main deadlines for self-assessment tax payers. The first is on 30 September. This is the date by which you must file your tax return if you want the Revenue to do your tax calculations on your behalf. If you miss this deadline, there is no need to panic, because you have until 31 January to send in your completed form, having done the calculations on your own, and with it the payment that you owe.

Self-assessment taxpayers now have two ways of filing their tax return: by filling in the paper form or by filing online. If you are in any way computer-literate, or mathematically challenged, you will no doubt prefer the electronic method, since the computer calculates how much tax is owed automatically. However, if you wish to file online, you first need to register. HMRC will then send you an activation PIN by post, which could take up to five days (or more, depending on how rubbish your local postal service is). So you cannot decide on 30 January that you want to file your return electronically.

Having made up your mind when you plan to send back your return, and by what method, you can then rest easy until the time comes. So long as you keep the right records, the actual process of filling in the form should not take more than a few hours and at the very most half a day.

However, if you have very complex tax affairs – for example, if you own more than one property, have a large range of investments, run your own business and so on – it is definitely worth paying an accountant to do your tax for you. It will cost you upwards of £450, but is likely to save you at least that much in tax, not to mention time and hassle.

But back to those of us who do not own several properties or our own businesses. Nikki came around for dinner on the Tuesday after our spa experience. She was very impressed that I had invested in a few scented candles and some fresh flowers to spruce my place up, and I was very impressed that she was taking her tax form so seriously this far before even the first deadline.

'It's not like you,' I said.

'I know. I'm becoming organized and tedious just like you, aren't I?'

I glanced at the folder full of documents I had asked her to bring along. Most of them appeared to be covered with tea stains or were partially torn.

'I wouldn't worry too much about being organized and tedious just yet.'

Which documents you need to hand when filling in your self-assessment tax return depends on your circumstances. For example, if you are an employee, you need your P60 form, which details your income, how much tax has been deducted and your National Insurance Contributions, as well as your P11D form, which gives a statement of benefits. If you don't have these, contact your company's payroll department and they should be able to give you copies. If you are self-employed, you will need details of income and expenses, and possibly a balance sheet, if you have one. If you have savings and investments, you will need bank statements, statements from unit trusts and investment trust companies and share dividend tax vouchers.

Once you get down to filling in the form itself, you should cast your mind back to your schooldays, when you had to write exams. If you can think back that far, you will no doubt remember that the point the teachers always stressed *ad nauseam* was that you must read the questions carefully. The same goes for your tax return. Read it very carefully before you write anything down. And when you do start writing things down, do it in pencil. You can (and must) come back and write your figures in ink later.

On the first page of the main tax return, you will see that it tells you to complete any supplementary pages first. The supplementary pages are colour-coded (red for land and property, pink for employment and so on). If you don't have all the forms you need, these can be downloaded from the Internet or ordered from the special HMRC Orderline.

Don't worry if once you start filling in the form, you find that very little applies to you and that much of your form is blank. If you're an employee, you should probably have around forty boxes to fill, whereas if you're self-employed with a turnover of £15,000 or more, you'll have around eighty boxes to fill in. (Some employed people, as well as pensioners and others with very simple tax affairs, will now receive a shortened, four-page tax return, instead of the usual twelve-page form.)

Doing the calculations is simply a matter of very carefully following instructions, but it can get complicated, particularly if you find yourself with lots of zeros, or negative numbers. There are various tax software packages, such as Taxchecker, Taxcalc and Taxcentral, that will help you figure out how much tax you owe. You can buy these online or order them on CD-Rom – they cost anywhere from £15 to £30.

If, when you have done all your calculations, you realize with horror that you will be unable to pay your bill, don't panic just yet. Contact your local tax office as soon as possible and explain the situation. There are no fixed rules, but in most cases the taxman will try to work out a payment schedule with you so that you can avoid paying fines and surcharges.

Finally, before you send your form off, check it very carefully and then make sure you sign it! And remember to sign your cheque too. A huge number of penalties are incurred simply because people fail to sign their forms.

KEY TAX DEADLINES

6 April. This is the date on which a tax year starts, so when you calculate how much tax you owe, the relevant period is always 6 April to 5 April of the following year.

31 July. This is a penalty date. If you have not paid the tax that was due back in January by this date, you will be fined £100.

30 September. This is the date by which you must file your tax return if you want HMRC to calculate how much tax you owe. Since this will save you loads of hassle, it's a very good idea to return your form by this date.

31 January. This is the final date by which you must file your tax return and pay any tax you owe. If you miss this deadline, you will receive an automatic £100 fine. If you have not paid your tax, interest starts accruing from this date.

28 February. Another penalty date – you will be fined a 5 per cent surcharge if you have not yet paid your tax.

Note that HMRC reserves the right to fine persistent late-payers £60 a day for every day that they do not pay their tax.

What Do You Have to Pay?

Tax rates and allowances are set every year by the Chancellor of the Exchequer in either his main budget, which is usually presented in March or April, or in the Pre-Budget Report (PBR, also known as the Green Budget), which is usually in October or November. Most Chancellors are reluctant to raise income tax rates, since this is politically very difficult, but you can be sure that they will find other ways to screw us for cash. Whichever party is in opposition, the media call the sneakier measures 'stealth taxes' and you can be equally sure that both main political parties are guilty of raising revenue this way.

Income Tax

Income tax is levied on anything that pays you an income: in other words, not solely on the money you are paid to do your job. If you have investments that pay dividends or savings that pay you a rate of interest, this money is also subject to income tax. Everyone has a personal allowance, an amount of money on which no tax is payable. In the 2006/7 tax year, the personal allowance is £5,035. Personal allowances for older people are higher: £7,280 for those aged 65–74 and £7,420 for those aged 75 and over. Income tax is then levied in bands on any income over and above your personal allowance. In the 2006/7 tax year, the bands are as follows:

£0–£2,150	10%
£2,151–£33,300	22%
Over £33,300	40%

National Insurance

In addition to income tax, we must also make National Insurance Contributions (NICs), which go towards funding our state pensions, paying for the NHS and so on. There are various types of NICs: Class 1 NICs are paid by employees, employers and company directors; Class 2 NICs are paid by all self-employed people; Class 3 NICs are paid by individuals filling gaps in their contributions records; and Class 4 NICs are paid by some self-employed people who have made a profit.

Class 1 NICs. If you are an employee and earn more than the primary threshold, which is £97 a week in 2006/7, you will pay Class 1 NICs. These are payable at a rate of 11 per cent up to the upper earnings limit (UEL), which is £645 a week. Above that level, they are payable at 1 per cent.

Class 2 NICs. If you are self-employed, you must pay Class 2 NICs at a rate of £2.10 a week unless your income falls below £4,465 a year.

Class 4 NICs. If you are self-employed and you have made a profit, you will need to pay Class 4 NICs as a percentage of that profit. At present, you pay 8 per cent on profit of between £5,035 and £33,540 and at 1 per cent on amounts exceeding that.

Capital Gains Tax

You have to pay tax when you sell an asset or even if you give one away, if you have made a profit on that asset. For example, you might buy some shares for £5,000. Several years later, you sell them for £20,000. Capital gains tax (CGT) is payable on the profit you made of £15,000. However, in each tax year everyone has a CGT allowance, known as the annual exempt amount (AEA), which is £8,800 in the 2006/7 tax year. So in the above example, you would not actually have to pay CGT on £15,000 but on £6,200.

Certain assets are exempt. These include your home, so long as it is your principal private residence – the place in which you live most of the time – your private car, cash and foreign currency for your private use, and jewellery, paintings and antiques that are individually worth £6,000 or less.

There are three bands of CGT: 10, 20 and 40 per cent. The rate of CGT which you have to pay depends on the level of your income liable to income tax. How it works is that the amount chargeable to CGT (for example, the £6,200) is added to the amount of taxable income which you have earned in that year, and it is then treated as the top part of the total. So if your earnings are £40,000, you will pay CGT at 40 per cent on the extra amount.

You may not have to pay the full amount, thanks to something called taper relief. Taper relief, which is designed to encourage long-term investment, means that gains on non-business assets are reduced by 5 per cent per year once the asset has been held for three years, with the maximum reduction amounting to 40 per cent. For example, if you sell a painting which you have had for six years, making a capital gain of £20,000, your CGT calculation would look like this.

£20,000 – £8,800 (your CGT allowance) = £11,200
15% × £11,200 (your taper relief for three years) = £1,680
40% × (£11,200 – £1,680) = £3,808

Stamp Duty

Stamp duty is paid when you purchase stocks, shares and property. On shares, the tax is small: just £5 on share purchases up to £1,000, then rising by increments of £5 up to £50 on purchases between £9,000 and £10,000. Above £10,000, stamp duty is payable at a rate of 0.5 per cent, rounded up to multiples of £5.

On property, no tax is payable on properties worth up to £125,000. Between £125,001 and £250,000, stamp duty is payable at 1 per cent. It is payable at 3 per cent on properties worth between £250,001 and £500,000 and at 4 per cent on properties worth more than £500,001.

Stamp duty has become controversial because it now catches such a large number of people, many of them of modest means, because house prices have risen so much recently. In fact, the amount of residential stamp duty collected by the Revenue has increased roughly nine times since the early 1990s. And this is not a minor tax: it raises the cost of house price purchase considerably. For example, if you are buying a home worth £270,000, you will have to pay £8,100 in stamp duty.

Estate agents argue, moreover, that it creates odd distortions in the housing market, since the difference between buying a home for £249,000 and £251,000 is no longer £2,000, but more than £7,000 thanks to the difference in stamp duty. This means that there is an incentive for private deals to be done whereby the seller will officially accept a lower offer, provided that the buyer pay over the odds for 'fixtures and fittings', in order to help the buyer avoid paying stamp duty.

You need to be very careful about this, however, since HMRC has begun to scrutinize this area more closely. Since December 2003, buyers have had to fill out a form providing full details of the house sale, including exactly what they bought and what was paid. The Revenue then has nine months to investigate the sale if it is not happy with the sums, and if it believes that you've inflated the value of the fixtures and fittings in order to cut your stamp duty bill, penalties and fines will ensue.

Don't Pay More Tax Than You Have To

IFA Promotion, a group that promotes the use of financial advisers, says that we waste £5.7 billion every year because we don't plan our financial affairs in a tax-efficient way, because we don't take advantage of the tax breaks we're offered and because we do stupid things, such as missing HMRC deadlines. The figures are really quite alarming:

- Almost £90 million is wasted every year because people fail to send in their tax returns on time.
- £108 million would be saved if everyone used their ISA allowances.
- We pay more than a billion in inheritance tax that could be avoided.
- £315 million is wasted by non-taxpayers who don't fill in R85 forms – these allow interest to be paid free of tax on bank and building society accounts.
- £680 million could be saved if everyone took full advantage of the tax breaks offered on pensions contributions.
- Perhaps most depressing of all, £360 million more could go to good causes if we used tax-efficient means of giving, such as Gift Aid.

Tax planning is a complex subject, so if you do face a large tax bill every year, it is probably worth speaking to an accountant or a financial adviser about how best to organize your affairs. However, there are some basic steps you can take to reduce your tax bill.

If you are part of a couple, make sure that you use both your personal allowances and transfer assets into the name of whoever is in the lower tax bracket. For example, if your other half stays at home to look after the kids while you work, keep any savings in his name, since he will not have to pay so much tax on the interest.

In order to lower your CGT bill, you can sell your shares and then have your spouse repurchase them. If you do that every year, you are more likely to have a gain that falls within the annual exempt amount.

If you're single and you have a spare room, rent it out. Under the rent-a-room scheme, you can earn up to £4,250 a year tax-free.

Unmarried couples have one key tax advantage over married couples in that if you both own properties you are entitled to treat each as your principal private residence (PPR), so long as both are used as a residence. So, for example, if one of you has a house in London and one in Cornwall, and you divide your time between the two, then both would count as PPRs, which means that when you come to sell one or other, you would not have to pay Capital Gains Tax. If you are married, you are entitled to only one PPR per couple.

You can also save money by being aware of the tax breaks that are available to you and finding out whether you qualify. Everyone is entitled to things like ISAs, but there are other tax reliefs available to parents and pensioners. Some of these are means-tested credits, so there is a fair amount of form filling involved, but it is worth it in the end.

Benefits and Tax Credits

In the past, marriage used to be rewarded with tax breaks. Nowadays, it is parenthood that wins you points in the tax system.

Child Benefit

This is available to anyone who is bringing up a child under the age of sixteen, or under the age of nineteen if the child is still at school or in vocational training. This is not a means-tested benefit: you could be a millionaire and you would still be entitled to claim Child Benefit. Nor do you even need to be the child's parent, but you must be the one who is caring for the child.

For the eldest child who qualifies, Child Benefit is £17.45 a week; for every other child you get £11.70. When you think about it, that's a pretty decent amount of money. For Jackie and Sam, for example, that's an extra £1,516 a year. To claim Child Benefit, you must contact the Child Benefit office as soon as the child is born or comes into your care.

Child Trust Fund

There is now an extra incentive to claim Child Benefit: if you claim it, you will also be entitled to receive a voucher for at least £250 to be saved in a Child Trust Fund (CTF). These are a relatively recent invention of the Labour government, designed to offer every child savings with which to start adult life.

Child Tax Credit

The Child Tax Credit (CTC) is yet another financial aid offered to parents, designed to help those on low incomes, although you can actually have a fairly high household income and still qualify for some help. Anyone with at least one child and a gross household income of less than £58,175 qualifies, although rates become much less generous once your household income passes the £20,000 mark. To claim the full CTC, which is worth £2,310 if you have one child, your household income must be less than £13,910 a year.

You do not have to be married, or even part of a couple, in order to claim the CTC, but if you are part of a couple you must apply for it as a couple – you cannot make individual claims.

How much you get depends on how much you earn and how many children you have. For example, a family with a household income of £15,000 and one child would get around £1,600; with two children the family would get around £3,200 and with three they would get £4,860. However, a family with an income of £25,000 would get just £545 if they had one or two children, or around £1,160 if they had three children.

To complicate matters further, the CTC is made up of two parts: a family element, payable to any family responsible for at least one child, and a child element for each qualifying child. The family element will be higher if you have a child under the age of one, while the child element is paid at a higher rate if your child is severely disabled. The CTC is paid directly into the bank account of the main carer in the family and can be paid either weekly or every four weeks.

Working Tax Credit

The financial assistance does not stop there. Parents may also be eligible to claim the Working Tax Credit (WTC), though the poor and childless will be pleased to hear that you do not have to be a parent in order to qualify. You can claim WTC if:

- You are aged sixteen or over, are responsible for a child and work at least sixteen hours a week.
- You are aged sixteen or over, work sixteen hours a week and have a disability.
- You are aged twenty-five or over and work at least thirty hours a week.

Once again, the amount you receive is based on how much you earn, and the rates are not particularly generous for single, childless people. A single person without children aged twenty-five or over and working more than thirty hours a week with an income of £8,000 a year would receive £1,125. If that person earned £10,000, they would get a mere £385. Above that level, you get nothing.

If you are poor and childless, you might find it something of an affront that a family earning close to £60,000 gets money from the government simply because they have children, while someone earning £12,000 a year gets nothing simply because they don't have kids, but that is the way the system works.

There is yet more help for families with children as part of the WTC if you pay for 'approved childcare'. The childcare element of the WTC is worth up to a maximum of 70p for every £1 paid in childcare costs, up to a limit of £175 a week if you have one child or £300 a week if you have two or more children. In other words, the maximum childcare element you can receive is £94.50 a week if you have one child or £140 a week if you have two or more kids. Again, this is means-tested, so if your family income is relatively high, you will receive less. Note that your children must be in 'approved childcare' – you cannot pay the in-laws to look after the kids and then claim back the cost. You need to leave the children with a registered childminder, nursery or playscheme, or an out-of-hours scheme on school premises.

Pension Credit

Older people on low incomes may also be eligible for help from the government in the form of the pension credit. The pension credit is paid to people over the age of sixty and is designed to ensure that, if you are single, you have a weekly income of at least £114.05, and if you are in a couple, your income is at least £174.05 a week. See Chapter 5 for details.

Once we'd sorted out her bits of paperwork, it took us almost no time at all to do Nikki's self-assessment form. I was even inspired to do my own once she had left. I was right in the middle of getting my paperwork together when the phone went. It was Mel.

'How do you fancy a business-brainstorming weekend in Bath?' she asked me.

'That sounds lovely,' I replied, 'but I'm kind of busy for the next fortnight.'

'Oh, not just yet,' Mel said. 'It won't be before then. Susannah's arranged meetings with lawyers and financial advisers for the next couple of weeks. She's got her settlement.'

'Is she pleased?' I asked, realizing as I said it how stupid that sounded. 'I mean, not that she's divorced, but with the settlement.'

'I think so,' Mel said. 'I haven't really asked. It's kind of difficult, isn't it? I know she's been pretty upset.' There was a pause. 'Uncle Ed's asked his other woman to marry him.'

'Jesus, that was quick. That must be horrible.'

'Yeah, well, they're all shits, aren't they?'

It seemed the right moment to mention Michael. I didn't tell her what he'd said, but I told her that he'd been asking after her.

'That's over now, Tash,' she said softly. 'I thought we could try to make it work, but he's just incapable of not hurting me. He doesn't know what he wants, or if he does, he doesn't want me. I can't be dealing with it.'

She said it with so much conviction that I just let it go. I felt oddly bereft, much sadder than I had been to end my own relationship with Mark, and quietly furious with Michael for not seeing how perfect they were for each other a little earlier. But I knew from Mel's tone that there was nothing more to be done.

9. For Richer, for Poorer: Money and Relationships

I was writing a story for one of the nationals when the phone rang.

'Yeah?' I answered, a bit short – I was right on deadline.

'Tash?' whimpered a voice at the other end of the line. 'Tasha?'

'Amy?' I asked, relieved that at least it wasn't yet another of Nikki's crises. 'What is it?'

'I think the wedding's off,' she said, and burst into tears. My relief dissipated.

'No, Amy! What happened? It isn't really, is it?'

'I don't know . . .' she started, but I interrupted her.

'You're not going to believe this but I'm bang on deadline. Give me twenty minutes, will you? Make yourself a cup of tea and give me twenty minutes. I'll call you right back.'

I finished my story as quickly as I could, writing a somewhat cursory conclusion. By the time I rang back she seemed a little calmer.

'Have you had some tea?' I asked.

'Shot of vodka,' she replied. 'I needed something a little stronger.' It was three o'clock in the afternoon.

'Aren't you at work, Ames?' I asked.

'No, I'm at home. I took the day off because Ade was flying out to Lagos at lunchtime and I wanted to see him off.' She started to cry again.

*

It turned out that Amy was being a little melodramatic. The wedding wasn't exactly off. It's just that Amy and Ade don't argue much, so when they do she tends to panic. What had happened was that a few hours before he jetted off to Lagos, Ade had discovered some receipts that Amy had left lying around. Not all of the spending was wedding-related. Sure, she'd bought herself a pair of killer heels for her going-away outfit, but there was also some jewellery, a handbag and – inexplicably given the time of year and the fact that they were not planning any trips to the beach any time soon – a bikini. Immediately after discovering the receipts, he opened their phone bill and his jaw dropped.

'Who have you been calling?' he asked her, exasperated. 'It's a £400 bill.'

'Not all of it is me,' Amy said defensively. 'There's calls to Africa there too.'

'None of those are mine, Amy,' Ade pointed out. 'None of those are to Nigeria. In fact they're all to Cape Town.' Which is where Amy's older sister lives. 'And one of them is forty-five minutes long,' Ade continued. 'There's also a couple of hour-long calls to New York.' Amy's brother, James, had been working out there for the past few months.

Amy brushed his concerns aside, but the phone bill, coupled with the receipts, had got Ade worried.

'I think it's time we pooled our money,' he announced. 'I think we should open a joint account so that we can keep everything in one place.'

'That'll just mean that I have access to your money, Ade,' Amy pointed out. 'Which is maybe not something you want to give me,' she added, giggling.

'I'm serious, Amy! You can't just spend money like water. I think we should pool everything so . . .' He tailed off.

'So what? So you can keep an eye on what I'm up to?'

'Yes, actually! Yes, I think I should be keeping an eye on things,' he replied. Seeing how cross she was getting, he tried a more conciliatory tone. 'I know there's the wedding and everything, but we can't just spend like there's no tomorrow. There is a tomorrow and I want there to be kids in it. Lots of them.'

'Ade, we can think about all that later . . .' she started.

'No, we can't!' He was raising his voice again. 'Do you have any idea what raising kids costs? I don't think you do! I don't think you're taking this seriously! I think you think I'm just made of money and you can just spend all you like and I'll bail you out. I want us to have a joint account so that I can keep an eye on things.'

'Well, you're not bloody going to get one!' she'd yelled at him as she stormed out of the front door.

By the time she'd calmed down and returned to the house, he'd left for the airport. She'd tried to call but his phone was off. Sitting in her home alone, with no way of talking to him, she convinced herself that he was going to call the whole thing off.

'Have I been incredibly stupid?' she asked me in a tiny voice. 'I know I've been spending too much and everything, and I just thought I'd rein it all in once the wedding was over. And I really don't like the idea of pooling everything. I know it sounds silly, but when I buy him a birthday present, I want it to be from me, not from us. And when I go and spend a couple of hundred quid on some cute shoes, I want it to be my money, not his. I don't want to have to justify things, or to hide receipts, or any of that kind of crap.'

'I think you're absolutely right, Amy,' I told her. 'But it sounds as though he thinks you're just going to spend all your money and then get him to bail you out.'

'Well, there was this one thing . . .' she said.

'Mm-hmm?'

'I couldn't pay off one of my cards last month, so he did it,' she admitted. 'It was just the one time.'

'Yes, but then he sees the receipts and the phone bill and he thinks that's what it's going to be like all the time.'

'I know.'

'I think you should stick to your guns on the joint account front, but don't take the piss. You've got to pay your own credit card bills. You can't have it both ways.'

'I know,' she said again, sounding like a chastened schoolgirl.

'And he is right about the kids thing . . .'

'OK, OK, I know!' she said plaintively.

'Are you really going to have lots of kids?' I asked her.

'Four,' she said, and I could almost feel her smile. 'Four or five.'

What's Wrong with a Joint Account?

Joint accounts are very useful. Holding an account with your boyfriend or husband makes life a great deal easier when you live together, since all the household bills can be paid out of the account. It can also make sense to set up joint savings accounts for specific things, such as the 'we want a new kitchen' account or the 'we're going on holiday to Thailand' account, so that you both have control over your savings.

However, I believe that it is foolish in the extreme to lump everything into one account. Amy's reasons for not wanting a joint account are perfectly valid, but there are other, more compelling reasons to make sure that you always have control over your own finances. Banks will not freeze an account without a court order. This means that if you and your partner split up, there is nothing to stop him (or you for that matter) clearing out the account and running up a huge overdraft for which you will be jointly and severally responsible. You will have no way of recovering the money he has taken from the account.

Moreover, if you have your own personal savings or current account at the same bank as your joint account, the bank can actually take money out of your account to cover any debts incurred on the joint account. Pooling all your money in one joint account makes both of you vulnerable. Now obviously no one believes that their partner will steal from them and leave them in debt. But it happens, more often than you might think. In the very worst cases, the wronged party is left with crippling debts that can take years to pay off.

Women tend to be more reluctant to pool their finances than men are, with around half of women polled saying they would not like a joint account, while around a third of men said they would rather not pool their finances. I'm not sure whether that's because we are cleverer with money, because we're more suspicious than our trusting partners or because we know that the feckless bastards will just try to scrounge our hard-earned cash given half the chance.

It's my view that women are right to be a little circumspect. It might not seem terribly romantic or trusting, but I think that ideally every woman should have a running-away fund. Or a walking-out fund. A declaration-of-independence fund perhaps. Whatever you like to call it, knowing that you have the means to support yourself if push comes to shove is very reassuring.

Who Controls the Purse Strings?

This is a tricky area. Money and relationships are a minefield to negotiate, because who controls the household finances is such a critical issue in our lives. And that is because who earns the money, who spends it and who ultimately controls it are not just matters of financial management but of power, equality and fairness. It is striking that where men earn more than women, that difference is noted, and is used to the man's advantage. However, where the woman is the high earner, the difference is often glossed over, minimized. The woman will downplay the difference in order not to emasculate her man.

In traditional arrangements, men have earned the money, while women have stayed at home to raise the kids. In some households the women managed all the finances, paying bills out of an allowance given to them by their husbands. There is nothing wrong with this of course, and the woman in fact has quite a high level of control with her hand on the purse strings, but in most households the allowance given covered bills and essential expenses. There was no room for her to buy luxuries.

This remains the case, whether women work or not. Research by Jan Pahl at the University of Kent has shown that in half of all British marriages men have significantly more money to spend on themselves than their wives do. She also notes that women often take control of the family finances in times of difficulty, when managing money is a chore, not a means of exercising power and influence.

Many men will argue that they are the ones who go out to work, that they work bloody hard and that it is therefore unfair for a woman who stays at home to complain. But the problem with that is they do not think about the monetary value of the work their wives or girlfriends do. They take it for granted.

Yet cooking, cleaning, bringing up kids – these are tough occupations and you can place a monetary value on them. I'm not saying you should present him with a bill at the end of the month, but you must be aware of the value of your labour. A good (if morbid) way to look at it is like this: if you were run over by a bus tomorrow, how much would he have to spend to get someone else to do the cooking, cleaning and child-rearing? A cleaner might cost around £1,200 a year. God knows what a cook costs! And childcare? Well, the Daycare Trust says that nursery costs for a child under two are more than £7,000 a year, but in London you could expect to pay around £10,000 a year. Nannies cost anything from £150 to £400 a week – that's up to £18,400 if you had a nanny for forty-six weeks of the year.

Most women who stay at home to look after their children think about what they are doing in terms of how important it is for their kids, not in terms of the financial value of their labour. However, it helps to look at things in a more mercenary way sometimes – for example, when you're negotiating a household budget with your other half.

Living in Sin

In many ways, life get simpler when you marry. It's cohabitees who have to watch their backs, since they are not protected in law the way that spouses are. The 'common-law wife' is a myth, she does not exist. If you live together and your partner dies without leaving a will, you will not inherit his estate. It will pass to his next of kin – his children, his parents or his siblings. This can be contested in the courts, particularly if you have been making a financial contribution to the mortgage, but this is costly and obviously unpleasant. Nor will you usually receive a pension if your partner dies and you are not married, although it may be possible in some schemes to pay death benefits to an unmarried partner.

Fortunately, death is not the usual end of cohabitation! Unfortunately, though, relationships where couples live together don't tend to last very long. The average cohabiting relationship lasts a mere nine months. So what happens if you split up? The harsh truth is that unless you have children, you will usually walk away from your relationship with exactly what you brought to it. Even if you do have children, and you have stayed at home to bring them up, you will not automatically be entitled to half of your combined wealth when you split up.

The courts have become more generous to cohabiting partners, but there are still plenty of grey areas, and plenty of circumstances in which you could leave a relationship with nothing.

Let's say that a couple decide to move in together and the male partner, who works in the City and has just earned a huge bonus, puts down the deposit and raises the mortgage. His girlfriend is still studying and as such is unable to make a financial contribution to the home. If the couple split up, the girlfriend will have no rights over the property unless she can point to a Deed of Trust whereby her partner unequivocally promised her an interest in the property.

But how about if the girlfriend – a bit of a dab hand at DIY – has spent every weekend since they moved in sanding floors, stripping wallpaper, painting bedrooms and building walk-in wardrobes? The answer is that she may be able to establish an interest in the property, but then again she may not – the success of her claim would probably depend on whether there had been an agreement, express or implied, that she would be entitled to a share in the property if she made some contribution to its maintenance or improvement.

And what if, after six months, the girlfriend starts to work and then starts to pay half of the mortgage each month? If she has made a financial contribution to the property, her claim becomes stronger still, but it is still not certain that she will be entitled to something. The male partner could argue that his girlfriend's payments simply constituted rent.

There are steps you can take to make living together a more secure arrangement for both of you. To make sure you are 100 per cent secure, you could also ask a lawyer to draw up a deed of trust and cohabitation agreement, which allows each partner to state the proportion of their holdings, not just in the property but in all your other assets too. You can detail who keeps which assets if you split up, as well as detailing what will happen to assets that have been purchased jointly in the event that you separate. The agreement is binding on both parties and can help you avoid costly legal wrangles.

If you are purchasing a property together, the legal side of things becomes all the more important – this applies not just to cohabitees, but to friends buying together and, to a lesser extent, to married couples.

Under a joint-tenancy arrangement, each person pays half the mortgage and household costs, and gets half the profit (or bears half the loss) when the property is sold. Neither party can sell without the other's consent, and should one partner die, the other will inherit their share. This is the most popular type of arrangement for people who choose to live together.

If you choose a tenancy in common, the terms of the tenancy are defined by the percentage of the property each person owns, which will depend on how much of the deposit each person paid and how much of the monthly mortgage repayments they cover. Unless there is a will stipulating otherwise, should one partner die their share of the property will go not to the other partner but to their next of kin.

If you are tenants in common, then you are jointly liable for the mortgage, which means that if one person defaults (scarpers with his secretary to Brazil, for example), the other partner will be pursued for the full amount of the mortgage loan.

Civil Partnerships

When the actor Sir Nigel Hawthorne died in 2001, his partner of more than twenty years, Trevor Bentham, had to contend not only with his grief but with a six-figure Inheritance Tax bill on his lover's share of their home, a fifteenth-century manor house in Hertfordshire. Had they been a heterosexual couple, married just a week, that bill would not have been levied thanks to the spousal exemption. But Hawthorne and Bentham's long-term commitment to each other meant nothing in the eyes of the taxman.

This iniquitous state of affairs, where gay couples have had no legal recognition no matter how long they have been together or how committed their relationship, has at last been addressed. The introduction of civil partnerships in late 2005 has meant that gay people can now have secure pension rights, be exempt from paying IHT on the death of their partner if they inherit his or her assets and be recognized as their partner's next of kin. Heterosexual couples who wish to enjoy those rights have no choice but to marry.

The day after her crisis call, Amy rang me again to say that she had been woken that morning by the Interflora delivery man, who came bearing a dozen long-stemmed red roses. The wedding, it seemed, was very much still on. She'd rung Ade in Lagos and he'd apologized profusely (as if the flowers weren't enough!) and declared that he would happily bankroll Amy's bikini purchases for the rest of all time. (It has to be said, the girl looks damn good in a bikini – I went on holiday to Greece with her a few years back. It was very demoralizing.)

Anyway, Amy was heading off to Wales for a long weekend to 'do wedding things' and stop in on her parents in Colwyn Bay, and she wondered if I fancied coming with her. Since I didn't have too much work to get done, and in any case could take the laptop with me, I agreed.

We set off early on Saturday morning. The plan was to head to Colwyn Bay, spend the night there and then drive down to the Snowdonia National Park on Sunday, where Amy had some wedding preparations to finalize, and I could go for long, bracing walks in the Welsh countryside.

On the way, Amy began fretting about some article she'd read which claimed that the cost of bringing up a child was around £150,000 and that if she planned to have four she'd need £600,000.

'Unless of course you feed them on bread and water, and deny them their fundamental right to play PlayStation,' I pointed out. 'Seriously. You don't have to have the 600 grand upfront! And at least you and Ade are thinking about this early. That's pretty rare.'

Research shows that, in general, we don't plan for life's big events. Around one in ten singletons make financial provision for the cost of marriage, while just 14 per cent of young people have given any thought to the cost of starting a family. It's just not something we tend to consider until it's about to happen, until the engagement's been announced or until you're actually trying for a baby. By which point the actual baby's arrival could be less than a year away! We prepare for other hypothetical events – holidays we haven't yet planned, for example – so it shouldn't seem that weird to prepare for a hypothetical child.

Perhaps less surprising is that fact that precisely 0 per cent of married people make any financial preparation for divorce. In fact, only a quarter of separated people prepare for it. Which is why it is always such a nasty financial shock when it comes. Most people divorce young: the most common age to get divorced is between twenty-five and thirty-four. Even if your divorce does knock you for six financially (it inevitably will emotionally), at this point there is still plenty of time for you to recover and start over. However, the number of people getting divorced much older is growing rapidly and for this group of people the recovery process can be a lot more difficult.

Research from Saga shows that the divorce rate among the over-fifties has soared in recent years, rising to almost 18 per cent. Experts put this down to the erosion of any stigma attached to separation and divorce, even among an older generation, as well as the all-important right of a wife to claim part of her husband's pension.

'Maybe you're lucky,' Amy said to me, out of the blue.

We were just leaving the motorway at Stoke-on-Trent, heading up towards Chester.

'Lucky how?' I asked, yawning. It had been a long drive.

'That you're single. You don't have to worry about all this stuff. You're so independent. You just do what you want, whenever you want. Like today – you can just up and leave with a friend whenever you please. There's no one to ask if that's OK, no one to get all sulky because you're going away without them, no one to get jealous wondering where you've been and who you're with –'

'No one waiting for me when I get home,' I interrupted. 'Just an empty flat and, if I'm really lucky, a blinking answer phone.'

Amy turned and looked at me with huge, sad eyes. 'Sorry,' she said softly, 'I just meant.'

'Watch the road,' I said, laughing. 'I'm only joking. Well, partly joking. I do love living alone actually, but that doesn't mean I want to do it for ever. It is great to have all the freedom, but there are plenty of drawbacks – even if you discount the obvious one of not having sex on a regular basis.'

Amy giggled.

'There's never anyone to go on holiday with, and when you go on your own you get hit on by all sorts of lowlifes and you have to pay through the nose for the pleasure thanks to the great single-room supplement.'

'True,' Amy agreed. 'And couples always buy you one birthday present and you've always got to get them one each! I remember what it's like. I've not been almost-married for ever, you know.'

'Oh, and talking of marriage, couples get to give one wedding present, cost split between two. I've got to shell out all by myself.'

'You certainly do,' Amy said forcefully.

'You have the same or almost the same rent to pay, you pay pretty much the same gas, electricity and water bills as a couple would, you get just a 25 per cent discount on your council tax and you have to pay full-price gym membership,' I went on, fully warming to the theme.

'God, being single's crap, isn't it?'

'It really is.'

We arrived in Colwyn Bay in late afternoon. Amy's parents, Euan and Carlotta (he's Welsh, she's Italian), had booked a table for us at a local seafood place that evening, so having caught up (and listened to seemingly interminable wedding chat), we got settled in a spare room each and I took a much-needed shower. Nothing like spending an entire day in a car eating endless packets of Mini Cheddars to make you feel grubby.

I emerged from the shower wrapped in a rather small towel and returned to my room, which, to my horror, now contained someone else. Sitting on the swivel chair at the desk, reading a magazine, was a dark-haired young man, who swung lazily around in his chair before I could back out of the room.

'Hello there, Tasha,' James said, a devilish little grin playing around his lips. 'Nice outfit.' He got up and crossed the room to give me a kiss. 'Long time no see.'

I couldn't think of a single thing to say. I blushed to my roots.

'This is my old room, y'know,' he said, still smiling, still enjoying my just-out-of-the-shower-and-wrapped-in-a-small-towel discomfort, 'but I'll let you have it for tonight.'

He disappeared. I shut the door and leaned against it. Oh, the horror. So the first time in several years I see James, Amy's brother, the really cool guitar-playing one on whom I'd had a huge crush when we were at college, I am wrapped in a towel with my hair scraped on to my head, speechless and blushing like a fool. Crap, crap, crap.

James is lovely. He's dark and skinny and high-cheekboned and bad. He used to come to visit Amy at college occasionally and shock everyone with his prodigious alcohol and drug intake. There was usually some scrawny blonde on his arm too, looking oh-so-hip and aloof, who would whisper in his ear occasionally but refuse to talk to anyone else. I fancied him something chronic.

I threw open my overnight bag in disgust. Why the hell hadn't Amy told me he'd be here? Then at least I'd have packed at least one halfway decent item of clothing. As it was, I had to make do with my unflattering jeans (ideal for bracing walks in Wales, not ideal for impressing hip musicians who've just spent the last six months in New York, surrounded by Carrie Bradshaw types) and a T-shirt with a velvet jacket and boots.

Tentatively, I made my way down the stairs.

'I liked your other outfit better,' a voice said. There he was, at the bottom of the stairs, smiling that smile at me again.

'Oh, fuck off,' I replied, finding the power of speech at last.

'Charming,' he said laughing. 'But honestly, you look good. Really well. Did you always look this good?'

I could feel myself blushing again and was hugely relieved to see Amy's mum emerge from the living room.

'Jay,' she said in a stern voice. 'Why do you have our guest cornered on the stairway? Don't you think you might offer her a drink?'

James disappeared into the kitchen to get me a glass of wine and Carlotta and I joined Amy and Euan in the living room.

'I didn't know James was going to be in town!' I said loudly, shooting Amy an evil look.

'He got back last week,' Carlotta said. 'We actually didn't know he was going to be here at home until yesterday.'

'We hardly ever know where he is,' Euan muttered darkly, 'or what he's up to.'

'Yes, what are you up to, Jay?' Amy asked as the topic of conversation re-emerged, glasses in hand. 'Why aren't you in New York?'

It turned out that James's band had suffered from an outbreak of artistic differences Stateside, so he had decided to return to Wales to regroup. He was thinking of moving down to London for a bit.

'Really?' I asked, a little too quickly, my heart skipping a beat. This was ridiculous.

Ridiculous it was, and my flustered demeanour did not go unnoticed. The next day, driving down to Snowdonia, Amy shot me a sly grin.

'How much were you two flirting last night?' she asked.

I blushed to my roots again.

'We weren't!' I shot back, again much too quickly.

She smirked for a while, then added, 'Just be careful with him. He's rubbish when it comes to being reliable.'

How refreshing, I thought.

A couple of days in the Welsh countryside did me no end of good. Well, a couple of days in the Welsh countryside and one night's outrageous flirting with James anyway. I returned to London with a spring in my step and a bunch of estate agents' details – I had decided to renew my property search once more.

I was not the only one who had rediscovered their *joie de vivre*. There was a near-hysterical message on the phone from Kate, who had found the perfect (perfect, perfect, perfect) house in a small village about fifteen miles from Oxford. It needed work, she told me, but it was within their budget and had three bedrooms.

'I really, really want it,' she told my machine.

I crossed my fingers and hoped they would get through this one without being gazumped.

10. Go It Alone: Setting up Your Own Business

'People might say that selling handbags is not a particularly original business idea, but then neither is selling knickers, and look how Agent Provocateur is getting on,' Mel commented to me as we rattled along the M4 in her ancient Mini on our way to Bath, where we were planning to spend the weekend with Susannah, developing a business plan. 'You just have to make them *the* handbags, don't you?'

'Absolutely,' I agreed. 'The only question is how to do that.'

Agent Provocateur is an excellent example of a successful business grown from scratch on the basis of a good idea and a clever marketing strategy. The lingerie retailer, which started with just a single store in Soho in 1994, is now a cult brand with a celebrity following and stores in London, Las Vegas, Los Angeles, Moscow and New York, to name but a few.

Agent Provocateur's founders, Joseph Corre and Serena Rees, may not have come up with a brilliant new invention, but they still came up with something unique. They wanted to coax British women out of their boring cotton pants and into something altogether more alluring. Now, until AP came along, sexy lingerie in the UK was the preserve of Ann Summers. It was all dodgy PVC outfits and red satin crotchless knickers. Lingerie, in other words, which would appeal to a certain sort of man (let's face it, most of them), but which many women found ugly, uncomfortable and faintly ridiculous. Rees and Corre wanted to get away from that whole British weirdness about sex being sleazy and smutty, so they came up with lingerie which was sexy as well as being pretty, glamorous and beautifully made. AP made knickers that appeal to the wearer, not just the audience.

So they got the product right. But developing a good business proposition is about more than just product. Agent Provocateur's marketing strategy was also spot on, designed to get maximum media attention. In 1995, the firm launched the Agent Provocateur girl search. The twelve finalists paraded, in their lingerie, outside London Fashion Week, holding banners declaring 'More S&M less M&S!' That sort of thing makes the papers.

The stores themselves are works of art, staffed by girls dressed sexily enough to arouse male interest without intimidating female shoppers. And AP has not rested on its laurels: in addition to lingerie, it now sells books, music, shoes, jewellery and perfume.

'Of course, Joseph Corre has certain advantages that you don't,' I pointed out to Mel. 'You not being the child of one of Britain's most successful and ground-breaking fashion designers ever.'

'You really think that having Vivienne Westwood in the family helped?' Mel asked sarcastically.

'Still, just because you don't have that sort of clout doesn't mean you can't get people's attention if you go about this the right way. You've got to exploit contacts,' I said.

'Like Amy,' Mel said with a grin.

'Exactly.'

The Feminine Entrepreneur

Female entrepreneurs are few and far between – just four out of every hundred women own their own business. But the number of women going into business has shot up in recent years, with a Barclays study revealing a growth in start-ups by women of 28 per cent between 2000 and 2004. Experts say this is probably due to the fact that banks are now more likely to accept that a business can successfully be run from home (an arrangement that tends to suit women, for obvious reasons), and also thanks to the higher profile of successful female entrepreneurs such as Linda Bennett, founder of L. K. Bennett, and Sahar Hashemi, the co-founder of Coffee Republic.

But few of us are going to end up with a success like Coffee Republic on our hands. Starting a business is one of the toughest things you could ever choose to do. No one goes into it on their own for an easy life – the average entrepreneur works sixty-three hours a week. And even with that work rate, many fail. One fifth of new businesses fold within a year of starting up, while just 50 per cent are still trading after three years.

So Why Do It?

One reason is that you've had a really good business idea. Perhaps you've thought of a gap in the market you can fill, or you want to go it alone in the field in which you already work. Maybe you think you can provide a service more efficiently and cheaply than the company you work for does. Or maybe – like Mel and Susannah – you want to turn a hobby or interest into a full-time career.

If you think you've just invented the next Post-it or Tetra-

Pak, or come up with a concept for the next eBay or Last minute.com, be sceptical about yourself. Rigorously test your idea. Are there similar products on the market? What could possibly go wrong?

Another motivation for you might be that you want to purchase an existing business, or buy out your employer or take over a family business. There are great advantages to this: the company will already be up and running, for starters, so you will have a ready-made pool of customers and you will find it easier to raise finance. However, businesses come up for sale for a reason. Often they are struggling, so you need to find out exactly why the current owner wants out. Buying a ready-made business is also expensive, and you may not be able to put your own personal stamp on things in the way you would have done if you had built it up from scratch.

Some people go into business because of a change of circumstances, such as redundancy or, as in Susannah's case, divorce. This might be the ideal time to start a new project, but then again it might not. Upheaval is stressful. If you are going through dramatic changes in your life, you might not want to rush into anything that you will regret later. Susannah felt comfortable because she'd had plenty of time to get used to being by herself and coping on her own. She had been working and living alone for months now. It was a steep learning curve, but she was dealing with it. At some moments, when she and Mel were deep in discussion about their ideas and their possible new lives, Susannah caught herself enjoying it.

Lots of people go into business for themselves because they want to be their own boss and take control of their lives. This too is a good reason for going it alone, but the problem is that people underestimate how tiring and time-consuming it is to work for yourself. All the problems of the business are yours alone to solve, and while you can take a sickie if you've got a hangover, you're the one who'll be paying for it. You lose your perks too. You can bid farewell to the generous corporate pension plan and six weeks' paid holiday.

Will It Work?

Sitting in Susannah's small rented apartment in the centre of Bath that evening, we did a quick progress report. Mel had been flat out at work, so Susannah had been doing a spot of research. She'd been reading up on the sector in trade publications, checking out the competition in magazines and on the Internet, and searching through all the official market research she could find. She'd trawled the shops of Bath, finding out what sold and what didn't (and for how much), and believed that she and Mel could fill a specialist niche.

She'd also decided to try selling the bags at the art college, with some success. The response from her students had been really positive and two had actually bought them, which was hugely gratifying. Even better, she'd got a strong response from two of the boutiques she had approached, with both saying they would be prepared to place small orders if Mel and Susannah could deliver before the Christmas shopping season got into full swing. One of the boutique owners had even asked whether Susannah would be prepared to make a bag of a particular colour and style – she wanted a pink one to go with a particular outfit.

'I was actually thinking that going down the bespoke route might be ideal for our purposes,' Susannah said.

'Great minds,' I said, looking over at Mel, who informed Susannah of her only slightly dastardly plan to use Amy's wedding as a marketing opportunity.

'Her actual wedding dress and accessories are all sorted,

but I was thinking of a bag to go with her going-away outfit, as well as some little purses for the bridesmaids, to give as gifts,' Mel explained. 'You see, the place is going to be packed with fashionista types from Amy's work, so it would be an ideal time to show off some of our stuff.'

'Aren't you a bridesmaid?' Susannah asked Mel.

'Well, yes, I am, but I'm sure we can get around that. Obviously we'd give the lot to Amy as a gift – if we get 'em done on time, we could give them to her at her hen night. I just need to find out what she's wearing for her going-away outfit and match it all up.'

'Easily done,' I said. 'Nikki's been working as her unofficial fashion consultant – she knows everything Amy is wearing at this wedding, right down to her knickers.'

But one wedding would not be enough to get the ball rolling. They needed to set up a website on which they could advertise their wares and take orders. And they needed to get some coverage in the papers and glossy magazines. Fortunately, they did have contacts. I knew a couple of fashion people at the newspapers and Amy of course knew people at the glossies. They also came up with the idea of 'handbag parties' – like Tupperware parties, but a little more glamorous. Mel figured that if they could invite a few friends round, and a few friends could bring their friends for a couple of drinks in the evening, they might be able to drum up some business that way.

'The key thing is that we've got to sell this stuff as unique, one-offs,' Susannah said. 'So we've got to be able to show people something exquisite and then say they can have one, only theirs will be their very own, no two alike.'

'And if you're going to do that, they're going to have to be expensive,' I pointed out.

'So we've just got to get them into the magazines and on to the arms of the girls who count,' Mel said. 'Girls who get their pictures taken.'

The Name Game

We agreed that getting the bags out to girls of that sort might take Amy's expertise. In the meantime, we could grapple with something more manageable: what they were going to call the business. It was all very well trying to get the word out about their products, but they needed to know what the word would be first. The name thing was something we'd talked about before, though we'd come to no conclusions. It turns out that naming a business is about as tricky as naming your firstborn.

'Harder,' Susannah said to me through a mouthful of salad. We'd adjourned to the dinner table by this point. We were eating delicious steaks with salad and drinking a rather lovely Merlot. 'You don't have to invent children's names,' she went on. 'Well, some people do, I suppose, like Frank Zappa. But most people just pick one, from a stock of names. There is no stock of business names, is there? Not in the same sense. This is definitely more difficult.'

Picking the right name is important. You want it to be memorable for all the right reasons. In some cases, a descriptive name is best. Carrie's Cleaners. If Carrie cleans, then it does what it says on the tin, which can be ideal. However, for something like a jewellery or clothing business, an abstract name might work better. Then you need to think about whether you want to sound traditional or modern. If you're going for modern, be careful – try not to pick something that's going to date easily. If you're going to be trading abroad, make sure your chosen name doesn't mean something rude in Czech or Japanese or wherever you're planning to market your goods, and watch out for oddly spelt names that may make it difficult for your potential customers to track you down.

If your business is web-based, or is likely to be relying heavily on the Internet, check whether the domain name for your business is already taken. Say, for example, that you want to call your company Tasha's Tiles and the domains *www.tashastiles.co.uk* and *www.tashastiles.com* are already taken, you might want to rethink.

If you're forming a limited company (see below), you will have to register the name of your firm at Companies House and you will have to follow its rules. That means that your company's name must end with Limited (or Ltd) or PLC. The name must not be the same, or very similar to, any other name on the register, it must not be offensive and it should not use any 'sensitive' words or expressions unless you have permission to do so. Sensitive words include things like British or European (suggesting your company has national importance), Authority or Society (suggesting a special status), Royal or Government (suggesting certain official connection) and so on.

Susannah liked Eye Candy, but Mel thought it sounded too American. Mel liked Miss Susie but Susannah didn't see why it should be only her name on the letterhead. All the abstract names we came up with just sounded odd, in a kind of 1980s way. I quite liked Susie + Melanie, but they preferred plain and simple S+M, which I thought was good. Not S&M, but S+M. We decided that it made a good working title for now, in any case. And then we called it a night, since it had been a pretty productive evening.

Susannah and Mel had gone some way towards addressing a few of the key questions that every prospective entrepreneur should be asking herself. Is there a market for the product? Will people pay good money for it? How do you spread the word about your product? Can you reach your intended market? What's so special about your idea? What will make it stand out from the crowd? And how do you plan to fund it? Once you have satisfactorily answered these questions, you can move on to the next phase of the start-up: writing a business plan.

The Plan

Writing an effective business plan is essential when you're in the early stage of starting up a new business. A good business plan describes your business, its objectives, its strategies, the market and your financial forecasts. It should be written in as lively and clear a manner as possible. Consign excess detail, such as CVs, technical information and market statistics, to appendices.

A business plan is not just there to help you secure external funding. Although this is one of its prime functions, it has other roles to play too. It can help you spot any potential pitfalls before it's too late, it focuses your mind on the challenges to come and it ensures that you structure the financial side of the business in the right way.

The Executive Summary

This outlines in broad brushstrokes what will follow in detail. It should not just be a table of contents, nor should it be an introduction to the business. It is a synopsis of your entire business plan and should include selected highlights designed to arouse interest in the business without overhyping it.

The Introduction

As the name suggests, this gives the reader a taste of what the business will do, as well as its short- and longer-term objectives.

Products or Services

This section addresses the products themselves. You need to explain how they are made and explain why anyone would want to buy them. What makes your product or service unique? And how is it likely to develop? If you believe you have invented the next Post-it note, you would need to say at this point whether you have trademarks or patents in place. And if you have invented something complex – say, a groundbreaking bit of software – you need to keep things simple. Don't blind people with science and try to steer clear of jargon.

Marketing

Here you need to analyse your customers and your competitors. Who are your customers and how do you plan to reach them? How do you intend to promote your products? Where in the market will they be positioned? Are you going for high end or the mass market? To answer all these questions, you will first have needed to develop a marketing strategy – of which, more later.

Operations

This section covers the physical location of your business, as well as you and your team. Here you need to detail where your business is based, and whether you own or rent the property, as well as detailing the equipment you own and what you have yet to purchase. You also need to talk about your staff and future personnel requirements.

Financial Forecasts

This is probably the trickiest bit of the plan, particularly if you haven't got a head for numbers. The main things to think about are how much money you need to borrow, what security you can offer lenders, how and when you plan to repay your debts, and what are your sources of revenue.

You'll need to do a forecast for at least the first three years of the business, although some plans run to five years. How much detail you include will vary with the sophistication of the business, but you should try to make forecasts for the first twelve months as detailed as possible.

Your forecast should include:

- Cash-flow statements, which will show your monthly balance and cash flow for the next year to eighteen months.
- A profit and loss forecast.
- A sales forecast.

A common mistake people make when drawing up financial forecasts is to construct them from the top down: that is, starting from the potential size of the market. It works better to analyse the amount you want (or need) to earn, then add in your costs and then work out how much you will need to sell. At the end of this section should be your funding requirements, if you have any.

Fortunately, for the moment Susannah and Mel didn't have any funding requirements. Susannah had decided to sink a small portion of her divorce settlement into starting up the business and was also planning to move to London, where she would buy a place for herself, preferably with room for a home office. Mel had a small amount of savings that she was willing to contribute, but she would also be taking out a personal loan – they wanted to be able to start the business on a fairly equal footing. Susannah had also decided to apply for some teaching jobs in London, while Mel would continue to work full-time until they were sure that they had a steady stream of orders.

Money Matters

Business Accounts

Banks are the most common source of funding for small businesses: around 60 per cent have an overdraft and 35 per cent have a bank loan. All the large high street banks, as well as a host of smaller ones, and even some ethical banks, offer business bank accounts of various types. Business bank accounts work in much the same way as personal accounts, although you will find that you have to pay for services that you get for free if you're a personal customer.

For example, drawing a cheque can cost as much as 78p (at Coutts). A direct debit or standing order can cost as much as 55p, while each time you make a deposit at Barclays you are charged 75p. However, there are some business accounts with low charges. Alliance & Leicester, for example, levies no charges for the first eighteen months on its Business Builder account. There is no minimum balance or restriction on the number of transactions per month. After eighteen months, your account is automatically transferred to one of its other tariffs.

The no-minimum-balance stipulation can be useful for businesses starting from scratch, since some minimum balances are rather high at around £10,000 or a minimum turnover of £100,000. To find the best business account for you, check out the Business Account Finder on the British Bankers Association website, which is run by Moneyfacts and has all the info you need.

Personal Accounts

Don't think that you have to keep your business and personal finances separate. In many cases, people will fund their business partly out of their own savings, or by personal borrowings such as a personal loan or mortgage. This is perfectly legitimate, although you have to be very careful about how much debt you take on, since if your business fails, your home could be at risk too.

Business Angels

Don't let the name fool you. Business angels are not angelic in the slightest. They are not altruistic souls out to make life easier for the small businesswoman but hard-headed, experienced, successful business people out to make a second fortune through investing in start-up companies.

The term 'business angel' was first coined to describe investors who put their money into the theatre in the 1920s. In those days, investors may well have been parting with their cash not just to make a profit but also because they loved the stage. Times have changed. Now what business angel is looking for is entrepreneurs with a solid track record and a brilliant, marketable idea: a product with a unique selling point and a market with growth potential.

Business angels generally invest anything from £10,000 to £250,000 in small companies, though the usual amount is closer to £25,000 – a pretty tidy sum for anyone starting out. The question for the small businesswoman is how to find the right angel for their business.

The answer is to go to the corporate equivalent of a dating agency, a business angel network such as Beer & Partners or the National Business Angel Network. You present your business plan and, if it makes the grade, the network will help to fix you up with potential investors.

Grants

Various institutions, including the government, the European Commission, local authorities and chambers of commerce, offer grants to small businesses. But don't imagine that it is easy to get a handout: competition for money is fierce, eligibility is limited and you must adhere to strict terms and conditions if you are to keep the money. If your company is involved in research and development, if it is located in a deprived area, if you are a young entrepreneur or if you are planning to train and develop staff, then you stand a chance of being given a grant. Grants are almost always awarded for specific purposes: to buy a certain piece of machinery, for example. There is no point in applying with just a vague notion in mind.

Business Link offers a Business Support Directory, which can help you to find a grant for your business.

Loan Guarantees

If you do not have enough security to get a conventional bank loan, you may be eligible for the government's small firm loan guarantee scheme. Under the scheme, the government will guarantee loans from £5,000 to £250,000. You need to prove that you have a viable business proposal and must have a turnover of less than £1.5 million, or £3 million if you are a manufacturer.

Teething Problems

The first year of running your own business is likely to be a tough one, so you need to make sure you're financially prepared. You will have to figure out how much you'll need to live on, as well as to run the business, and then figure out whether you'll be able to cover your costs. Before you quit your day job and launch yourself into the world of entrepreneurship, make savings. Save up enough money to keep your essentials covered for at least six months before you take the plunge. Make as many savings as you can: switch to the cheapest utilities providers and remortgage to a cheaper lender if needs be.

What Sort of Company Do You Want to Run?

There are various legal structures you can adopt for your business. Which one you pick will affect how much tax and National Insurance you have to pay, the financial liability if your business runs into trouble, the way the business can raise funds and who takes the management decisions. Most small business will be sole traders or partnerships – it is not until a business grows to a certain size that people start to think about incorporation.

Sole Trader

At the most basic level, you have the sole trader. This is the simplest form of business structure. You don't have to pay registration fees, you take all the management decisions yourself and all profits come to you. You will raise the money against your own assets, you pay tax as a self-employed person and must keep records of your business income and expenses. You personally bear full liability for any debts incurred by the business.

Partnership

On the next rung of the ladder is the partnership, in which two or more people share the costs, risks and profits of the business. A partnership is not a legal entity distinct from the people which make it up, however. If one partner decides to leave the partnership, if she goes bankrupt or dies, the partnership is dissolved. Each partner is personally responsible for all debts incurred by the company.

Limited Liability Partnership

Setting up a limited liability partnership (LLP) allows you to limit your liability to the amount of money you have invested in the business and to any personal guarantees given to raise money. This gives the partners an element of protection. If the company runs into trouble and fails, the partners' homes need not to be at risk. LLPs must be registered at Companies House and the members should have a legal agreement drawn up, outlining partners' rights and responsibilities. Usually, partners will share the profits equally, although this could be varied as per the partners' agreement. Each year, the business must file an annual return to Companies House, along with a fee.

Limited Liability Company

A limited liability company exists in its own right: it is not simply the sum of its shareholders. Its finances are separate from those of its shareholders, who may be its founders, but may be other individuals or companies. Limited companies can be either private or public – in the latter case, their shares are offered for sale on the stock exchange. Public companies must have issued shares up to a value of £50,000 before they can trade on the stock exchange.

Limited companies must be registered at Companies House (this is also known as incorporation) and must have at least one director, or two if it's a public limited company (PLC). Profits are distributed to shareholders in the form of dividends. Shareholders are not liable for the company's debts but they may lose money if the company fails.

The tax situation becomes a lot more complex when a business is incorporated: Corporation Tax is payable to the Inland Revenue, while National Insurance Contributions may be payable on behalf of employees.

Working for Yourself

Even if you are just a sole trader or a partner, there are certain legal and administrative matters you will need to clear up. First, if you are a sole trader or a partner, you will have to register as a self-employed person. This means that you must register with the Inland Revenue and must fill in a self-assessment tax return for each tax year, by 31 January at the very latest. You will have to pay Class 2 NICs and may have to pay Class 4 NICs too, if you make a profit.

If your business has a turnover of more than £61,000 a year, you will need to charge your customers VAT and send it to HMRC. Some goods – such as children's shoes, for example – are zero-rated for VAT purposes (in other words, no VAT is charged). HMRC will be able to tell you whether or not you should be VAT-registered.

If you are using your home as an office, you may have to pay business rates on the part of your home that is used for work, although this will depend on the degree of commercial use.

Note that if you work from home, it is possible that you will have to seek planning permission. This is true if your home is no longer used mainly as a private residence, if your business activities will lead to increased traffic in the area, if your business will affect your neighbours or if you need to alter your home in order to use the place for work.

Growing Your Business: Employees

For people planning to start up a business in the spare room of their house, hiring staff seems a long way off. But if your business is successful, it is likely that before too long you may need to recruit employees. Perhaps you'll need someone with skills that you and your partners don't have, or perhaps your workload will simply increase to a level that you can no longer manage.

Hiring people is a tricky business. There are practical issues to consider first of all. If you have been running your business from your spare room, where will your new employee sit? Do you have to think about moving premises as well? Remember that once you have employees, you will need to start thinking about access, as well as health and safety regulations.

There are various types of employee contract:

Temporary staff. The advantage of going through a temp agency is that much of the legwork is done for you. The agency will already have checked out the person's CV and chased up references. They also deal with payroll and all related issues, such as NICs, so all you have to do is pay the agent a fee. The drawback is that the agency has to make a profit, so you will be paying over the odds for your new employee. However, if all you need is someone to come in to take care of administrative or secretarial duties, a temp is probably your best bet.

Freelancers. Another relatively hassle-free way of employing someone is to use freelancers, since in most cases they take care of their own tax and NICs, and you would not be required to give benefits such as holiday pay.

Part-time, full-time or fixed-contract workers. If you employ people on these terms your obligations to them become more complicated. You will need to provide a statement of employment and an itemized pay slip, to register with the Inland Revenue to set up a payroll (to allow tax and NI deductions), to give your employees paid holiday, statutory sick pay, maternity leave and, if you have more than five, to offer them a pension plan.

Insurance

If you work from home, you will need to arrange specialist insurance, since running a business from your home will invalidate a home contents insurance policy. Instead, you will need to take out home business insurance. Obviously if you have separate premises for your business you will need contents and buildings insurance for those premises too. The insurance needs of the small business person do not stop there, however. If you have employees, or a commercial vehicle, there are certain mandatory insurances that you must take out. The first of these is Employer's Liability (EL) insurance, which covers you in the event that one of your employees is injured in the workplace. If you have a company vehicle (even if it is just your own car which is used for work), you need to make sure that your car insurance covers both types of use. If you have a vehicle that is used for commercial purposes only, then you must take out commercial vehicle insurance.

There are various other types of insurance that the small business owner should consider. These include business interruption insurance in the event of fire, flood or theft, deterioration of stock, portable equipment, goods in transit and public liability insurance.

Professional Advice

It is a mistake to imagine, just because you are going it alone, that you have to do everything yourself. In fact, one of the major reasons why small businesses fail is because entrepreneurs try to save money by shunning lawyers and accountants, preferring to do all the paperwork themselves. This is a false economy. Much of the administration and many of the tax issues are complex, so you must find yourself a decent lawyer and accountant, and possibly a financial adviser, before you start up.

If you are opening a business bank account you will get some help from the bank, since you will be assigned a relationship manager who will be able to advise you on basic legal and administrative concerns.

If you are planning to sell products or services online, get a professional to design your site and make sure all the IT works. Don't try and save on this – home-made sites look unprofessional and are full of glitches.

Free advice is worth embracing when it comes along too. Business Link is a hugely useful information service backed by the Small Business Service, a division of the Department of Trade and Industry. It has a brilliant website, *www.businesslink.gov.uk*, which covers a huge range of issues, as well as a helpline on 0845 600 0787. The Business Link website has tools such as the regulations checklist, an interactive section that allows you to describe your business and then goes on to tell you about all the regulations with which you need to comply. It covers everything from the basics of starting up to employment issues and international trade.

Why Do Businesses Fail?

For a huge range of reasons, most small businesses don't make it – around half fold within three years. Some failures will be due to the fact that the product or service on offer just wasn't good enough. But in many cases small-business owners create their own problems.

Lack of preparation is a key reason for failure. If you don't do your homework before going into business, it is likely that you won't get very far. You need to know how big the market is, what your competitors are up to and what others really think of your products or services. You need to ask around, get feedback. Don't be too secretive about your plans – others might be able to spot flaws that you cannot, so wrapped up are you in your idea.

Poor financial planning is also a killer. You have to make sure that your sums add up, that you will have the cash flow when you need it. And if you don't have the necessary funds just yet, then wait. You need to have a contingency plan in place too, just in case things go wrong, which they invariably will. Think about the implications of interest rate increases, transport or postal strikes – the kind of difficulties which businesses have to deal with all the time: how would they affect your new venture? You should also think about exit strategies. That may sound defeatist, but if it all goes horribly wrong within a year, would you be able to walk back into a job?

Many businesses run into trouble because of unreliable suppliers, so choose your business partners very carefully. The same goes for staff. Another key reason for failure is the business owner trying to do too much all by herself. Get help if you need it, even if it costs you – the alternative is likely to be more expensive in the long run.

Successful entrepreneurs say the same things over and over. You have to be very passionate about what you do, because it's going to take over your life. You need to stick with something you know and love. You need to be flexible: if something isn't working, think about how you can change it to make it work a little better. And you need to be realistic. You're not going to be a millionaire by this time next year.

11. The Hen Night

We were lounging by the pool on a freezing night in November. Fortunately, the pool was inside and nicely heated, so we were blissfully oblivious to the incipient snowstorm outside. Eight of us – Amy, her sister Ceri, Kate, Mel, Nikki, Jackie, Susannah and I, had decamped to the Royal Crescent Hotel in Bath for an extremely civilized hen night. Amy had insisted no dodgy strippers or L-plates, so Mel had organized a weekend of luxury instead.

The Bath House spa, behind the eighteenth-century façade of the Royal Crescent, is something else. Dark and gothic, with a beautiful pool, hot and cold tubs, sauna – the works. We were all feeling suitably soft and scrubbed after our afternoon treatments, and were relaxing around the pool sipping champagne.

'God, this is the life,' Jackie sighed, stretching her legs out in front of her. 'I haven't felt this relaxed since before the kids were born.'

Nikki giggled, a little nervously I thought. 'Is that the last time you were allowed to get stoned?' she asked.

'Stoned?' Jackie asked aghast. 'What, me? Never.'

Then everyone giggled. We were all in exceedingly good moods. Nikki was in her element – she hadn't enjoyed luxury like this since before her debt crisis, which she was well on her way to overcoming. She looked wonderful, glowing with health. Susannah and Mel were looking pleased with themselves too, if somewhat overworked. They had been deluged with orders since we'd managed to get one of their hand-painted bags featured on the fashion pages of the *Sunday Times Style* magazine – a huge coup. And they had presented a gorgeous deep-red bag to Amy that afternoon – to match her going-away outfit – as well as a couple of tiny silk purses for the bridesmaids. Amy was so touched she started to cry, and for some bizarre reason Nikki did too. She really does get worked up over fashion.

Kate and Alex had exchanged contracts just the day before and Kate was ecstatic.

'I'll be doing DIY for the rest of my life, but I just don't give a damn!' she announced gleefully on arrival.

'I'll help you out, Kate,' I said to her.

'You?' she asked, surprised. 'Are you any good at DIY?'

'No, I'm rubbish, but I think I might need the practice,' I told her. 'I'm seriously thinking of putting in an offer on a cottage near Caernarfon.'

'No way!' Amy squeaked excitedly. 'That's really near to my parents!'

'It is – and only a couple of hours' drive from your wedding reception too. If I'm successful we can drive down and visit afterwards.'

'I'm there,' Nikki said, bouncing over to give me a hug. 'I can even afford to take you out for lunch in the pub.'

Nikki wasn't quite ready to be taking me out to lunch yet, but she had managed to clear an impressive portion of her debt in a year. The fact that Andrew had had a promotion at work had helped, since he was now fully equipped to spoil her, so she didn't have to spoil herself.

*

At the pool, the conversation turned to what everyone would be wearing at the wedding. Nikki was torn between a simple strapless dress with fake fur stole and a more glamorous halter cocktail number. I definitely thought simplicity was the way to go.

'The wedding is in the daytime, you know,' I pointed out.

'The service is at three, and we won't be out till three-thirty at the earliest, by which time it'll be starting to get dark, or at least dusky,' Nikki said. She had clearly thought this one through. 'And then the reception is the evening and that's when everyone gets to see what you're wearing,' she said.

'Are you buying new things?' I asked, slightly warily.

'No,' she said, sighing dramatically. 'They're both old dresses that I bought at the height of my spending bonanza and have never worn. I was going to sell them on eBay, but I decided to hold a few numbers back for this type of thing.'

Susannah was going for a more tailored approach, wearing a black shift dress with a red floral silk coat over the top.

'I hope I'm not going to look too . . . dull,' she said, fiddling with her dressing-gown cord.

'Oh, God!' Amy suddenly cried out, almost causing several of us to choke on our champagne in fright. 'I totally forgot!'

'What?' Kate asked, alarmed. 'What did you forget? Flowers? Rings?'

Amy looked at her as though she were mad. 'No, you idiot, Susannah!'

'You forgot Susannah?'

'To ask Susannah,' she said with a huge smile, 'who she's bringing to the wedding.'

Mel's mouth dropped open slightly. 'You're bringing someone to the wedding?' she asked.

Susannah looked a bit sheepish. 'Well . . . you see . . . I met him at the shop.' As if that explained anything.

'And?' Amy asked. 'Who is he? Where's he from? Is he fit?'

Everyone laughed, except for Mel, who was just looking flabbergasted.

'You're bringing someone to the wedding?' she asked Susannah again, and I thought I could detect just the merest hint of menace in her tone.

Susannah had noticed this too.

'Mel, I'm sorry,' she said softly. Then, addressing the rest of us, 'Mel and I had made a pact to go the wedding dateless. And then I went and got myself a date.' She turned back to Mel. 'I was just waiting for the right moment to tell you.'

'Traitor,' Mel muttered under her breath, no longer able to suppress her grin. 'I'll have to hang out with Tasha now, since she's always single.'

'Cheers,' I said, draining the last of my champagne. 'Anyway, who is this man?'

Felix was one of Susannah's customers at the art store. 'He's fifty-ish, I think, but looks very well on it. You know how some men do.'

'Silver fox?' Nikki asked.

'Exactly,' Susannah said with a smile. 'But he doesn't look overly groomed. He is a painter, after all.'

'Oh, yes?' Mel prompted her.

'Moderately successful, mostly abstracts. I really like his stuff.'

'And what's going on with you two, then?' Mel asked. 'Why haven't I heard about this?'

'Well, I've been keeping it all under wraps,' Susannah admitted. 'I mean, not that it's anything serious. We've been out to dinner a few times, that's all. We haven't even . . .'

She blushed and everyone else giggled. 'And I haven't told the kids yet. What with Ed proposing to that hussy, I didn't want to upset them any further.'

Nikki moved among us, topping up glasses of champagne.

'I think they'll be really pleased you've met someone actually,' Mel said.

'To Susie and Felix,' Nikki toasted raising her glass. 'Felix,' she said a moment later, 'cool name.'

12. The Wedding

'It couldn't be any more idyllic, could it?' I said to Kate as we approached the church.

Amy had pictured the perfect winter wedding and she had got it. The snow had been falling for three days, miraculously ceasing the night before the service. Snowdonia was coated with a thick blanket of white, dazzling bright even in the wintry December sunshine.

'It is lovely,' she breathed.

The service was taking place at a small stone chapel which was, quite literally, decked with bows of holly.

'I think I preferred Jackie and Sam's,' Alex grumbled, shivering. 'It's bloody cold. And I bet there's no heating in there.'

'Oh, shut up whining,' Kate replied. 'At least you're not wearing a bloody dress.'

It was chilly. I was thankful for the white cashmere coat I had bought to wear over my dress (a dark green velvet number with fitted bodice) – who cared that it was the least practical item of clothing I had ever purchased. As we approached the doorway to the chapel, my heart skipped a beat. James was standing on the steps smoking a cigarette, looking incredibly dashing in his tux.

'Greetings,' he said with a smile. He kissed Kate and shook hands with Alex, then gave me a peck on the cheek.

'You alone?' he asked. 'Dateless?'

'Afraid so,' I said, shrugging stupidly.

'Excellent.' He grinned. 'Me too.' He took my arm and ushered me in. 'This is what I'm here to do, you know,' he said. 'Usher. Save me a seat,' he added, before returning to his post at the doorway and lighting another cigarette.

I didn't save him a seat. Nikki and Andrew turned up and squeezed in on the end of our row and there was no way I was going to tell them to move. Particularly as Nikki was dabbing at her eyes with a tissue. I held her hand.

'Have you two had a row?' I asked in hushed tones.

'No, no, nothing like that,' she said, smiling at me through her tears. 'It's just all so beautiful.' Then she asked, 'Do I look like a panda?'

'I'm sorry?' I asked, looking at her outfit, which was dark red and sleek as anything.

'My face!' she said, starting to giggle. 'Do I have mascara everywhere?'

'No,' I whispered. 'You look beautiful.' She did too. Absolutely radiant, and not quite so thin as she had been of late.

Nikki sobbed all the way through the ceremony, which I thought was weird, since she's not usually like that at weddings. I was starting to feel suspicious. Perhaps she and Andrew had had a row. Although he certainly didn't look troubled by anything. So perhaps it was her debts. Had she fallen off the wagon? Had she been a little economical with the truth about the dress she was wearing? Perhaps it was new after all. Or was it the shoes? I didn't recognize them, but since she owns about eighty pairs, that's not really all that surprising.

The ceremony was lovely. Amy looked ravishing in a pure white velvet sheath with a stole around her shoulders, her blonde hair piled up on her head and threaded through with flowers. She cried a little too and even Ade shed a couple of very dignified tears. But most of the time the two of them just couldn't stop beaming at each other.

Later, at the reception, I was just ordering myself a peach bellini when someone sidled up next to me.

'Don't you scrub up nicely?'

It was Michael, who was looking pretty dashing himself. I ordered him a drink and we leaned on the bar, surveying the scene.

'How are you, Mike?' I asked him.

'I'm really shit actually. I don't think I've ever felt so low. Over a woman I mean. I probably felt worse when West Ham got relegated, but this is the worst I've ever felt over a woman.' He looked like he meant it too. 'And why is it,' he asked, 'that she has to look so bloody amazing today? Is that just to piss me off?'

'Probably not, Michael, though I accept that it's difficult for you to realize that you're not the centre of the universe,' I said sarcastically.

He made a small noise, like a whimper.

'He whimpered,' I told Nikki over dinner. Amy had very kindly sat me between Andrew and Alex. James was out of bounds, on the top table. 'He actually whimpered.'

'I don't believe it,' Nikki said with her mouth full. 'Do you think he's actually changed?'

'No way,' Alex said. 'She's better off out of it.'

'Usually, I would agree with you, but I'm actually not completely sure,' Kate said.

For Kate to stick up for Michael was frankly astounding, but I didn't really have time to think about it for a second, because something else, something momentous, had just dawned on me. As Kate was saying that she wasn't completely sure, I saw Nikki put her hand over her glass, preventing the waiter from pouring her some wine. This in itself was weird, since she drinks like a fish. But then it struck me – I hadn't seen her light a cigarette all evening. In fact, I was now struggling to remember the last time I'd seen her with a fag in her hand. There could only be one possible explanation, and there was no way I could wait to find out for sure.

I wolfed down the rest of my starter, got up and whispered in her ear, 'You and I are going to the loo. Now!'

She looked at me with a small smile. She knew that I knew. I knew it! It all made sense: the weight gain, the tears, that odd little quip about Felix being a cool name. She was pregnant!

In the safe sanctuary of the loo, we both burst into tears.

'I'm so happy,' she blubbed at me. 'We're so happy! I didn't think I could ever be so happy about getting fat and giving up smoking!'

I couldn't say anything. I just hugged her for ages and sobbed. Eventually, we pulled ourselves together and set about trying to fix our faces – no mean feat.

'You can't say anything,' Nikki said to me. 'I'm sure everyone's going to guess once they notice I'm not smoking, but I'm only nine weeks, so it's too early to say anything.'

'Nine weeks!' I was flabbergasted. I couldn't believe she had kept it a secret this long.

'Well, I didn't actually know until a couple of weeks ago. I didn't even notice that I was late,' she admitted. 'It was the throwing up in the morning thing that gave it away.'

'That'll do it,' I said.

'Well, actually I just thought that I must have a bug. It was Andrew who made the suggestion.' She smiled at me. 'He's just so happy it's ridiculous.'

We had to repair our make-up yet again after that, but eventually made it back to our table.

The rest of the evening passed in a blur of champagne, hard liquor and some very bad dancing to 1980s pop, mostly with James, but also with Michael, who was hanging around gloomily, casting furtive glances over at Mel, and Ade, who had clearly made it his mission to dance with every single guest at the wedding, male or female, infant or octogenarian. At around one in the morning, slightly later than scheduled, Amy and Ade appeared in their going-away outfits and bade us dramatic farewells, despite the fact that they were only going upstairs and we would all see them at some point the following day. They were not due to leave for their honeymoon (in the Seychelles, natch) until Monday morning. Those of us who were still standing by one then retired to the drawing room with a couple of bottles of whisky, determined to see the night out. Needless to say, I was fast asleep by two.

As I write this, a month after the wedding, a couple of things have changed. It's a new year, for starters. Everyone knows Nikki and Andrew's news, though only I know that he's planning to propose, at La Mamounia, on Valentine's Day. Kate and Alex have started work on their new place near Oxford. They reckon it'll be finished by the summer; I reckon this time next year is more likely. Michael turned up uninvited at Mel's office Christmas party and declared undying love for her. She's thinking about giving it another go.

As for me, I've thrown caution to the wind, not only buying an isolated cottage in North Wales but also acquiring a half-Welshman, in the form of James. He's totally unreliable, disorganized, shambolic, completely unsuitable and therefore perfect for a slightly neurotic personal finance journalist who lies awake at night worrying whether she's got the best mortgage rate and always pays off her credit card debts on time.

Resources

Chapter 2. Shopaholics Anonymous: Debt and How to Survive It

Consumer Credit Counselling Service:
www.cccs.co.uk

National Debtline:
www.nationaldebtline.co.uk

Financial information providers:
www.moneyfacts.co.uk
www.moneysupermarket.com

Information on the cheapest gas, electricity and phone suppliers in your area:
www.uswitch.com
www.buy.co.uk

Chapter 3. Useless Bankers: Current Accounts

Ethical banking:
www.co-operativebank.co.uk

Chapter 4. Rainy Days: Saving and Investing

Compound interest calculator:
www.moneychimp.com

Fund performance statistics:
www.morningstar.co.uk
www.trustnet.co.uk

Information on ethical investment – Eiris:
www.eiris.co.uk

Chapter 6. First-time Blues: Buying Your Own Home

Key worker schemes:
www.odpm.gov.uk

Chapter 7. Holidays in Hell: Travel and Other Insurances

Insurance quotes:
www.insuresupermarket.com
www.confused.com

Chapter 8. Death and Taxes: Benefits and Taxes

Online will-writing sites:
www.bequest.co.uk
www.willwriters.co.uk
www.willwrite.co.uk

Information on tax from HM Revenue & Customs:
www.hmrc.gov.uk

Information on benefits from the Department for Work and Pensions:
www.dwp.gov.uk

Chapter 10. Go It Alone: Setting up Your Own Business

Professional advice:
www.businesslink.gov.uk

Index